Harold Holt

Harold Holt

Always One Step Further

ROSS WALKER

LA TROBE
UNIVERSITY PRESS

IN CONJUNCTION WITH BLACK INC.

Published by La Trobe University Press in conjunction with Black Inc.
22–24 Northumberland Street
Collingwood VIC 3066, Australia
enquiries@blackincbooks.com
www.blackincbooks.com
www.latrobeuniversitypress.com.au

La Trobe University plays an integral role in Australia's public intellectual life, and is recognised globally for its research excellence and commitment to ideas and debate. La Trobe University Press publishes books of high intellectual quality, aimed at general readers. Titles range across the humanities and sciences, and are written by distinguished and innovative scholars. La Trobe University Press books are produced in conjunction with Black Inc., an independent Australian publishing house. The members of the LTUP Editorial Board are Vice-Chancellor's Fellows Emeritus Professor Robert Manne and Dr Elizabeth Finkel, and Morry Schwartz and Chris Feik of Black Inc.

9781760643836 (paperback)
9781743822555 (ebook)

A catalogue record for this
book is available from the
National Library of Australia

Cover design by Akiko Chan
Cover photo © Leonard Burt, Hulton Archive / Getty Images
Text design and typesetting by Typography Studio

Printed in Australia by McPherson's Printing Group

For Anne Mancini and John Gellie

Contents

Prologue   1

PART ONE – UPHILL

1. Another World   7

2. Dislocated Lives   16

3. Harold Holt Goes to Wesley   22

4. Harold and Zara   36

5. Third Time Lucky   52

6. New Connections   57

7. Accidental Father, Accidental Lifesavers   61

8. From Gunner to Godfather   66

9. Americans Down Under   74

10. Married and Back in Government   81

11. Childe Harold's Pilgrimages   94

12. A Lucky Escape   107

13. Another Jolt   112

14. Unleashing the Furies   122

CONTENTS

PART TWO – THE NEW PRIME MINISTER

15. A Death and a New Beginning 131

16. Early Days as Prime Minister 137

17. At Home and Abroad 151

18. Turnbull Returns 155

19. One Dead – How Many More? 158

20. A Shot in the Dark 162

21. A Sharp, Compelling Cry 164

22. August 1966, Bingil Bay 175

23. August 1966, South Vietnam 177

24. The Return of LBJ 182

25. Off to the Races 187

PART THREE – NINETEEN SIXTY-SEVEN

26. The Prime Minister and the Artists 201

27. Testing the Water 206

28. A New Voice 209

29. Back to Asia 212

30. The *Voyager* Case 217

31. A Bad End to a Bad Week 227

32. Two Referenda 229

33. Shadows in the Rose Garden 236

34. Far From Lotus Land 243

CONTENTS

35. Treading Water   249

36. Man Wasn't Made to Live Like This   255

37. Down to Portsea   270

38. The Last Day   275

39. Missingness   285

40. In Memoriam   290

41. Enduring Memorials   294

Acknowledgements   299

Bibliography   301

Image Credits   311

Index   313

Prologue

MY AIM IN WRITING THIS BOOK HAS BEEN TO STRIKE a midway point between biography and narrative non-fiction – history told as a story. It is the story of Harold Holt's public and personal life. Though Holt was happy to talk about his love of the sea and about his life in politics, he said and wrote little about his most personal feelings. When he travelled he kept diaries, but in these he focused mainly on the people and places he encountered along the way rather than on his thoughts and feelings. Little of what has been written about him to date has given much idea of the inner life of the man.

This book is an attempt to fill that gap. It asks how Harold Holt may have become the man he was and why he may have done some of the things he did. There is a caveat here, however: 'Who knows why any man does anything?' asked John Jess, one of Holt's parliamentary colleagues. Holt's friend and president of the Portsea Surf Life Saving Club, Milton Napthine, implicitly asked the same question: 'He knew damn well that the surf was too high. God only knows why he went in for a swim.' 'Indeed,' agrees Tom Frame, after quoting this statement in his biography of Holt.

Harold Holt was a man of contradictions. He was mild-mannered yet passionate; his wife Zara said that 'everything for Harry has to be lived with his whole heart'. He was measured, but he sometimes exceeded sensible limits and could not leave well enough alone – hence my subtitle, *Always One Step Further*. When considering a course of action in politics, he often asked the question: 'Does it make good sense?' Yet he often acted in ways that did not make good sense. He was an extrovert who enjoyed parties and other social life, yet he savoured the solitude of the underwater world. He was life-affirming, yet sometimes he seemed self-destructive, as if inwardly compelled to imperil his physical safety. These are the tensions which drove his life, and which drive the narrative of this book.

No individual can be fully known. When we try to understand the motives underpinning a person's behaviour, we are always operating in the orbit of surmise. And so I have sometimes taken the liberty of surmising, using words such as 'perhaps' or phrases like 'he might have' or 'he must have' to indicate this. That said, I have based any surmise on objective sources; I have never bent the known history.

Readers may ask: 'How do we know the author is not making this up?' To this I reply that all events and incidents related in the book are factual and all the people about whom I have written actually existed. This is not a work of fiction. I have drawn my material from books and articles about Holt and Australian politics and history; from the Australian parliamentary record, Hansard; from Australian daily newspapers and magazines; from the Holt collection in the Australian National Archives in Canberra; from the archives of Wesley College and the archives of Queen's College at the University of Melbourne; from the travel diaries of Harold and Zara Holt; and from discussions with people who met or knew Holt. I have taken all dialogue from what has previously been printed, or related to me in the course of interviews.

Keeping in mind Søren Kierkegaard's comment that though life must be lived forwards, it can only be understood backwards, I have given considerable attention to Holt's early years, before his public career began. We cannot understand people without trying to understand the wider context of their lives, including those around them and the times in which they lived. Therefore, I have included some detail about those close to Holt in these early years, many of whom later became part of his life in politics.

I hope that this book will read as a snapshot of earlier times in Australia and, though non-fiction, will read like a story. Robert A. Caro, multi-volume biographer of Lyndon Johnson, discusses his methodology as a biographer thus: 'You've got to have the facts, and you've got to get them right, but you can't forget that you're telling a story . . . Are you making the reader see the scene? Can you see the scene?'

This objective holds good, I believe, whether one is writing fiction, non-fiction, or any genre between the two.

PART ONE

UPHILL

1

Another World

The sea, once it casts its spell, holds one in its net of wonder forever.
—Jacques Cousteau

It is a strange necessity to dive
Beyond the comfortable land, to seek
Among strangers where your nakedness is weak
And graceless. Well, go. What is it to live
And nothing taunts your nerves?
—Thomas Shapcott, 'Skin Diver'

HAROLD HOLT INHABITED TWO WORLDS: THE WORLDS of politics and of the sea. By the time he became prime minister in January 1966, he had already spent three decades in public life. In the course of his duties as a federal minister, he had travelled widely. Wherever he went, he felt the strong pull of water. 'In every part of the world I go,' he explained, 'I try to get my head underwater.' He might have amended Tennyson's declaration 'I am part of all I have met' to 'I am part of all the waters I have met'.

Rarely was he interested in just going for a swim; his true passion was seeing what went on beneath the surface of the water – he enjoyed spearfishing, snorkelling and scuba-diving. Over many years, he built up a pearl fisher's capacity to stay submerged – even as prime minister, he made use of the more tedious periods in parliament to try to lengthen the time he could hold his breath. Perhaps he was trying to distance himself from his immediate environment, anticipating the next time he could escape the chafing ties of land. As if to challenge the laws of nature, he was adapting himself to spend as long as he could in, and preferably under, his favourite element.

He seemed to scoff at the limitations of the mammalian body, the boundaries that being human imposed. One day his wife came into the bathroom to find him submerged in the bath, lying quite still. She let out a shriek of horror, and with a signal from a raised finger he reassured her that he was still conscious. He had been testing himself to see how long he could remain submerged. He continued this practice regularly, each time checking with a stopwatch to see how long he had endured. Eventually, he reached two and a half minutes of submersion.

He considered his body a major asset and he had always looked after it. Having been endowed with the gifts of a fine constitution and handsome looks, he meant to keep them. Physical skill and fitness he valued highly; he shared the Ancient Greek admiration for the perfect human physique, and the ballet beguiled him for its grace and beauty, as well as the fitness and agility demanded of its dancers.

Holt claimed that politics was all he had, but, whether he acknowledged it or not, he also had the water, which eased the tension of political life. The time he spent in the water was 'the refreshment'; without it, he claimed, 'I would go bonkers.' Once he became prime minister, he needed this refreshment more than ever.

He felt a sense of comfort and ease in water. There was something in his make-up, too, that answered to the nature of water; as a man, Holt was fluid, often gentle, oriented towards harmony and union, and capable of deep feeling.

The sea to which he kept returning encompassed the waters of Port Phillip Bay, which surrounded the coastal towns of Portsea and Sorrento, at the southern tip of Victoria's Mornington Peninsula. These waters had flowed into and around his earliest memories. He got to know these seaside towns as a young man, when he holidayed with Zara Dickins and her family. At Sorrento, Zara's parents,

Sydney and Violet Dickins, owned 'Chattanooga', an attractive house with a fine garden. To Zara and his other intimates, he was Harry.

While in his late thirties, he became Zara's second husband and found himself with three growing boys in his care: Nicholas, the eldest, and twins Sam and Andrew. They introduced him to spear-fishing. At first he was reluctant, but Zara encouraged him; the boys would teach him, she said, and they did. He soon became addicted and he could never get enough of the excitement this sport brought him. Often he would wake the boys early in the morning, rousing them from their beds with the words: 'Come on, boys, we want to go spear-fishing.' Sometimes suffering with hangovers, or having other plans in mind, they were not always immediately responsive to his enthusiasm.

They would set out together in a battered old boat. The boys were struck by their new father's risk-taking attitude; he would often stuff fish into his wetsuit jacket, ignoring the perils of sharks smelling a nearby meal. 'I've tried a lot of sports – and this is the daddy of them all,' he said of spearfishing. 'It requires physical skill, it takes you into a new world which is entirely different from the world in which you spend most of your time, it's stimulating – and I like fresh crayfish.'

Wasn't it surprising, he was asked, that a gregarious man such as he should have chosen such a solitary recreation? He explained,

> Mostly I do go on my own, that's true, and that's part of the attraction, because I'm away from noise and people and telephones and tensions. Down there there's drama of your own making. You can set your own pace . . . It's another world, as fascinating as I imagine travelling in space must be. It's so solitary.

He had long been accustomed to solitude. To be alone under the water was to be free, he said. 'There is the sheer exhilaration of contact with the sea – of being one with the ocean.'

*　*　*

Late in 1957, with money earned from Zara's fashion business, the Holts bought a block of land at Portsea, where an orchard once stood. The builders kept to such a tight schedule that the new house was built within six weeks. The sight of the house emerging in its various stages puzzled the locals.

One day Zara answered the telephone at home to hear: 'Look, we don't want to interfere in your private affairs, but someone has built a house on your block of land.'

'That's all right. It's ours,' she replied.

Their house, which the locals referred to as 'Holtsville', was part of the Weeroona Estate, a subdivision of eight houses near the gates of the Portsea Officer Cadet School. It was situated on top of a cliff overlooking the sea. At the front lay the garden, protected from the wind by a strand of tea-trees. The bay was so close that it seemed almost an extension of the house. Just two minutes' walk away was a private beach.

The Holts liked to collect Chinese sculptures and figurines. At their house in Melbourne they displayed statues of the eight Chinese virtues; near the edge of the cliff at their house in Portsea, staring out to sea, stood a Confucius-like Chinese statue. This may well have represented Mazu, the Chinese goddess of seafarers, whose spiritual power was said to be able to save swimmers from drowning. Mazu would indeed have been a suitable goddess to represent Australia, an island country surrounded by wild oceans and inhabited by hardy swimmers and seafarers.

The house at Portsea was nineteen squares, flat-roofed, split-level, with casual furniture, cane matting on the floors and knotted pine-panelled walls. It had many bedrooms, so that the boys could come down to visit with their families. Colourful shells fished from the water or gathered from the beach adorned some of the tables in the main living area, where the walls were decorated with cartoons and photographs depicting Harry's life, both public and private: photos of the boys at various stages of their lives to date; of grandchildren, Christopher and Sophie; of wetsuited Harry emerging from the water, proudly showing one of his spearfishing catches; informal photos of himself with Zara; formal photos of him with various dignitaries; and many cartoons of himself and Zara, her mouth always open in a wide, toothy smile. The modern paintings from her private collection contrasted with these decorations.

In this main living area were four unusual ornaments, which Harry described as his 'window on Australia'. Fixed on the wall, from the bottom upwards, were an iron ball and chain; a pair of handcuffs dating from the early days of Sydney; a rusted gold-panning dish which Zara had found on the bed of the Snowy River while fishing for trout; and a mirror of pioneer design, which he described as 'primitive but durable'.

From the Holts' house in the Melbourne suburb of Toorak it took less than two hours to drive to Portsea. Harry often made the drive alone down the Nepean Highway, in the process transforming himself from public to private citizen. His telephone and briefcase were always at his side to keep him anchored to his job, but nearby was the water to soften the sharpness of politics. 'A jack-knife dive into the depths' was to him 'an excellent cure for a man's jaded nerves'.

* * *

It seems fitting that the burrow of the amphibious rodent, the otter, shares the name holt. These animals build their holts under tree roots or rock cairns lined with moss and grass. In times of leisure, they play, frolic and tumble-turn in the water. When Harold Holt entered the water in a wetsuit, glistening like an otter's fur, he created his own world of play and drama. Here was his own holt, his own place of belonging, where he often spent two or more hours at a time. This was his way of temporarily going missing before resurfacing into the world. It was a place where he felt he truly belonged, a private world into which he could disappear. When he fitted his snorkel in preparation for an underwater plunge, his face displayed a sureness which countered the uncertainty always present in his life on land.

His wetsuit and extra-large flippers seemed to transform him, the flippers creating the closest possible equivalent to the webbed feet of amphibians. Over time he built up an extraordinary level of underwater endurance, generally fishing at a depth of ten to twenty feet, using only the air he could hold in his lungs. He always used a snorkel, never an aqualung, for he considered it unsporting to spear cray or other fish while wearing this apparatus.

Skindiving, he acknowledged, had 'an element of risk which is also part of the attraction' – it didn't give you any second chances. But he was a stoic who took everything as a matter of course. Experience had taught him that life was inherently insecure, so why not enjoy risk rather than fear it? He felt more alive when flirting with death, pitting his strength against an element which brought rewards despite its indifference to his welfare. Excitement lay in the thin partitions between life and death, and by putting himself on that line between the two, he affirmed life. He was a man of risks: just one step further, and another, and another . . .

In politics, he was measured and moderate, always seeking consensus among his colleagues by finding the middle-of-the-road solution to a problem. His judgement about whether or not a particular policy was worth following was often based on commonsense questions such as: Is it sound? Does it make good sense? But he revelled in danger and the adrenaline rushes it brought, to the point that he sometimes engaged in an addictive dance with death.

His aquatic adventures taunted his wife's nerves. 'He feels invincible in the water,' she told her friends. His cavalier attitude to hazards frightened her, for he rarely drew the line where most other people would, prepared to stay in the water even when there were sharks nearby. 'Everything for Harry has to be lived with his whole heart,' said Zara, and that was how he lived in the water.

In colder weather she waited for him on the beach, next to a fire burning in anticipation of his return from the water, often with his body covered in purple patches. Then, after his hours in the other world, he began the familiar process of re-entry to life on land.

He usually swam breaststroke, since the effects of a broken collarbone from his university football days hampered his ability with freestyle. As a swimmer, he was very ordinary, but as a skindiver, spearfisher and snorkeler, he excelled. His favourite waters for these sports were those of Cheviot Beach – a surf beach on the waters of Bass Strait near Point Nepean, at the very tip of the Mornington Peninsula. Cheviot Beach was a cove, curved like a closing hand, enfolding, inviting. When the sea was placid it was like paradise, but it was not always like that.

For Harold Holt, nowhere spelled Portsea like Cheviot, his personal fiefdom. He claimed to know it 'like the back of my hand'. To reach it he had to enter the gates of Fort Nepean, part of a network of fortifications which once protected the entrance to Port Phillip. As there was a quarantine station located within, it was closed to most members of the public, apart from people such as he who held a special pass.

From Cheviot Hill, above the beach, you could see the full expanse of Port Phillip Bay, including the gap of water between Point Nepean and Point Lonsdale, 2.7 kilometres away on the Bellarine Peninsula. This triangle-shaped gap is known as The Rip, or The Heads, the narrow waterway entrance connecting Bass Strait to Port Phillip Bay. When the tide turns, the Rip becomes a fierce confluence of moody, unpredictable waters – a hazard to the maritime transport passing through on the way to Victoria's two largest cities, Melbourne and Geelong. Very few swimmers have braved this stretch of water, and it was not until 1971 that Douglas Mew became the first swimmer to traverse it, taking sixty-one minutes to complete the crossing from Point Lonsdale to Point Nepean.

Harold Holt prided himself on his ability to read the water, the tides and the conditions at Cheviot. He knew parts of the beach – rock pools; passages of sea between rocks; caves and limestone holes – as well as he knew his own body.

Cheviot Beach could be ferociously wild, as it was on the night of 19 October 1887. In the midst of a violent storm, the propeller of the

English steamer the *SS Cheviot* broke, dashing the ship onto Corsair Rock. Within fifteen minutes, it broke in two and sank. The ship was tossed about on the water like a helpless log; the back beach was strewn with bodies. The skull of one of the dead had been crushed when the sea drove his body against the rocks, and all the fatal injuries were to the head. Several weeks later, another body was found, unidentifiable, a leg and an arm missing. Thirty-five of the crew of fifty-eight lost their lives in the wreck.

The rocks had done the damage. There were platforms of them, as well as reefs jutting out far into the water, ready to slice through any timber or flesh that collided with them. Rip-tides dominated the inner and outer bars and high waves were customary. The area was notorious for irresistible rip-tides known as runouts – they could easily catch a swimmer and in seconds he could be 100, even 200, metres out to sea. If that happened, he would have to go with the tide, hoping it would turn and carry him back. At high tide, the rocks and reefs lay immediately off the beach, and as the tide dropped, strong permanent rips intensified off the rocks and amongst the reefs.

The *SS Cheviot* was memorialised when the beach where it had met its end was given its name. Until December 1967, eighty years after the disaster, it was a largely unfamiliar name to the Australian public.

One of the beach's attractions for Holt was the site of the wreck. The ship returned to life as he dived down into its remains, embellished with coral and seaweed in its sea change. On one day in January 1960 he reached the wreck and located its engines, propeller shaft, iron beams and iron hull plating. He also found a coral-encrusted porthole lying loose and claimed it as a souvenir, making that patch of sea part of his own history, adding his own drama to the one from so many decades earlier.

He had two other favourite spots near Cheviot: Pope's Eye and Chinaman's Hat, both of which were popular with scuba divers and snorkellers. Pope's Eye was the uncompleted foundation of an island fort intended to defend the entrance to Port Phillip Bay. Chinaman's Hat, named for its shape, was an octagonal structure which served as a shipping channel marker, lying about three kilometres south-east of Pope's Eye.

While he was exploring the waters around Portsea, Holt was, in both mind and body, far removed from the institution of which he was one of the longest-serving members: Australia's Federal Parliament. In Australia's bicameral system of government, members of the House of Representatives, where he held a seat, often refer to the Senate as 'the other place', and vice versa. But for Harold Holt, the other place was the sea. This was his 'other world', and he had fallen under its spell.

2

Dislocated Lives

I am that father whom your boyhood lacked and suffered pain for lack of.
—Odysseus to his son Telemachus, in Homer's *Odyssey*

Whether he knows it or not, and no matter what his position in society, the father is the initiating priest through whom the young being passes on into the larger world.
—Joseph Campbell, *The Hero with a Thousand Faces*

FOR HAROLD HOLT THE ADULT, THE SEA PROVIDED a sense of emotional and physical anchorage. But for Harold Holt the child, flux was the only constant. By the time he reached the age of eleven, he had already attended four different schools.

Thomas Holt, his father, spent his earliest years on the family farm in the small New South Wales country town of Nubba, in the Harden–Murrumburrah district west of Canberra. By the time he turned twenty he had four siblings, some of them many years younger than he. As the farm was no longer able to support the growing family, Tom moved to Sydney, where he secured a position as sportsmaster and director of cadet training at the Cleveland Street School. He still seemed undecided about which career he would make his life's work, but he soon decided against devoting his whole life to teaching. Capable, handsome and charming, he was seeking a wider stage.

Near the school lived the Pearce family, owners of a hotel in nearby George Street. Olive Pearce, the daughter of the family, was slightly older than he and also a school teacher. Tom began to court her and a romantic relationship developed. It was not long until Olive found that she was pregnant, and a wedding quickly followed. The year 1908 must have been the most momentous one in their lives thus far, with a wedding in January and a birth in August. On the fifth day of that month, a Wednesday, their first child, Harold Edward, was born. Eighteen months later he was joined by a brother, Clifford Thomas.

With a growing family to support, Tom needed to find a suitable long-term occupation. Olive's family had connections in the hotel business, in Payneham, a north-eastern suburb of Adelaide. There he bought the licence to the Duke of Wellington Hotel and relocated with his wife.

With their parents in Adelaide, Harold and Cliffie, as he was known, remained behind in Sydney with Olive's brother-in-law, Harold Martin, known as 'Uncle Marty', and his wife, Ethel. A journalist whose special area of interest was the world of theatre, 'Uncle Marty' worked as the editor of the variety magazine *Everyone's*, which carried news about the latest plays and films, and gossip about the popular actors and actresses of the day.

The Holt brothers were shuttled from one set of relatives to another. They attended Randwick State School in Sydney until late in 1916, before moving to stay with relatives in Nubba, where they attended the local public school. Harold enjoyed some happy times in the small town, riding horses, catching rabbits and playing tennis. As he grew, he developed a fine physique, solid but not heavy, which enhanced his inherited good looks.

The inchoate outlines of his personality began to take shape. Already he was known for his charm and friendliness and the warm, disarming smile which created a bridge between him and other people. A reservoir of benevolence was deepening within him. When you had to keep re-establishing yourself in a succession of different environments, it was an asset to be able to please others. He was driven by a deep desire to be liked, and it was easy to like him. In each of his new schools he used his charm, and thus it grew strong, like a well-used muscle.

Though not endowed with outstanding athletic ability, he had great determination and undertook every activity wholeheartedly. Though always determined to win, he was a good loser, with a mildness which prevented outbursts of temper. Already he sensed that he would have to depend on his own resources, to stand on his own feet and make his own way, more or less alone. His life to date had been fragmented, but from within himself he wove threads to reassemble the pieces. He was learning to survive, to become, as far as he could, the architect of his own destiny.

Many people take their lives for granted. Others feel the need to struggle, as if to justify their being alive. Harold was like this, and sometimes he tried too hard, not knowing when to stop or pull back. He was like the servant in the Parable of the Talents, found in the Gospel of St Matthew, who expanded his talents by putting them to sound use, making the most of what he had. Already he was drawing up the blueprint for the rest of his life.

The constant movement from place to place, from one set of people to another, made demands of the Holt brothers. But against this rocky background, they built a solid sibling bond. They were close in age, temperament and physical appearance – so much so that they could have easily been taken for twins. Good-natured and accommodating, they avoided the rivalries common among siblings, freeing their energies to deal with the demands of the world outside the family.

*   *   *

For Tom Holt, hotel management proved to be another false start. So too, it seemed, was his marriage, which was not wearing well, the seeds of its ending sown in its hasty beginning. By the time Harold was eight years old, his parents were separated. By the time he was ten, they were divorced.

At last, Tom Holt found his long-term career in a quite different milieu – the theatre. This world contained variety, challenge, glamour and frequent travel, which was practicable for a newly single man. Once again, the Pearce family helped Tom, this time through Olive's family connections to the theatre. There was Uncle Marty, writing about the world of entertainment, and there was also Vera Pearce, Olive's younger half-sister, a well-known actress and comedienne.

Vera Pearce had already enjoyed a busy and varied career under the footlights, having spent her youth in Adelaide, where she had acted from her earliest years. At age five, she played the white rabbit in *Alice in Wonderland*; in 1910, as a teenager, she went to Melbourne to act in J.C. Williamson Theatre Company's pantomimes and musical comedies, winning acclaim for her role in *Our Miss Gibbs*.

Harry D. McIntosh, entrepreneur and manager of Melbourne's Tivoli theatre, signed her up. Aged eighteen, she travelled to London in 1914 to act, but later in the same year McIntosh persuaded her to return. In November, he signed her up for the *Tivoli Follies* revue, in which she became known as 'Queen of the *Follies*'. Her statuesque figure was a point of attraction, and she was billed as being two inches taller than the Venus de Milo, with 'all her other dimensions proportionately correct'.

Soon, she branched into the emerging world of film, and in 1916, changing style, she took the title role in the silent film *The Martyrdom of Nurse Cavell*. But comedy was her natural bent, for she possessed all the qualities of the true vaudeville comedienne: a compelling stage presence, a sharp sense of comedy and a commanding voice. According to *Truth* newspaper, she was 'as popular as pay day'. She was popular with her nephews Harold and Cliffie, too, showing them personal items like cigarette cards adorned with her face, and even a 'good luck boomerang' carrying her name, given to Australian troops going to war. After the war ended, she returned to England into an expanding career in film.

With her help, Tom Holt secured work at the Tivoli, managing the tours of famous female singers. He looked after the 'Spangles' world tour of Ada Reeve, as well as some of the tours of Dame Nellie Melba. Soon, as the Tivoli–Williamson travelling representative, he went to London and New York to study the entertainment business, both live entertainment and the new medium of cinema.

Before long, he secured the position of J.C. Williamson's manager and, specifically, of the Tivoli theatre in Melbourne, for which he toured the country as a talent scout. His job was one of constant movement, his life a collage of snapshots from many parts of the world.

During his sons' earliest years, Tom Holt's energies must have been largely absorbed by his continuing search for a career and by an unsettled marriage. Due to constant travel, he was only intermittently available to Harold and Cliffie. His absence created a large gap in their lives, but the brothers at least had each other. They were learning to survive and, beyond that, to be fathers to their own lives.

With their father interstate or abroad, the brothers divided their time in Sydney between their mother and Uncle Marty and Aunt Ethel. Their father's new financial success enabled them to attend the prestigious Abbotsholme College for day boys and boarders on Sydney's North Shore, in the affluent suburb of Killara. Standing five hundred feet above sea level, the school was an eye-catching landmark for miles.

Parents from all parts of the British Empire sent their sons to board at Abbotsholme, drawn by its reputation as an open-air school whose students had one of the lowest rates of illness in the state. It was one of the few Australian schools to stay open during the Spanish flu epidemic of 1919, the same year that Harold and Clifford Holt were first enrolled, aged ten and nine respectively.

At Abbotsholme, Harold met William McMahon, a short, thin boy with blue eyes in a head dominated by oversized ears. Like Harold, he'd had a childhood of frequent movement, shuttled between different sets of relatives. William's mother had endured years of illness with tuberculosis, which kept her separated from her four children. Now William was living with his maternal uncle and aunt, Sam and Ethel Walder. James, his elder brother, had recently died.

Young McMahon desired his father's attention, but William McMahon Senior gave him little of that, so the boy turned to other people. He was extroverted, voluble, sometimes undisciplined, and he already wanted to be noticed. Though smaller and less prepossessing than many of his peers, he was determined to find ways to compensate.

On the first anniversary of Armistice Day, 11 November 1919, Harold Holt and William McMahon marched together, side by side, seized by a sense of the occasion's solemnity. Like Harold, William could be charming, perhaps already understanding how charm could work to his advantage. He enjoyed being the centre of attention, and was dogged, determined and already ambitious.

3

Harold Holt
Goes to Wesley

You could see now that he might make a boxer, as far as width and heaviness of shoulders went, but there was a mildness about his mouth and eyes that proclaimed no devil.

—William Golding, *Lord of the Flies*

A NOTHER CHANGE OF SCHOOL WAS APPROACHING FOR Harold and Cliffie, an opportunity for Harold to take a hand in his own future. Young though he was, he knew that he needed to rely on his own resources, to struggle uphill on his own two feet. He was beginning to create his own personal myth.

Now that Tom and Olive Holt were divorced, they turned their attention to the question of their sons' long-term future. Tom would soon be leaving Australia for London, to serve as J.C. Williamson's representative there. Harold had already made up his mind where he wanted to go to school, having encountered a boy from Melbourne who attended Wesley College. He found it a tremendously exciting place to be and praised it to the skies. Harold found the lad so convincing that he asked his mother if he and Cliffie could leave Abbotsholme immediately and move to Melbourne to board at Wesley. His enthusiasm convinced his parents and they enrolled their sons at this, one of Australia's most reputable public schools. (The title 'public school' was misleading, as these schools were in truth private, non-government schools which charged substantial fees.)

Harold choosing to take it upon himself to determine which school he would attend was a sign of things to come – from now on, he would fight his own battles and make his own decisions with little outside assistance, apart from financial support.

At the time, Wesley College was known for its remarkable headmaster, Lawrence Arthur Adamson. He placed great emphasis on sports and games, fitting with the image of the outward, sporty nature of Australian masculine culture. The school was a place for healthy living, striving on the sports field and academic achievement in the classroom. It was close to the city centre and to trains and trams. If the boys had to find a home away from their parents, this looked like a sound choice.

The school's facade fronted St Kilda Road, a long, plane tree–lined boulevard which ran north towards central Melbourne and south towards its bayside suburbs. The school's bluestone in Italianate style gave the main building an air of permanence. The facade was flanked on each side by towers which, according to one of the school songs, watched over the school at night. Although they were known as 'grey' towers, the school's colours were purple and gold.

Lawrence Arthur Adamson, known as 'Dicky', was the most famous of Australia's public-school headmasters. He ran Wesley on the British public-school model, emphasising the importance of character, good manners, good citizenship and community service, as well as sporting and academic attainment. He was reputed to be a great man who could inspire young boys, and a champion of all sports. English by birth, he read classics and jurisprudence at Oxford and in 1885, aged twenty-five, he was called to the Bar. After he had endured a severe attack of pleurisy, his doctors advised him to move to a warmer climate. And so he emigrated to Australia to practise at the Sydney Bar, but the summertime humidity of the climate did not suit his condition. He then moved to Melbourne, where he was appointed headmaster of Wesley after he undertook financial responsibility for the school's growth. When the Holt brothers entered the school in 1920, he had already been headmaster for eighteen years.

The school was a world in itself, with its own distinctive culture. This included an ever-expanding book of school songs, many composed by the headmaster himself; others had been imported from the Mother Country, to bring the Old World near. The school offered the possibility of a surrogate family to those whose ties to their birth families had been severed, and the boarding house was full of such boys. The headmaster used the songs, the boat races, the other sports and the Great War as ties to bind his boys more closely to the school. Though nominally run by the Methodist Church, the school itself was the real religion, and the headmaster wrote its scriptures – the school songs – which promoted the virtues of character, team and sentiment.

Above all, the headmaster emphasised the team. You could never remain an isolated fragment when you joined your own exertions to those of a great throng striving together towards a common goal. Adamson often spoke of the importance of 'strenuousness and sentiment'. Henceforth, Harold entwined around his heart the colours of whatever team he belonged to, and the notion of loyalty to the team became as unchangeable as his blood type.

For four years of his childhood, the Great War had loomed in the background of Harold's life. During those years, Adamson made his presence felt on the public scene as one of the strongest advocates of support for the British war effort, and many of his songs encouraged patriotic support for the Empire. He urged his boys to enlist, argued for the introduction of conscription, and valorised the deaths of the 148 of 'his boys' who died in the conflict. He intoned their names at school assemblies, especially (after 1916) on 25 April – Anzac Day. And still the unfinished business of the war dragged on with the premature deaths of those whose mental or physical health it had ruined.

At the headmaster's request, sculptors were employed to create four lions from almost-translucent white pure Sicilian marble. Each of the lions stood on a plinth on the stairs leading up to Adamson Hall, with names of war dead engraved on the plinths. In this way, a pride of lions guarded the entrance to the hall – daily reminders of the cost of the war to the school and the country.

Adamson lived between two worlds, the Old World of England and the New World of Australia, still in some ways an antipodean outpost of Empire. From time to time, he left his school in the hands of his deputies and made the long sea voyage back to England, from where he returned laden with more of his beloved antiques. These, like his bust of Antoninus of Naples, often embodied male beauty.

The headmaster stood for both the solidity of the past and the glamour of the future. He owned a rebuilt Wright aircraft named *Stella*, which was stationed about twenty miles from Melbourne at the town of Diggers Rest. Adamson knew that Harry Houdini, the famous American magician and escapologist, was planning to make the first flight on the Australian continent during his visit there in 1910. Houdini's *Voisin* aircraft was stationed right next to *Stella* at Diggers Rest.

Adamson was adamant that the glory of making the first flight in Australian history should not go to an American magician, so he hired an Englishman named Ralph C. Banks to pilot his craft, and ordered him up in the air at the first possible opportunity. Banks had gone about three hundred metres when the plane suddenly spiralled towards the ground. The entire plane was demolished with only the motor and two wheels left intact.

Following Banks' failure, Houdini completed fifteen flights over the next few days at Diggers Rest, including a flight that lasted more than seven minutes and spanned six miles. So, to Adamson's chagrin, an American magician did become the first person to fly successfully in Australia.

Houdini's best-known tricks involved escapes from water, including his famous Water Torture cell, or 'Upside Down' act, in which he freed himself from a tank full of water while standing on his head. While in Melbourne, he showed off another of his trademark aquatic escape acts: plunging into the murky waters of the Yarra River manacled, liberating himself and then resurfacing, on the way up dislodging a corpse from the muddy riverbed. An audience of twenty thousand was there to watch him. Undoubtedly, news of this and other exploits reached Adamson and his pupils.

Adamson's presence dominated his school and Harold soon fell under his spell, as did many of his peers. An oil painting of Adamson by the portrait painter William Beckwith McInnes hung in the corridors at Wesley, a tangible reminder that this was *his* school. The colours were sombre, chosen to emphasise his natural gravitas. His head and shoulders looked as if they had been chiselled out of the bluestone of the school itself.

His height was average, but his girth was impressive. With a mountainous stomach, he looked as wide as he was long. He was anchored in the world as solidly as the Moreton Bay Fig trees in the grounds near his house, whose trunks and networks of roots stretched out for yards while their shelves of dark-green-leafed branches headed skyward.

The headmaster drew the attention of his pupils to the beauties of nature – to the swallows that built their nests under the eaves of the college front; the magpies and magpie-larks that wandered on the cricket ground looking for whatever scraps they might pick up; the wattle birds in June and the mopokes towards the end of August.

Adamson loved animals, especially dogs, and he encouraged his boys to love them, too. He believed that children should be trained as early as possible to have a love for animals and beautiful things, whether made by man or by nature. He felt that the education of a dog should run on the same lines as those of a boy, remembering that one year of a dog's life equalled seven of a boy's. A dog should be the constant companion of the master; the more he is talked to, the more understanding he gains. You could even tell a dog stories about himself or about other dogs, and by the tones of your voice he would soon pick up some understanding of what you were saying.

Adamson had established a dog cemetery under the Moreton Bay Fig tree where, beneath special headstones, Paddy Adamson and

Nancy Adamson rested in peace. When one of Adamson's canine companions died, the boys gathered with their headmaster to observe funeral rites, thus acknowledging a death in their wider family.

Although not a father himself, Adamson was a father-figure to many at Wesley. The school was his family and the boys were his adopted children. He was especially gifted at talking convincingly to individual students, and he encouraged both day boys and boarders to think of their school as their home, and the masters to feel that they were part of an extended family. For boarders, with parents sometimes on the land in rural Australia or overseas, the idea that school was family took on a more powerful emotional colouring, as the headmaster watched over his 'fatherless boys'.

Even from this early stage of his life, Harold had begun gravitating towards men with strong personalities and paternal characteristics. For young Harold, Adamson was a ready-made father substitute, a man in the twilight of his life urging his pupil towards his sunrise. For his part, the headmaster saw young Harold as diligent and dedicated, successful in both sport and studies, courteous, even urbane. His succinct assessment of him was 'a fine boy'.

Harold must have looked forward to the occasions after school hours when the headmaster, royally purpled in his dressing gown, invited some of his favourite pupils into his living quarters. On Saturday nights there were lessons in Bridge or in the social graces and skills that would enhance their later lives. Adamson told stories of events on the other side of the world, with readings from his favourite books, such as Robert Louis Stevenson's *Treasure Island*, Stanley John Weyman's *A Gentleman of France* and Rudyard Kipling's *Stalky & Co*. The headmaster especially admired Kipling; for Adamson the British Empire was a male hunting ground, as it was for Kipling. Sentimentality, camaraderie, an emphasis on the primacy of The Team: these were central.

So too were the virtues of a gentleman, who, according to Adamson, never gave needless trouble to those who served him, and knew how 'to win decently and to lose decently'. The game was more than the player of the game, and as for victory or defeat, you heeded Kipling's advice to 'treat those two impostors just the same'.

Adamson also emphasised the importance of the school's own motto, *Sapere Aude* – 'dare to be wise'. Harold was so impressed by this motto that he signed a photograph of himself and Cliffie to a friend: 'To Jim – Sapere Aude. See where it gets you!'

*　*　*

At Wesley, in acknowledgement of his determination and persistence, Harold acquired the nickname 'Tiger'. As time passed, 'Tiger' evolved into a more benign feline; presumably in recognition of his smile, he became known as 'Cat' or 'Puss'. Perhaps he reminded his peers of the Cheshire Cat in *Alice in Wonderland*, whose smile remained behind even after the cat itself had gone. Harold wanted and needed the love and approval of others, which he had no trouble attracting.

Wesley was a place where he could be a participant – a sports-mad school that rewarded endeavour, goodwill and good character. Here he could be part of a family, albeit an unconventional one. Since he was old enough to remember, he had been moved from one environment to another; each time he entered a new school, he had to re-establish himself. But Wesley offered a sense of permanency. Even if the bluestone buildings were forbidding rather than friendly, they embodied a reassuring solidity, as if to say: *Here you can build into the future.* The school was well organised, with clear boundaries. Harold had already lived in three different states; now, at last, he thought of Melbourne, and more precisely, Wesley, as his home.

But the school was not a home with all the things that most teenagers desire, such as the softer comforts of the middle-class home, which in other circumstances he might have enjoyed. Instead, there were Spartan dormitories with little furniture apart from iron-framed beds; a wrought-iron fence that protected the Mowbray Street and St Kilda Road sides of the school, with its spear-shaped spikes ready to castrate any lad foolish enough to try to climb over them; and the Assembly Hall, where the headmaster presided over morning assemblies of the whole school. There he addressed the boys in his voice of perfect clarity, its measured cadences emphasising the most important words, as if each distilled a lifetime of careful thought.

Adamson encouraged Harold's natural eagerness, inspiring him to participate. He threw himself into many activities, sporting and cultural. Facing the camera for the Prep. School football team photo, he posed with his hands folded across his chest, as if nurturing his strength so that it could go to work for him. His face was serious, with no trace of a smile. Not commanding, but determined, he gave the impression of a small boy marshalling his resources to confront the world around him and to defend the interests of the institution with which he now identified himself.

Every couple of weeks, the Wesley boys made the fifteen-minute walk from St Kilda Road to the St Kilda Beach Sea Baths situated on Port Phillip Bay, which was almost surrounded by the city of Melbourne and its suburbs. Nude bathing was commonplace, unless, as the regulations put it, 'there were ladies present'. Without reaching the speed or fluency of the best swimmers among his peers, Harold learned to live and move in water, developing some facility with breaststroke and the 'Australian Crawl' – also known as freestyle – made famous by the Australian Olympic swimmer Andrew 'Boy' Charlton.

Harold was a handy tennis player and soon became friendly with John Busst, one of the stars of the Wesley team. Johnnie, as he was known, was a fellow boarder from the regional city of Bendigo. He had an engaging and forthright personality, and he was developing a strong enthusiasm for painting. Harold's main connection with the arts at Wesley was as a member of the dramatic society, which made sense in light of his family's theatrical interests. Johnnie watched him take the stage in his hometown, in the role of a policeman in W.W. Jacob's play *The Monkey's Paw*.

But it was in cricket and football that Harold really made his mark. Though he lacked the quick reflexes, natural balance and fluency of movement of the natural athlete, he was sturdy, robust and determined. By the time he reached his senior years of school, he had won places in the cricket team, where he both batted and bowled, and in the football team, where, as a nuggety back-pocket player, he kept opposition rovers out of the game while they were 'resting' from chasing the ball, and drove the ball out of defence into attack.

One of his young teachers, Arthur Phillips, questioned the football coach, Mr Kelly, over the wisdom of placing him in that position, saying, 'I know he'll give you four quarters of hard trying, but he's pretty clumsy, isn't he?' But Kelly reassured him:

> Ah, but that's just the point, you see. 'Puss' would never do anything unsporting or against the rules of the game, but when he's going through for the ball, no one can get near those naturally flailing elbows.

Harold's name began to appear in sporting reports. He was an untiring defender of his team and, by extension, of his school. 'Xavier were aggressive from the bounce,' ran one report, 'but Holt was there.' His unfailing *thereness* made him an asset to the team.

As a member of the football team, Harold established a close connection with Reginald John David Turnbull, known as 'Spot'. With his brother, Reg had entered the school as a boarder around the same time as Holt. His father had been a journalist at the *North-China Daily News* in Shanghai – one of the 'foreign brigade'. Reg's life to date had been jolted by bereavement: his father had died when the boy was still in his early childhood. But the weight of his loss was lightened when his mother remarried Enos Soren Thellefsen, whom Reg came to idolise.

Reg's sobriquet, 'Spot', referred to a prominent birthmark on his forehead, right between his eyes. He must have believed that his distinctive feature set him apart in a positive way, for in a community often marked by rigid conformity, he was *sui generis*, very much his own person. Nevertheless, he could conform and fit in with others when necessary. He was both graceful and forthright.

Young Turnbull was six feet tall, with a champion sportsman's physique, lithe and lissom. He was Captain of Boats and prominent in athletics, and he played alongside Holt on the back line in Wesley's senior football team. He was often mentioned in match reports, his name paired with Holt's, who was said to 'ably second him with splendid judgement'. On another occasion: 'Holt, on the full back line, excelled himself, marking like a veteran and coming away with great dash, while Turnbull on the other wing was always sound, and at times brilliant.'

In sports photographs, the tall and slender Spot wore an expression of solid self-assurance, as if he were holding all the aces. This made his face stand out, even more than the fact that as team captain he was front and centre. His smile was both restrained and confident.

Second only to his love for his stepfather was Spot's love for his headmaster. Mr Adamson saw his potential and encouraged him, especially in his ambition to become a medical practitioner. With his confidence, trim body and mellifluous voice, Turnbull was clearly leadership material. Adamson, who always recognised quality, made him senior prefect. But in doing so, the headmaster advanced Turnbull ahead of Holt, feeling that the leadership position would help compensate him for the absence of his far distant parents. Holt was appointed Turnbull's deputy, but as he felt he had the better claim to the top position, he was hurt.

But he grew used to holding second position. He had also been deputy house captain to Turnbull. As time passed, a pattern developed regarding the scholars at the top of the senior classes at Wesley. A boy named John Cumpston was usually first, Holt second and Turnbull third. Holt became accustomed to this, almost as if it were the natural order of things.

In their final years at Wesley, Spot and Harold shared a dormitory. They played alongside one another on the sporting field, now spending their non-waking hours together as well. From time to time, Spot sailed by steamboat to Shanghai to reunite with his parents. The Holt brothers often called by the Tivoli theatre seeking news of their father. When Tom Holt was back in Melbourne, they collected their pocket money from him there.

Early in 1925, Cliffie Holt turned fifteen. He decided to take up an offer from Uncle Marty to work in Sydney as a journalist on *Everyone's* magazine. His brother, though surrounded by many friends, must have been disappointed to learn that his only sibling would no longer be at Wesley.

Soon after Cliffie's departure, Harold was confronted with a new anxiety. Though she had only just turned forty, his mother was seriously ill. Now his tenuous link with her was about to be cut permanently. His school friends knew that his mother was unwell, and concluded that his recent absence from school could be explained by this. After Harold returned to school, a friend enquired, as casually as he could: 'How's your mother?'

'She's dead,' was his curt reply.

So that was that. None of Harold's friends said any more about the matter. Harold had received the news from Sydney that, in the early hours of Thursday 2 July, his mother had 'quietly passed away' from pneumonia, after 'a very brief illness'. On Wednesday she had still been alive; on Thursday she was dead; on Friday she was buried. There was no time for Harold to travel from Melbourne to Sydney for the funeral. He had seen little of his mother since moving to Wesley. She had flickered in and out of his life, and now the flickering flame had gone out. One death notice stated that she was remembered for 'her manifold kindnesses and personal charity'.

Harold's aunt Vera was on the other side of the world, as was his maternal grandmother, and his brother Cliffie was in Sydney. Harold had relatives nearby, but their homes were not his. He celebrated his seventeenth birthday on 5 August in the boarding house, which was familiar, but without the warmer, more intimate comforts of a family home.

In learning to adapt to bereavement, he was acquiring the habit of taking things as a matter of course, willing himself to go on and to give his energies to the world around him. Besides, he lived in a country and in a school which valued stoicism. So he struggled on, enjoying his relationships with his peers and teachers, for here was his home now. But he wished that he and Cliffie had more photographs of their mother to keep alive the memory of the time they had shared.

Sometimes throughout the school holidays he remained at Wesley; sometimes he stayed with relatives in Nubba or with Uncle Marty and Aunt Ethel in Sydney. Tom Holt, though still alive, was largely absent from his son's life. Perhaps Harold felt a pang of longing when the gathered school reached the final verse of 'Lord, Behold Us With Thy Blessing', the hymn which welcomed each new term:

Keep the spell of home affection
Still alive in every heart;
May its power, with mild direction,
Draw our love from self apart,
Till thy children, till thy children
Feel that Thou their father art.

* * *

Having been elected form captain in most of his years at Wesley, Harold had originally set his heart on being senior prefect, but resolved to play his part as deputy – until Mr Adamson called him into his study one morning to impart some news.

The headmaster's study inspired awe. It was crammed with classical antiques, paintings and sculptures, so many that they nudged against each other, as if jostling for space. Bric-à-brac covered every horizontal surface. On the walls hung paintings: a still life of wattle in a vase, an English rural scene of a lake and hills, and a triptych. An antique glass-enclosed cabinet teeming with weighty tomes occupied almost the entire length of one wall. On top of the cabinet were antique vases, both oriental and European, and a row of sepia photographs. On the wide timber desk lay piles of yellowing papers held in place with a stone paperweight, and a silver tray supported by legs and containing pens, pencils and bottles of ink.

Here Mr Adamson explained to him that Spot Turnbull was sailing to China to visit his family, and that while he was absent from school he wanted Holt to be school captain. Even if he was technically only acting captain, Harold must have been delighted to be recognised for his good character, ability and devotion to the school.

In the study balmed with the scent of Turkish cigarettes, the headmaster and the acting school captain sat and talked. Barney the Airedale, Adamson's current canine companion, nuzzled his head against his master's trouser leg.

Perhaps they talked about Kipling, Harold speaking of his fondness for his poem 'If', a literary example of Victorian era Stoicism which took the form of paternal advice to the poet's son John, including the injunction to 'fill the unforgiving minute / With sixty seconds worth of distance run'.

School Speech Night for 1926 was held at the concert hall in the eight-storey Auditorium building near the top of Collins Street. This was a special occasion, for it marked the close of Mr Adamson's twenty-fifth year as headmaster. He thought of it as his 'silver wedding'.

Harold had been named Alexander Wawn Scholar and was to be presented with this award during the evening. Each year, the honour was bestowed on a sixth-form boy who had best attained, in equal measure, outstanding achievement in the areas of academic work, sport and general character. As acting school captain, Harold had two main tasks at Speech Night: to present the headmaster with a Wedgwood vase, and to sing a solo, the School Leaving Song.

As a boy with ambitions to become a public man, this would be part of his education for the role. But as the night of his public appearance drew near, he realised that no one from his family would be present to acknowledge him.

To mark his silver anniversary, Harold presented the headmaster with some specimens of old silver, including a Queen Anne paten and tankard from 1712 and a George III salver from 1779. Mr Adamson was touched by these symbols of the school's esteem, saying that 'usually presentations such as these are embarrassing, but these plates and this vase are so beautiful that they overcome my embarrassment.' Harold felt the headmaster's warm hand in his as he presented him with the vase, but it was a poor substitute for the presence of a blood relation.

Finally his turn to sing arrived. All evening he had felt anxious about this moment, his nervousness deepening as the minutes passed. He felt the absence of the faces of family members to encourage him, but he dived deep into his own reserves of courage as he sang the words:

Adieu, adieu old school, adieu, adieu
And if I never more see you, see you
Although the time has come for us to part
You've still your corner in my heart.

The words were cloying, but to him they were true. Wesley had supported him when he most needed it and so he sang with conviction. But as he stared out into the sea of faces, people almost all secure in their family bonds, he longed to have someone present who shared a corner in his own heart.

Standing on stage, Harold felt the drift towards isolation, and he never forgot the feeling of loneliness he experienced that night. He took with him the applause of the audience and the certificate which was tangible evidence of the esteem in which he was held. But he left the auditorium alone, set apart from his classmates and their warm family groups.

4

Harold and Zara

When I was a child I was simply mad about any sort of physical
beauty, or what I considered physical beauty, and my parents were
endlessly kind.

—Zara Holt, *My Life and Harry*

AFTER GRADUATING FROM WESLEY, HOLT FOLLOWED
the path taken by many of the school's alumni and became
a resident of Queen's College, a Methodist-run residential
college attached to the University of Melbourne. The young men
of the college were known as Wyverns, after the mythical beast.
From Wesley, Johnnie Busst, John Cumpston and Spot Turnbull all
followed Holt to Queen's. As he had long intended, he enrolled to
study Law.

Although life at Queen's was constrained by the rules of the
Methodist Church, such as a ban on all forms of alcohol, it was a
freer, more mature version of life at Wesley. The college was widely
known for housing young theologians intending to enter the Methodist ministry, but there were also students of many other disciplines,
such as Medicine, in which Turnbull enrolled, Engineering, Arts,
Science and, of course, Law. Women students, known as Wyvernas,
were not allowed to live at the college, but could attend meetings and
tutorials as non-residents.

Holt shared a room with Johnnie Busst, who was studying Arts
and Journalism. Through his friend's influence, Holt's interest in the
fine arts began to develop. They also shared an interest in sports.

Holt was a competent tennis player, but Busst was the champion and captain of the college team. He was also becoming a source of amusement to others because of his dogged campaign for the installation of a second toilet in the college's south wing. When it was finally installed, the Sports and Social Club named it in his honour, attaching a plaque naming it The Johnnie Busst Memorial Lavatory.

Cumpston and Turnbull joined the college rowing crew and Holt the cricket and football teams. Wesley alumni had scored the trifecta: Turnbull was captain of rowing, Busst of tennis, and Holt of cricket. Holt opened the batting and was a handy bowler. As a batsman, he had the dubious honour of being run out in both innings of one match – indeed, he was dismissed more often than usual in this way. As a footballer, he was again anchored in the back pocket, as he had been at Wesley.

Posing for photos in his striped college blazer made of fine Florentine cotton, he was prepossessingly handsome. Now that he had crossed the frontier of adolescence, he looked less like a boy and more like a man. The boy was still visible in the smile which exposed his uncapped, bright white teeth, but the man was emerging in the eyes that looked out into the world with greater certainty. He was trying to follow Kipling's injunction to 'fill the unforgiving minute with sixty seconds worth of distance run'. He followed Aunt Vera's advice and tried himself out as an actor in college plays, such as A.A. Milne's short farce *The Man in the Bowler Hat*, in which he played one of the lovers.

One night, when Holt was in his first year at the university, his old school friend Norman Mussen arranged to pick him up in his car to attend a dance in the city. The collection point was the corner of Toorak and St Kilda roads, south of the CBD, near the bluestone buildings of Melbourne Grammar. While Holt waited, the familiar green trams trundled past in both directions.

Finally, with a peremptory honk, Mussen's tiny Morris car pulled up. Although the car was designed for only two, three were already squeezed into it – the driver and two young women, one of whom was perched on the hood at the back. Holt's attention at once gravitated to the other woman, who was sitting in the front seat. This was Zara Dickins, one of Mussen's current girlfriends.

As a result of a seating rearrangement, Harold and Zara ended up sitting together on the hood at the back of the car. They both felt the electricity as their smiles met and connected. Zara was wearing Norman's top hat. Harold soon saw that she had a flamboyant streak and a strong measure of *joie de vivre*. Like him, she had a sense of theatricality, but the role she played was always herself. They had each been brought up to value graciousness and consideration towards others. Each enjoyed the other's sense of humour; each released the other's springs of happiness. They were both disarming in their friendliness, welcoming others with the warmth of their smiles. Zara's extraversion cut through her more private side, though she often guarded this.

Both were in their late teenage years, just seven months apart in age. Zara, slightly the younger, had both the youthfulness of a teenager and the worldliness of a mature woman. She seemed to know who she was and what she was about. At the core of her being she had a sense of fun, a spirit slightly off-kilter. Her face was never still, for she talked with her eyes, which danced, and with her mouth, which creased readily into a smile.

Her voice seemed to emerge from somewhere at the back of her throat. Often it floated above the trouble of the world, in clear, light brushstrokes. Her speech was chatty and unfiltered; she often spoke without weighing her words. When she was excited, her words emerged with a gush; when she was surprised, there was a hint of a gasp.

Under this slightly daffy exterior, she was anchored by a steadiness born of feeling comfortable in her own skin. As Harold seemed not always comfortable in his, he may have sensed that some of her sense of security would rub off on him. She had the amplitude and affection of a warm, nurturing mother. Her new friend aroused her latent maternal instincts; sympathy stirred within her when she learned that his mother was dead, his brother in Sydney and his father in London. She warmed to his robust good cheer which had already survived many challenges.

For the rest of the night Zara forgot about Norman as she and Harold spent almost the entire time together. She had started the evening by taking Norman's top hat and wearing it; by the end of it she had returned the hat but thrown over its owner for Harold.

Harold may have hoped that he could fill the gap left by his mother's death with Zara's vital, living presence. He suffered from the lack of a stable home with the intimacy and attention which Zara and so many others like her had taken for granted as children. It may have appeared to an observer that she had been overprotected in her early childhood, cosseted while being homeschooled. But this was her choice – she had managed to impose her own will on her parents, Sydney and Violet Dickins. She disliked school, she said, because she liked to dream, and the school authorities disapproved of dreamers. So a governess took charge of her earliest learning, and later Zara attended Ruyton Girls School in the comfortable middle-class Melbourne suburb of Kew.

The Dickins family was prosperous, for Sydney Dickins owned a successful chain of supermarkets in Melbourne that carried the family name. The family house at 17 Ridgeway Avenue was an elegant Queen Anne–style residence with an ornate facade, classically adorned hallway, plenty of living space and a sun-filled garden. Living there must have deepened Zara's feeling for beauty.

Zara had grown up confident that she and her way of seeing the world were validated. She was grateful to her parents for their endless kindness in encouraging her and her siblings to develop their own personalities. She had been shy, but she had conquered her shyness, as her parents showed her how to give herself to others. Close to her heart and her inward eye she held the image of them walking in their garden near the end of the day, arms entwined in a statement of unity and love.

When she left school, Zara wanted to become a painter. 'I haven't got an exercise book that isn't drawn all over,' she said. Harold told her about his friend Johnnie Busst and his artistic aspirations. It was clear that he found artistic types attractive: Johnnie and Zara with their painting, Aunt Vera with her acting.

Zara sought patterns of order and beauty in her art, perhaps seeking to replicate the image of stability modelled by her parents. She was finding it difficult to make her mark in the art world, but lately she had developed ambitions to start a career as a designer and manufacturer of women's clothing, where she saw artistry and beauty, too. Often she found ideas for clothing in the natural world, weaving them into the patterns of her designs. Clothes were not just about appearance; they could also make a spiritual statement, gracing the earthly with touches of the ethereal.

From the beginning of her life, Zara had tried to surround herself with the beautiful, seeking it wherever she went. At the age of four, she had painstakingly cut the tulips from her mother's bedspread, one by one, and then pasted them on her bedroom wall.

Her father claimed to be distantly related to Charles Dickens, the famous novelist. This, she told Harold, was why he had a love of storytelling. Somewhere in the years between Charles Dickens' life and his, the *e* in the surname must have been changed to an *i*. Perhaps the story was apocryphal. But, whatever the truth, she was already showing something of the flair and imagination of a creative artist. Charles Dickens would have found her interesting, perhaps writing her into one of his novels.

She had something else in common with her near namesake: like him, she had developed the habit, wherever she went, of looking at the world around her. The novelist used his eyes to imprint on his mind an ever-growing gallery of characters and scenes; the future clothing designer and manufacturer used hers to create patterns and designs. Already she had developed unusual powers of observation, which her parents cultivated by stopping the car many times during a journey to allow her to look at something she had noticed along the way.

In one of the family photographs of Zara as a child, she and her sister Genevieve were decked out in identical white lace dresses and black polished shoes, sitting side by side on a small settee decorated with gold brocade stripes. 'Vieve' was older and looked it, but their faces were so similar that they could readily have been taken for twins, as could Harold and Cliffie.

Each had dark hair with pigtails, and their little legs dangled from the settee. The expression on Zara's face was dreamy, but also suggested a growing sense of purpose, as if she were waiting to give something of herself to the wider world beyond that sitting room. Her face had a sweetness that said she would do no harm, but also a firmness that said she would not endure harm either.

Speaking of her parents, she said that 'they taught me manners, how to be nice to people, how to cultivate them and get along with them. I used to be shy. But after I learned to get along with people I got over that.'

Harold and Zara began to seek out each other's company increasingly, going out together four times a week. But Harold seemed to think of his time with her as less than permanent: 'You'll do me for a few weeks,' he told her.

This was not wholly encouraging. Even if his tongue was somewhere in his cheek, he may have been stating truthfully something about himself. He was not ready to give himself to any one person. But Zara liked the way he was always cheerful, good-natured and happy. They were both that way.

They were keen partygoers who enjoyed social life. Some evenings they went to a play at one of Melbourne's theatres or dined at one of their regular haunts, Florentino's restaurant near the top of Bourke Street. For half a crown they could buy a three-course meal with wine. But with the Depression on, money was scarce for a student like Harold. His budget was two pounds a week. To economise, he usually walked back from the city to his room at Queen's, a much shorter walk than the one from the Dickins' house in Kew, through Studley Park, to Collingwood and Richmond and thence to the city.

Once while he was returning home late in the evening, Holt was startled to see a young man's body hanging from one of the

41

gum trees in Studley Park. There had been an alarming upsurge in suicides after the onset of the Depression. Perhaps this man had been the breadwinner of a family and had become unemployed and unable to endure the shame of no longer being able to provide.

Holt dealt with jarring events such as these by returning as soon as possible to the flow of life. There were always new activities in which to engage. He became a member of the 'High Court', a group of senior Law students who sat under the window at the west end of the university library and occasionally handed out advice to new students, such as, 'Now, the way I always failed at Property Law was to . . .'

Cecil Gribble, a fellow resident of Queen's, who was studying for an Arts degree while a candidate for the Methodist Ministry, found Holt to be friendly, likeable and sociable, even to the extent of neglecting his studies. But Gribble observed that Holt, though not brilliant, had a quick, able brain. On one occasion Holt borrowed some notes of Gribble's, read them quickly and swept through the examination based upon them.

Gribble observed that Holt, though outspoken, argued with a smile, even if he disagreed with the person with whom he was discussing an issue. Given Holt's interest in ideas and current affairs, it was not surprising that he joined the Willie Quick Club, the college debating society. He became known as an orator, developing a light, engaging style of speech, enlivened with touches of humour. His voice was pleasant and well modulated and his diction sometimes sparkled with oratorical flourishes. He had a reputation for rising to the occasion, as he did when he defended college initiation activities and won over a sceptical audience. Against Trinity College he and his fellow debaters sought to argue 'That life is not worth living', but they failed to convince the Rector of Newman College, who awarded the debate to Trinity.

Holt represented Melbourne University in the annual Intervarsity debates, opposing the motion 'That the cinema is pernicious'. This time, the adjudicator awarded the debate to his team. Holt had the benefit of personal knowledge of the topic, which, given his family background, was probably of special interest. When Queen's visited Trinity to oppose the motion 'That modern civilisation is headed for disaster', he was praised for his contribution: 'The outstanding feature of this debate was the concluding speech of Mr Holt, who impressed most favourably each of the adjudicators.'

In 1930 he won the Queen's College Oratory Award – a handsome gold medal. At Queen's, he was preparing for a wider stage, while making a solid impression among his peers. He could win people over with his disarming friendliness and ability to understand viewpoints unlike his own. He put himself forward as a candidate for president of the College Sports and Social Club and was elected. Now his name was carved in golden letters on the honour board of the student common room for all, present and future, to see. In a life composed so much of the temporary, this was something permanent.

His political acumen as a negotiator began to show. He and Johnnie Busst were two of the four representatives on the At Home subcommittee, formed to initiate social events at the college. At Home had run into difficulty over reports that alcohol had been consumed at one of the meetings, a serious matter in a college run by a bastion of temperance like the Methodist Church. So Holt brought along a theology student to meet with the master and got him to affirm that he had seen no evidence of drinking. The master was happy to let the matter rest, though perhaps not entirely convinced. Tactful interventions like this built Holt's popularity and confidence as a negotiator.

Often he talked with Zara about his plans for the future, after he had finished his studies and qualified as a solicitor. This would be the first step into a life of politics. When there was talk between them about getting married, he warned her, 'I'm not interested in making money. Never think you're going to have any. I don't care about it. If I've got it, I spend it.'

If Harold had little ambition to make money, Zara would have to be the one to do so. She was ready to step out into the world, and she felt she could make her mark in fashion. Her friend Betty James, who had played opposite Harold in *The Man in the Bowler Hat*, shared her interest in this field, and they decided to go into business together. Before that could happen, Zara had to work hard to convince her father to lend her the 150 pounds she needed. Though he thought it foolish to enter such a chancy business, Zara persisted, and eventually he yielded. 'I harried him into giving me the money,' she told her friends. With Betty James, she opened a dress shop in Little Collins Street, in the centre of town. For a young woman just short of nineteen, this was a bold move.

* * *

Though Holt was short of money, he had much else to give and politics was where he felt he could give it. Wesley had emphasised the importance of service to one's community and the responsibility of the privileged to give to the less well-off. 'From him to whom much is given, much will be required', ran the scripture from the Gospel of St Luke often quoted in Methodist institutions. In politics you could help people in their daily lives, make a difference, and thus give and receive at the same time. Besides, he liked the theatre and in politics he could occupy centre stage.

He won his Law degree, left Queen's College and moved into a small flat at 2 Parliament Place, Melbourne, at the top end of Bourke Street. He shared these lodgings with Johnnie Busst and Arthur Munday, his aspiring artist friends, each of them paying two pounds a week for rent. Holt served his articles with the law firm Fink, Best and Miller, while Busst and Munday set out to find their place in the art world.

Holt set himself up in his own practice as a solicitor. His rooms were just one block south of the lodgings he shared with Busst and Munday, at the top end of Collins Street, where plane trees formed a canopy above the street, creating an interplay of light and shade along its length from east to west. This was an auspicious setting, but it was an inauspicious time to establish himself in a new occupation. With the world in a depression, it was hard to secure briefs when potential clients had little money to spend on solicitors.

Short of money, Holt moved to a nearby boarding house. Those of his friends who could afford to take sympathy on him in his straitened circumstances came to visit with ready-made meals. Though money was tight, he was cavalier about it. If you had life, you lived it; if you had money, you spent it. He followed that pattern even as a hard-up student. The temptation of the horse races was irresistible; when he had a few extra quid, he went to Flemington for a punt. The element of risk got his adrenalin pumping. He started to become known around the racetracks, more for his charm than for his success.

Both Holt brothers were strengthening their connections in the entertainment industry. With the assistance of his father, Cliffie secured the role of publicity officer for Hoyts theatres, a role which enabled him to provide Harold with complimentary tickets to the cinema – one of his passions. Harold became Secretary of the Victorian Cinematograph Exhibitors Association, the lobby group for the film industry, appearing several times in this capacity before the Commonwealth Court of Conciliation and Arbitration. At last he had a role which helped him in his law practice, as he started to make a name for himself.

Meanwhile, Johnnie Busst and Arthur Munday had joined with Justus Jorgensen to start construction of a new colony for artists at Eltham, in Melbourne's outer north. The builders used mudbrick, granite, limestone and bluestone. Set among lush gardens, the colony, named Montsalvat, grew into a place with more than a dozen buildings.

For his part, Holt was determined to make politics his long-term career. At school he had shown that he was leadership material. People had confidence in him, while he had the confidence to organise people and the solicitude to look after their interests. He talked to Zara about the things he wanted to do if he won a seat in parliament: 'There are so many things that should be done in this country. It's a wonderful country, and we've got to open it up, expand it.' For her part, Zara had her own ideas about what should be done in Australia:

> The government should pay to protect people from the costs of the different stages of life – I mean, infancy, childhood, sickness, old age and death. It should raise taxes to pay for the costs, and everyone in the country would share the burden. That way, the wage or salary earners would have money free to spend on the fun things of life.

He questioned these ideas. He thought they sounded dangerously close to socialism, a philosophy which had appealed to him at one stage of his thinking, until he studied it carefully and rejected it. 'If you ran things that way,' he concluded, 'you'd end up breeding a race of shiftless men and women.' His old school's motto encouraged people to act wisely; in keeping with that, he intended to promote policies which he felt made good sense.

* * *

Meanwhile, Tom Holt had returned from London to become the right-hand man of Frank Thring, a theatrical impresario, speculator and now manager of Efftee Studios – a new filmmaking company whose title Thring had derived from his own initials. Thring sold his large holdings in the Hoyts theatre chain to Fox Film Corporation and sank his personal fortune into Efftee, banking on it becoming Australia's first 'talkies' studio.

Given the context of the stock market crash in October 1929 and the world depression which followed, this was a huge gamble, but Thring trusted that Efftee would transform the role of motion pictures in Australia. He chose a distinctly Australian logo for his company – a koala munching on a sprig of eucalyptus. This endearing marsupial was clearly based on Blinky Bill, the anthropomorphic central character of Dorothy Wall's recent children's book *Blinky Bill: The Quaint Little Australian*. Thring asked Tom Holt to become general manager of Efftee. He then sent the already well-connected Holt to America, armed with a cheque book to buy recording equipment and to bring back directors of comedies and dramas, as well as up-to-date knowledge of what was happening in the motion picture industry.

Through his connections in the theatrical world, Harold Holt had come to know Thring's daughter Viola, known universally as Lola, and although he still was involved with Zara, the two began to date. Three years younger than Harold, Lola was a handsome rather than beautiful young woman, slightly gawky and unusually tall, towering over most women and many men. She was reserved, and innocent in the ways of the world.

Like Harold, Lola had suffered bereavement early in life. Her mother, Grace, died when her daughter was only nine. Until then, Lola had lived with her mother and her maternal grandparents in the South Australian town of Gawler, 450 miles away from her father in Melbourne.

Barely three months after his bereavement, Frank remarried. At once Lola was dispatched to Melbourne to live with her father and his new wife, Olive Kreitmayer, who resented the presence of her stepdaughter. Lola had little time to grieve before having to navigate a new life with this formidable and domineering woman. Olive's influence pushed Lola to the margins of her new family, and she spent most of her time, including holidays, as a boarder at St Catherine's, an Anglican school for girls in Heyington Place, one of the most desirable addresses in Toorak. St Catherine's became her de facto family, as Wesley had been Harold's. Frank and Olive soon left Australia for their honeymoon, leaving Lola to celebrate her tenth birthday at school.

Lola's experience of childhood and adolescence had certain similarities with Harold's. Both had lost a parent early in life; both had gone to boarding school; both had been popular with their peers, were sporty and enthusiastic about school activities. A head taller than most of the other girls, Lola made herself useful in basketball, netball, baseball and tennis.

But perhaps more than anything else, Lola and Harold had shared a lonely childhood marked by the loss of a mother and by the hunger for a closer relationship with a physically and emotionally unavailable father. Both were driven by a need to fill these deep emotional gaps.

Like Harold, Lola dabbled in theatre, strengthening her connection with her father through this interest. For her eighteenth birthday present, he invited her to accompany him on a business trip to the United States, where they visited film sets and watched auditions together. As a bonus, Frank allotted some time for travel in England and France.

Lola was becoming far more actively involved in her father's career than was her stepmother. Thring rewarded her with the position of editor for Efftee, and she quickly learned her work on the cutting room floor. Her father's cameraman, Arthur Higgins, was duly impressed – rather than nepotism, employing Lola turned out to be sound business. She was present at the Sydney opening of two films – *A Co-Respondent's Course* and *Diggers, Everyone* – at the Hotel Australia, when Tom Holt invited some film and newspaper people to supper. Lola had won her father's attention at last. She wanted never to lose it again.

* * *

After a few years, operating her business had run Zara down. She loved having the shop and was pleased that the human interactions forced upon her had helped her overcome her shyness, but eventually the work drained her. Her mother was with her in the shop one morning when a prospective customer walked in. Presumably seeking to protect her daughter from any further work, Mrs Dickins walked up and slammed the door on the customer, declaring that 'this shop is closed'. The force of her mother's response made its mark on Zara, as she never forgot the woman's face.

Zara sold the business, emerging with a handy profit of £1500. Though she had bought herself some freedom for a while, her heart was still set on Harold, but it was not long until she found out that he was seeing Lola Thring, among other young women. She was furious. Apparently he had not been joking when he had told her that she would do him for just 'a few weeks'. While she wept copiously, he retreated to his law books, adding fury to her distress.

Zara was prepared to be a solid fixture in his life, but Harold gave her some terse advice: 'Go away and stand on your own two feet.' She marshalled the energy she was spending in anger and channelled it into the wider world, using some of the profits from the business to buy a passage to the United States on the new American passenger ship *Monterey*. She loved the wallpaper on the ship, pale green and patterned with white magnolias. She bought a round-the-world ticket, intending to disembark in London.

On her way home from there, she met a young English cavalry officer stationed with his regiment in India as a representative of the British Raj. Tall, with a long, angular face and good looks, Colonel James Fell possessed some of the qualities of the ideal Boy Scout: willingness to help out others, practical skills and general know-how. At the same time, he had a sense of fun and enjoyment which resonated with Zara's. He was about five years older than she, not a vast difference, but enough, she felt, to give him an edge in experience over her.

If she had felt sure of a solid future with Harold, she may not have looked twice at this man. But there she was, away from home, free and ready to stand on her own two feet. James Fell was to leave the ship at Bombay to rejoin his regiment. He wired his Commanding Officer's wife, who invited both of them to spend some time with her and her husband in their quarters at Poona.

Zara jumped ship and began her first, brief sojourn in India. Fell proposed to her. It was all quite sudden and unexpected. She wired her family with the news. 'Wiser come home,' they wired back.

When Harold greeted her at Port Melbourne he was happy enough to learn of her shipboard romance. Such liaisons were common among travellers, but they seldom lasted long. He told her that this one had better not last long either: 'You're not going to see that Indian type again. If you do, you'll never see me again.'

Another row followed. Before the sparks had settled, Zara had resumed contact with her 'Indian type'. From Jubbulpore, in the state of Madya Pradesh where his cavalry regiment was stationed, he stepped ashore in Sydney for a week's holiday and went off whistling in the rain. He regaled the local press with a brief report of the high spots of his holiday:

> Your weather really is wonderful. Went to the races in Adelaide. Never been so cold in my life. Got wet through, too. Marvellous. You see, in Jubbulpore, at the best of times it is very, very hot.

The real high spot of James Fell's holiday was his wedding. He and Zara were married with Congregational forms at Kew on 4 May 1935. Two days later, the Melbourne newspaper *The Argus* reported that this wedding had been 'quietly celebrated' and that the newlyweds would leave Melbourne for India the following day, sailing in the British ocean liner *Maloja*.

It was indeed hot at Jubbulpore. Later, the couple moved much further south to Meerut, in Uttar Pradesh state, about forty miles north-east of Delhi, where early in the previous century the British had built a large cantonment. Restless ghosts haunted this place, for the initial uprisings of the Indian Mutiny of 1857 had occurred there, when some sepoys attacked and killed their British officers before marching on Delhi.

Once in India, Zara felt she had entered a volume of Kipling. Harold had encountered that writer at Wesley through L.A. Adamson; now Zara was encountering him through Colonel Fell. Sometimes she must have felt as if she had been suddenly transplanted into the life of a quite different person.

The heat wore her down. From time to time, the sky suddenly turned black and the monsoonal rains swept in, soaking and bringing relief to all in their wake. But then the heat returned.

Her fellow Anglo-Saxons also wore her down. She was troubled by the arrogance, the born-to-rule mentality and the insular mindset of the British. It was clear to her that they hated India and were contented only in the small Anglo-enclaves they had created. Zara, too, felt exiled from her peers. Her husband shared the arrogance of most of the British colonial masters, and Zara felt the need to escape the net of prejudice in which he was caught. She liked the Indians, but she was troubled by their poverty and sense of hopelessness, and she was angered by the caste system. The idea that some people could be classed as 'untouchables' seemed to her an act of mental cruelty.

Her parents had taught her to get along with people wherever they were and to make herself useful. But in her exile she must have thought nostalgically of home, of her parents and siblings, and of Harold. The time they had spent together had been more than an interlude, a self-contained episode; it had to be stitched back into the wider integrity of her life. The man who occupied the special corner in her heart was not her husband.

Around Christmas, before she had completed a year in India, she found that she was pregnant. She decided to return to Melbourne to have her baby and show it to her family. Seeing Harold again must also have been foremost on her mind.

5

Third Time Lucky

It is not often that one has an opponent as able, as courteous and as decent as you were, and I wish you well in the future.
—John Cremean, Harold Holt's opponent in the State Election, 1935

WHILE ZARA FELL WAS STARTING A NEW LIFE AS AN Australian wife in India, Harold Holt was seeking a new career as a member of parliament. He brought to his quest certain advantages, both innate and acquired. Press reports credited him with having all his father's charm and good looks, as well as being a smooth ballroom dancer and a shrewd bridge player. Though below average height, he had a beautiful physique and a tanned face which beamed with robust health. Aunt Vera had told him that he had the qualities necessary to make a career of theatre: 'You've got the figure, the voice and the looks.'

As for his looks, in some quarters he was now known as Handsome Harold. But although he enjoyed the theatre, it held no glamour for him as an occupation, for he had already seen too much of its hard side when visiting his father at the Tivoli.

He was aiming to make his debut on a wider stage. His face was that of a man who felt much more secure about his place in the world. His hair gleamed like the sun on the surface of the ocean and his sartorial sense enhanced his good looks. His smile was enchanting when the line of his lips curved upwards and set his white teeth flashing.

For him, the practice of law and advocacy for the Cinematograph Exhibitors was a sideline to the main show – his campaign to win a seat in parliament. When he had first became interested in politics, he leaned towards joining the Labor Party. Some who knew him described him as 'parlour pink', a socialist or fellow traveller with socialism. But his political views were not yet fully formed, and his political leaning shifted. He became friendly with a young Law graduate named Douglas Menzies, who took him to a meeting of the Young Nationalists Association at Healesville, north of Melbourne.

There he met Douglas's cousin Robert Menzies, a rising figure in Australia's second major party, the United Australia Party. He discovered that Menzies had been a star pupil at Wesley College a decade or so before he had been there himself. Menzies had come to Wesley from the small Victorian country town of Jeparit and made a lasting impression, having his name displayed in golden letters on the school honour boards after becoming Dux of Humanities for 1912. At school, he showed outstanding skill as an orator and a deep love of literature and language. He had a prodigious memory which enabled him within the space of a few weeks to memorise between 8000 and 9000 lines of Shakespeare.

Menzies made a powerful first impression on Holt. He was fourteen years older and endowed with an imposing physique, a formidable personality and immense self-assurance. Here was a man under whose tutelage Holt could learn the art of politics and make his entry into that profession. Impressed not only by Menzies but by what he saw as the United Australia Party's easy tolerance of all political beliefs, Holt joined the Prahran branch of the party. Soon he was ready to take the plunge as a candidate. As was the usual practice with aspiring politicians, he had to cut his teeth by standing in a seat that safely belonged to Labor.

The next federal election was set for 1934, and the safe Labor seat which the party had chosen for Holt to contest was Yarra, held by the former prime minister James Scullin. Holding power in the midst of the Great Depression, his Labor government had been routed in the previous federal election.

For Holt, there were the inevitable outdoor meetings with audiences of workmen in hats and overcoats. He campaigned at midday meetings in downtown Melbourne, speaking against a background of solid opposition, gaining practice in dealing with interjectors, one of whom he successfully challenged to debate the problem of unemployment.

He took the inevitable defeat in his stride. In March 1935, he made his next attempt. A vacancy had arisen in the state parliament, to be filled in a by-election. This was another safe Labor seat, Clifton Hill in Melbourne's inner north. He lost again, but he won the admiration of his opponent John Cremean who, with a warm handwritten note, thanked him for the exemplary manner in which he fought the campaign.

By now he had jumped through the hoops of two campaigns. Upon the death of George Maxwell, a lawyer and the member for the electorate of Fawkner, another opportunity arose. As an inexperienced young lawyer, Holt had made his first appearance at the bar as a junior to Maxwell, and he remembered gratefully the courtesy and consideration he had shown him; now he was chosen as the UAP candidate to replace him. Fawkner included the prosperous suburbs of Prahran, Malvern, Caulfield and South Yarra, making it one of the UAP's safest seats. The by-election was set for 17 August, just after his twenty-seventh birthday.

The third-time candidate campaigned from the back of a motor truck, enjoying good-humoured badinage with interjectors in the audience, developing one of his favourite forms of debate.

'During the Depression —' the candidate began.

A burly man in shirt sleeves interjected, reminding the candidate of his youth.

'You were at school then,' he taunted.

'I hope I learned more than you,' the candidate rejoined.

The shirt-sleeved interjector was undeterred: 'You are one of those parliamentary parasites!'

'Thanks. I am not in parliament yet,' the candidate shot back, 'but your assurance of success is welcome.'

Within a matter of days, he was indeed in parliament. At twenty-seven, he held one of his party's safest seats. On the Monday following the election he smiled at the newspaper's headline: 'Well done, Harold!'

But he did not see himself as an antipodean Franklin Roosevelt, the president whose 'New Deal' promised sweeping social reforms for the United States. Holt's goals were modest: 'I have no New Deal to take to Canberra but there are many problems facing parliament and I am particularly interested in that connection with the employment of youths.'

*　*　*

Canberra now became Holt's new home, at least during the periods of the year when parliament was sitting. Like Washington, DC, Canberra is an artificial city whose construction arose from a dispute about where the national capital should be situated. After Federation in 1901, Melbourne became the temporary Australian capital, with Sydney also laying claims to the honour. To settle the dispute, the new city was created from a slice of bushland which had previously been a sheep station, about 180 miles south-west of Sydney.

The idea was to use the intrinsic beauty of the natural world as a backdrop to the new city. The new Parliament House, opened in May 1927 by the Duke and Duchess of York, was built in neo-classical style and was demure in appearance. So too were the new hotels, the Canberra and the Kurrajong, built to accommodate the influx of politicians and other public servants. Such buildings looked like intruders in the rural setting. The air was the cool fresh air of the mountain country; the dominant scent was of eucalypt trees, some slender, some imposing, with branches spreading in all directions, providing homes for the families of birds which flourished in the area, such as magpies, white cockatoos and galahs.

On the edge of the parkland beside Kings Crescent stood an enormous bunya pine tree, planted to commemorate the visit of the

Duke and Duchess of York. Forty metres high, with a dead-straight trunk and symmetrical dome-shaped crown, it embodied the permanence which the new national capital was intended to acquire.

For many of the politicians who now found their new home here, Canberra might well have felt like the site of a school camp in their childhood days, or perhaps a boarding house. So it might have seemed for the new member for Fawkner, as he set himself up in the Hotel Canberra. In the early days of Washington, DC, a posting to that city afforded a hardship allowance. There was no such allowance for public servants in Canberra, lonely and isolated though they may have felt. But Harold Holt was used to boarding houses. The chance of a settled home with Zara had escaped him, but he had what he wanted most of all – a safe seat in the national parliament.

6

New Connections

He was brave and foolhardy and took everything as a matter of course.

—Mabel Brookes, speaking of Harold Holt in
The Sydney Morning Herald, 19 December 1967

AROLD HOLT NOW HAD A NEW CAREER TO LEARN about; a new place of residence to get used to; new colleagues and opponents whose measure he had to take – in short, a new life. From time to time he took the train back to Melbourne to meet with his constituents and friends, including Lola Thring. But now that he was establishing himself in his new career there was less time to spend in social life.

In 1936, the year after Holt won his seat in parliament, Lola's father died after a short and sudden bout of cancer, aged only fifty-three. Lola was bereft, having lost, regained, and then lost again the most important man in her life.

After her father's death, her need for emotional support grew more pressing. Holt was mostly in Canberra, but his father was still very much on the scene. Lola must also have seen in Tom someone who could help fill the sudden gap in her life. Twenty-five years older than she – almost exactly twice her age – he was a ready-made father substitute. Besides, he was still handsome, though in a craggier way than Harold, with dark, wavy hair and piercing eyes.

By now, Cliff Holt was a prominent labour organiser in the theatre industry, and his father's responsibilities with Efftee had expanded. In 1935, Frank Thring acquired the Melbourne radio station 3XY for Efftee and asked Tom Holt to manage it. Its programs were provided by Efftee Broadcasters Pty Ltd, and its licence was held by the United Australia Party.

Tom Holt claimed to know not much about politics but everything about plays, and he knew how to make Lola feel as if she were centre stage in his life. More than anything, she needed a sense of security. Tom knew that as well as playing the role of substitute father he could make a satisfactory husband. He'd had plenty of experience as a suitor and fancied his chances with Lola.

So it was not really surprising that soon after he had begun to court her, she accepted his proposal of marriage. Her father was dead and her stepmother paid her little attention, but Tom could provide the security she craved. He had been one of her father's close associates, and she must have hoped that some of her memory of F.T. might be preserved in the form of his friend T.H. She appeared to have made a seamless transition from her father to a husband who held for her many of the characteristics of a father.

Tom was a smart operator with a proven record of success in a field which keenly interested Lola. For Tom, the marriage would probably be his last chance to make a match with an attractive young woman. For him, it must have represented a chance to erase some of the disappointment over his first marriage. At fifty, he was still handsome and charming. He shared with his elder son a reputation as a ladies' man, but Lola must have felt confident that at his age he was at last ready to settle down again.

Harold's situation was very awkward. His relationship with his father had never been close. Tom had been absent from much of Harold's life and now he had made his presence felt more strongly than ever in a way that disgusted his son. Harold found it grotesque that he now had a stepmother who was younger than he, and one with whom he had already been romantically involved. In politics, he favoured decisions and policies which to him made good sense, and this did not make good sense at all. When he had played cricket, bowlers had delivered him more than the odd 'curved ball', as a tricky ball was known in the jargon of that sport, but he could hardly have expected one like this.

With his brother, he attended the wedding and reception, but it must have been galling to endure these events in the presence of his father and his new bride. After the ceremony, the bride's stepmother, Mrs F.W. Thring, invited a few close friends to extend their congratulations to the couple at Rylands, her home in Toorak Road, Toorak.

After this occasion, Harold tried to avoid his father whenever he could. If he ever saw him in the city, he changed direction or crossed the street.

*   *   *

Though he was shaken by his father's new marriage, Harold's natural extroversion enabled him to enjoy the company of a widening circle of friends. Among these was Mabel Brookes, a prominent Melbourne socialite and charity worker, whom he had met at a meeting of the Young Nationalists. Her husband, Norman Brookes, had been a champion tennis player, the first left-hander to win Wimbledon. During the war, he was appointed Commissioner for the Australian branch of the British Red Cross in Cairo. In 1915, Mabel joined him and helped set up a rest home for nurses. Later she became a patron of good causes, especially those connected with the prevention of cruelty to children and animals.

She had a talent for arranging grand social functions and for befriending other people. Perhaps her physical amplitude reminded Harold of Zara, but as she was almost two decades older than he, her role in his life was less romantic than motherly. She and Norman had three young daughters, Cynthia, Elaine and Hersey, whom Harold sometimes escorted to social functions.

He often visited the Brookes family at their property, Cliff House, at Davey's Bay in the Mornington Peninsula town of Mount Eliza. To one of the local papers, Davey's Bay was 'the Mediterranean of the

Southern Hemisphere', known for the placidity of its water. In the late 1920s, the Brookes built an 'outdoor dance pavilion' on top of the cliffs over the bay, a favourite spot for 'romancing'.

There were tennis matches, dancing and swimming off Davey's Bay pier. Harold began his swims by diving off the jetty at the western end of the bay. As a swimmer, he was more enthusiastic than accomplished. Worried by his vigour, the Brookes girls kept an eye on him when he dived into the water. Their mother also worried when he swam out far and alone, which she considered brave, but careless, too.

Harold Holt admired the Wesley motto – *Sapere Aude*, dare to be wise – because you did often need daring to uphold the cause of wisdom. But sometimes daring and wisdom are strangers to each other, and wisdom means knowing your limits. Sometimes, recklessness lies just a step or two beyond daring.

Mabel Brookes had a warm spirit which cheered those who were touched by it, so that they eagerly returned to her. She was formidable but kindly, commanding but welcoming. Harold would talk and confide in her – on personal matters he said little, but he spoke to her as one political animal to another. Twice she had stood for parliament as a 'liberal conservative'. Perhaps she was inspired by Napoleon, for she was an avid collector of artefacts connected with him and was a student of his final period of exile at St Helena.

She did not consider Holt a brilliant person; she thought of him principally as a very popular and charming young man, fundamentally honest and a very good lawyer. She found him a little naive, despite his legal training.

He told her that 'politics is all I have'. Perhaps she wondered why a man who seemed to have so much – good looks, charisma, friends – saw the hazards of politics as his sole *raison d'être*. After all, if anything scuttled his political career he could always return to the law. He had endured more than his share of losses in his personal life to date, but why did he see the field of politics, strewn with the wounded and the defeated, as his salvation?

7

Accidental Father,
Accidental Lifesavers

*I certainly wasn't built for the job, but managed to stay the distance
and eventually had the twins. It was a wonderful thing to have the
three children, the same sex and so close in age. They were all blond
and sweet, and I seemed to live in a deluge of orange juice and nap-
kins. My husband came to Australia again, stayed for a few months
and then returned to India alone. So ended my first marriage.*

—Zara Holt, *My Life and Harry*

*Had it not been for those few wonderful Australians at a dinner
party in South Yarra . . . I and my family would have finished up
in the gas ovens of Auschwitz with my aunt, cousins and family
members.*

—Walter Glaser, *Australian Jewish News*, 10 May 2018

THE SEPARATION OF HAROLD AND ZARA TURNED OUT
to be a mere intermission in their relationship. Their connection had been intense, so it was not surprising that
eventually they stitched together the loosened threads.

In 1937, Zara returned to Melbourne to have her baby. On 22 September, Harold cut out and kept the notice from that day's personal
section of *The Age* newspaper, confirming that Mrs J.H. Fell had given
birth to a son at the Mercy Hospital. Now Zara was back on familiar ground with the people who had given her such solid emotional

support in her life before India. There were her parents and siblings, especially Genevieve, and, of course, Harold.

Her marriage was not wearing well. She had married in a hurry and her impulsiveness had ended in tears. It had been a sidetrack from the real source of her happiness. But at least she had a child from the union.

When Harold scrutinised the features of Nicholas, Zara's new baby, perhaps he had fleeting thoughts that this child, or one like him, could easily have been his, rather than the child of 'that Indian type'. But with Zara's marriage seeming unlikely to last, he had a second chance with her.

*　*　*

As a cinema enthusiast, Harold may well have seen his Aunt Vera on the screen, as she was starring in a new British comedy, *Please, Teacher*. She was paired with Bobby Howes, who was billed as the man who 'takes on all comers, even the mighty Vera Pearce'. A highlight of the film was the song-and-dance routine she performed, to the tune of the quaintly misspelt song 'Exsersise'. At this time, Pearce was also appearing live with Bobby Howes at the London Hippodrome, in the long-running musical comedy *Yes, Madam?*

By now, the world outside Australia – and beyond the entertainment industry – was also making its presence felt. The coming of Hitler and the Nazis in 1933 was destabilising Europe and causing anxiety in the world at large. For the first time since Holt had entered politics, foreign affairs were eclipsing domestic politics. With the annexation of Austria in March 1938, the situation grew dramatically worse.

One night in July of that year, Holt joined friends, including one named Fred Ashworth, for a dinner party in the inner suburb of South Yarra. The party was held at the Park Street home of Holt's constituents Beatrice and Clara Dacomb, sisters and single women in their seventies. They had been teachers of shorthand to young women and had created a simpler form of this, which they called Dacomb Shorthand, and which they taught at the school they had established – Dacomb College.

Fred Ashworth brought with him a letter written in German which he wanted the Dacomb sisters to translate, for both were fluent in that language. Working together, they conveyed the message of the letter writer to the assembled guests.

The author was a man named Johan Glaser, a keen trout fisher and a banker by profession. He claimed to be the only Jew in the Austrian Fishing Club, and explained that a man in this club had warned him to get out of Austria as quickly as possible. This man was an undercover Nazi and the newly appointed District Commissioner for the Germans.

In advising Mr Glaser to 'get out of Austria fast', the Nazi had warned him that

> You will be top of the invitees to Dachau. I reckon you've got about three to four weeks. I was able to remove your records from the police department, but even I have no jurisdiction over the duplicates that the Gestapo have.

The gist of the rest of the letter was that Johan Glaser was desperate to get himself and his family to safety. He had a distant uncle in Australia, from a side of the family named Borer, and so he searched the Melbourne and Sydney telephone books at the British Embassy in Vienna. Six Borers were listed, one of whom he hoped might be his uncle. Johan Glaser's letter was addressed to 'Mr Borer' at the 'Borer and White Ant Extermination Company'. He speculated that this might have been his Uncle Borer, working in partnership with a Mr White. Thus the letter reached Fred Ashworth, the owner of the extermination company. It was a comical and lucky mistake.

The urgency of the letter-writer was plain, so the guests decided they would all be 'Uncle Borer' to help save this family. This was the first time that the Member for Fawkner had been confronted with such a pressing human need from his own electorate. Early the next Monday, he rang his colleague John McEwen, Minister for the Interior, asking for a permit for the Glaser family to come to Australia.

After that, things moved rapidly. The family received their permit, left Vienna, sailed to Marseilles, then to Batavia (modern-day Jakarta), and finally to Melbourne.

On 7 November, they reached Station Pier, to be greeted by all the dinner party invitees, apart from Harold Holt, who was in Canberra. A banner read 'Welcome to Dr. Glaser and Family'.

Two days later the news reached Australia of Kristallnacht, 'the night of the broken glass', when hordes of Nazis burned and sledgehammered their way throughout Germany, Austria and the Sudentenland, destroying hundreds of Jewish shops, houses and synagogues. Against this background of mayhem, hundreds of Jews throughout these countries committed suicide.

Few people in Australia or elsewhere had heard the story of the Glaser family. But as his feeling for these displaced people grew stronger, Harold Holt liked to think of himself as an 'Uncle Borer'. The Glasers were seeking a new place in the world, and that goal resonated with him. He was learning of some of the evils from which his country was insulated, and from which it could protect others in less fortunate countries.

In politics, you could get things done and see the results of your efforts. If you had power, you could help people and make a difference to their lives. You could even save their lives.

* * *

By the time the 'Uncle Borers' had done their work, Harold and Zara were lovers again, with a marriage in all but name. Early in September 1938, she told him that she was pregnant. After Harold had adjusted himself to this new reality, he coined a word to describe Zara's condition: she was *infanticipating*.

History was repeating itself. Perhaps Harold reflected on his parents' probably unplanned pregnancy thirty years earlier. Was this new pregnancy also unintentional? It may have been, but perhaps he and Zara unconsciously wanted to create some tangible, lasting evidence of their intimacy. The way things had worked out seemed entirely appropriate.

Whatever the truth, the reckoning with James Fell had to come. When he came to Australia to see Nicholas for the first time, he learned that Zara was pregnant. He returned to India without her.

In April 1939, Holt's mentor, Robert Menzies, was elected leader of the United Australia Party and thus became prime minister of Australia. In his cabinet of twelve ministers, four were appointed as 'Ministers without Portfolio', among whom was Harold Holt, whose job was to assist Richard Casey in the new Department of Supply and Development.

In Melbourne on 23 May, Zara gave birth to twin boys, named Andrew and Sam. She was now the mother of three boys under the age of two, and on her own. Genevieve helped her as much as she could.

Zara and Harold knew that eventually they would marry, but that it would take time. For a cabinet minister, marriage to a recently divorced woman would be bad public relations, so they would have to wait for a decent interval to elapse. At least publicly, Harold would be a father at one remove. Politics was about covering what lay under the surface, fashioning an image for the outside world. It had always been thus and always would be.

8

From Gunner
to Godfather

He swims in unknown waters, this Mr Holt from Victoria.
From their background, Melbourne political trainees cannot
understand the high powered unionism of Sydney, or that of
Queensland further north.

—*Smith's Weekly*, 25 January 1941

THREE MONTHS AFTER THE BIRTH OF ZARA'S TWINS, the world beyond Australia intruded dramatically. Prime Minister Menzies performed his 'melancholy duty', informing Australians that their country would follow Britain into war against Germany. In March 1940, six months after the start of the war, the Country Party entered a coalition with the United Australia Party and, as a result, four Country Party members were offered ministries. Harold Holt, Menzies' most junior minister, lost his place. He had regrets, but announced to the parliament that, in accordance with the demands of the times, he was seeking a new role: 'As the youngest member of the House, I could not feel happy in my position if I were not prepared to make some sacrifice and take an active part.'

So in May 1940 he enlisted in the Australian Imperial Force, with a new identity – Gunner Holt. After arriving at the Army base at Puckapunyal in northern Victoria, he spent his last night of civilian life sleeping in the privacy of his own car. It was cold, confined and lonely, but helped him savour what he imagined would be his last taste of private life for a long time.

He found ways of making the time in camp more tolerable than it might otherwise have been, such as by volunteering for latrine duty, an unpleasant but brief early morning detail. Once this was over, there was time to enjoy lying in the sunshine. He settled into his new identity, coming to terms with the idea of serving in an overseas theatre of war, as his unit was slated to do.

He had almost completed his training and was preparing for deployment overseas with the Australian Imperial Force, probably to Egypt or Palestine, when sudden disaster struck, destabilising the federal government and so ending his time in the Army. In Canberra on the morning of 13 August, a Lockheed Hudson plane crashed while its pilot was attempting to land. Turning away from the aerodrome after approaching to land, the plane wobbled in the air, then spiral-dived into a hillside two miles from the aerodrome. When the plane hit the ground, eyewitnesses more than a mile away saw a vivid flash a fraction before they heard the noise of the crash. The wrecked plane burst into flames; the victims were incinerated. Among them were three of the prime minister's most trusted ministers, all of them key war leaders: Geoffrey Street, Minister for the Army; Sir Henry Gullett, Information Minister; and James Fairbairn, Minister for Air.

Menzies feared that his government, too, might crash and burn. Three ministers dead could mean three by-elections – a scenario he ruled out, instead calling an early general election. The army gave Holt leave to campaign in his electorate, which he held with a comfortable majority. The Menzies government, however, retained power only with the support of two independents. In these circumstances, the prime minister proposed to Opposition leader John Curtin that a government of National Unity be established with the Labor Party. Curtin turned him down.

The deaths of Gullett, Fairbairn and Street may have indirectly saved Harold Holt from a premature death overseas. Menzies, having lost these three men, wanted Holt back as part of his government. The prime minister needed a Minister for Labour and National Service who could prevent industrial disputes from disrupting the war effort. On the docks, for example, waterside workers were refusing to load war materiel bound for overseas.

Menzies wanted a minister who could meet with union leaders and employer groups and secure their agreement with a stream-lining of the arbitration process for the duration of the war. With these requirements in mind, he asked Holt to return to the ministry. He knew that Holt was not only a capable administrator, but also a bridge-builder who could talk to an adversary as one human being to another.

Holt agonised over how he should best serve his country, through public or military service. But his true leader and master was Robert Menzies, and he could not turn him down. Besides, Menzies must have thought well of him to extract him from the army at such a critical time and he probably envisaged a time when his protégé would be worthy of far greater responsibilities.

On 28 October 1940, Holt was sworn in as the new Minister for Labour and National Service. Before long, the Sydney-based tabloid *Smith's Weekly* was expressing doubts about his ability to make a success of this portfolio. A headline declared 'Young Mr Holt Out of his Depth' and a sceptical profile followed of the new minister from Victoria who 'swims in unknown waters'. It was not long, however, until 'the baby of the cabinet' was winning praise for his deft handling of industrial conferences. After an agreement was reached with engineering unions, a high-ranking Commonwealth official was quoted as saying that

Although Mr Holt was a junior minister and considered inexperienced in such matters, I cannot remember in nearly thirty years of industrial conferences one handled so skilfully, so tactfully and so successfully as this one.

Soon the new minister was prepared to make his first major policy intervention. The national child endowment scheme would provide five shillings per week for each child under sixteen years of age after the first child, regardless of family income.

In his speech arguing for the passage of the bill, Holt announced the government's main intentions for it:

> Child endowment will help to ensure that the exigencies of war do not take away from our children necessary food and clothing . . . I offer this measure to the House, confident that members will welcome the opportunity of contributing to the welfare of the one million young Australians who will benefit directly from it.

On 3 April 1941, the *Child Endowment Act* rapidly passed through the House, cheered on by its members when the bill became law. Opposition leader John Curtin congratulated the minister on the work he had done, while Holt thanked the Opposition for ensuring its smooth passage. The following month, the *Adelaide News* acclaimed the bill as 'the greatest piece of social legislation of the present generation in Australia'.

On the day after the bill was passed, Holt's friend 'Uncle' Alex Isaacson, a long-time jeweller in the Melbourne suburb of St Kilda, sent him a telegram:

> MATTHEW 25 STOP VERSE 21
> SINCERELY UNCLE ALEX ISAACSON

The Biblical verse from the Gospel of St Matthew was part of Jesus' Parable of the Talents, which highlights the importance of fidelity to one's purpose and of the full use of one's innate gifts:

> 'Well done, my good and trusty servant!' said the master. 'You have proved trustworthy in a small way; I will now put you in charge of something big. Come and share your master's delight.'

It was ironic, the press suggested, that Harold Holt was the man to introduce the scheme. As the only bachelor in the cabinet, he was to become 'Godfather to one million Australian children'.

Holt was interested not only in his 'godchildren', but their parents as well. Where profits were high, he felt, wages should also be 'on the upgrade'. He was pleased that newspapers endorsed his efforts, even if the writers implied that these efforts were not disinterested: 'Even if this does annoy Very Big Business, it will help make his "political" reputation.'

Due to his political success, he was being featured in popular magazines, with attention given to his striking appearance – he was judged one of the three best-looking men in parliament – and his living arrangements. While in Melbourne, he lived in a flat which he had helped to design, built over a garage in Toorak. He had a housekeeper. Most evenings he spent at home dealing with official correspondence. He liked to collect books and had a growing library of classics, modern political commentary and parliamentary works. He was also a member of the theatrical Green Club.

Less than a week after the passage of the *Child Endowment Act*, Holt had a 'narrow shave', according to the headline of the Sydney *Sun*, 'when his car was struck by another which did not stop'. On his way to Sydney, near Gundagai, he dropped a burning cigarette in his car and alighted from the car to discover its whereabouts. While he was standing by the open door, a car travelling in the opposite direction struck the door. Holt was struck in the head by the door but was not seriously injured. He was able to continue his journey to Sydney. Would he seek the 'hit-and-run' driver? No – 'I am far too busy.'

* * *

Besides Labour and National Service, Holt held an additional job. John Curtin, though refusing Menzies' offer to have the Labor Party play a role in a government of National Unity, consented to the formation of a bipartisan advisory war council. This body usually met either at Parliament House in Canberra or at Victoria Barracks in Melbourne, and was designed to exist in addition to the war cabinet which Menzies had set up two weeks after his declaration of war.

The council was established on 28 October 1940, the same day that Harold Holt was sworn in as the Minister for Labour and National Service. Its objective was to draw all the major political parties in the Parliament of Australia into the process of making decisions about the country's war effort. Holt was the council's youngest member; the eldest was the septuagenarian former prime minister Billy Hughes, now attorney-general and Minister for the Navy. As prime minister, Menzies chaired the council; other members were Labor leader John Curtin, Labor deputy leader Frank Forde and treasurer Arthur Fadden.

*　*　*

For Australia, 1941 was to become a year of three prime ministers: one from the United Australia Party, one from the Country Party, and the last from the Labor Party.

Out of sight often means out of mind, but not in politics, where plotting and scheming are easier when the intended victim is away. And early in 1941 the prime minister was away from Australia for four months.

The war was going badly for Australia and its allies. With German bombs pounding British cities, Robert Menzies sailed to the Middle East to meet with Australian troops, then to London to consult with Prime Minister Winston Churchill. Armed with his movie camera, he intended to witness at first hand the travails of the Londoners enduring the Blitz. He would show the people back home that he was prepared to brave the risks of living in a city under siege.

'If you feel you must go, you will go,' his wife, Pattie, told him. But she foresaw a sting in the tail for him, adding, 'but you will be out of office within six weeks of your return.' This time it was Pattie Menzies who displayed the superior political acumen. Her husband was welcomed home unenthusiastically. Only half of his ministers were present in the House to hear him report on his trip, and one of them slept through his presentation.

The prime minister's hold on power was slipping. He was the head of a minority government propped up by the support of two independents; he was under attack over the failure of the military campaigns in Greece and Crete; he had been accused of not adequately preparing the country for war. He had made too many enemies with his dominating manner and caustic wit. Many of his colleagues felt that his popularity with the electorate was declining, and that his perceived arrogance was undermining solidarity within the coalition.

Once again, Menzies tried to establish a national government for the duration of the war. He offered the Opposition half of the seats in cabinet, including the prime ministership, believing this was a better arrangement than being forced to another election likely to result in defeat. Not many of his ministers saw things that way, fearing the loss of their jobs, and Labor leader John Curtin again turned down his offer.

On 27 August, the matter of his leadership came to a head in the party room. Holt was one of the first ministers to speak:

> The circumstances before us require candour. Greatly as I admire your work, Prime Minister, I feel bound to say that the prospects of government success will most likely be enhanced if there were to be a new prime minister. I would suggest that Mr Fadden would be able to fill this office appropriately.

John McEwen concurred: 'While I feel a deep sense of personal regret, I feel sure that a change of leadership would be beneficial.' Then Percy Spender, saying: 'Nothing could be more unpleasant for me, Prime Minister, than to feel bound to advocate a change of leadership, because I owe the whole of my political advancement to you.' Holt interrupted in agreement: 'I feel the same embarrassment, because personally I owe everything in my political life to you, Prime Minister.'

As a majority of cabinet members had now expressed the view that a new leader was needed, Menzies resigned, on 29 August.

Holt had agonised over the decision but finally cast his vote against his friend and mentor. As he saw it, this was in the best interests of the party, which was more important than the individual. But from this time onwards, he silently vowed that he would never again treat a friend this way, not even in the context of political life, where disloyalty was often par for the course.

So that was the end of Prime Minister Menzies – or so it then seemed. He advised the governor-general to send for Arthur Fadden and offer him a commission as the new prime minister. Fadden lasted just forty days before the two independent members of parliament voted against him in October, bringing down the government and making John Curtin prime minister and leader of a Labor government.

When Curtin became prime minister it was agreed that the advisory war council's decisions be automatically accepted as war cabinet decisions, with the council referring only some matters to the war cabinet. This gave the Advisory War Council a very influential role in the proceedings of the war.

Curtin had been prime minister for only two months before Japanese planes bombed the American naval base at Pearl Harbor in Hawaii on 7 December 1941, the date which President Roosevelt said would 'live in infamy'. As a result, the United States was in the war at last. Menzies had said he was 'British to my bootstraps', but now on the cusp of 1942, national survival was going to depend on Americans rather than Englishmen.

For the first time, Australia's national security was in direct and immediate danger as Japanese troops swept downwards towards the Australian mainland, conquering one Asian country after another on the way.

9

Americans Down Under

There can be no compromise. We shall win or we shall die, and to this end I pledge all the mighty power of my country and all the blood of my countrymen.

—Douglas MacArthur, quoted in Arthur Herman,
Douglas MacArthur: American Warrior

BEFORE GENERAL DOUGLAS MACARTHUR ARRIVED IN Melbourne in March 1942, few famous American visitors had stepped onto Australian shores. The general was the best-known American to arrive Down Under since Harry Houdini some thirty years before. The general and the magician were both showmen, but of different kinds. Each had a strong sense of drama and an ego craving the limelight. But unlike Houdini, MacArthur had come to save rather than to beguile Australia.

After the fall of Bataan in the Philippines, MacArthur hunkered down in his dugout at Corregidor, where he was known to the belaboured troops as 'Dugout Doug'. He was dramatically evacuated from the Philippines and ordered by Roosevelt to go to Australia to help hold the line there.

On 21 March he arrived by train in Melbourne. Deputy Prime Minister Forde and other members of the government were on the platform at Spencer Street Station to meet him. A roar of welcome from thousands of voices arose as he alighted from the train with his wife, Jean, their four-year-old son, Arthur, and the boy's Filipina nurse, or *amah*. Although he and his family had endured many trials in the previous days, MacArthur looked regal as he stepped onto the stage to begin his new role, his garrison cap with golden oak leaves glinting in the sun, his bush jacket open at the throat.

All the way to his new headquarters, crowds shouted and waved to the man sent to save their country. The general and his party established themselves on the third floor of the Menzies Hotel; he named his new headquarters 'Bataan'. Later, the family was welcomed at *Kurneh*, the South Yarra residence of Norman and Mabel Brookes.

In Canberra, the general met Curtin and threw his arm over his shoulder, commanding: 'You take care of the rear and I'll take care of the front.'

On 26 March, he attended a special meeting with the Advisory War Council in Canberra to discuss the problems associated with his command. Later, a special dinner was given in his honour at Parliament House. His voice rumbled with thunder as he assured the audience that would return to the Philippines as its liberator.

'I shall return' was a sentence typical of the general's rhetorical style. He made proclamations rather than statements. John Curtin thought him the greatest actor he had ever known, and General Dwight Eisenhower mischievously claimed to have studied dramatic art under him. MacArthur's gait and bearing seemed to say: 'You folks stop worrying, and let us do the fighting for you.'

To end the day, the general was ushered into the House of Representatives while it was in session, ensconsing himself beside the Speaker's chair, his legs crossed as casually as if he were in his own home. He heard a heated debate over the Opposition's motion, to disallow the government's waterside regulations.

Holt, now Opposition Spokesman on Industrial Matters, moved the motion, arguing that these regulations made no provision for representation on the committees of the Permanent and Casual Wharf Labourers Union. This union therefore had no voice in matters of vital importance to it, and was threatened with extinction. At issue was the preservation of the rights of minority groups such as this union. The regulations, Holt argued, jeopardised the industrial representation and employment of hundreds of workers in wartime, a serious matter, as it was not conducive to industrial peace. Further, the regulations involved 'arbitrary use of the emergency powers by the government in time of war in a partisan and political manner'.

Labor MP Bert James frequently interrupted Holt as he spoke: 'He doesn't realise there's a war on,' he interjected, referring to Holt's remarks and turning to MacArthur as he spoke. The House was in uproar throughout the debate, and the Opposition's motion was eventually lost on party lines. The general apparently enjoyed the experience of listening to the debate. 'If the men of Australia can fight as well as they can argue,' he concluded, 'we are certain of victory.'

Before long, one million American servicemen followed MacArthur to Australia to help defend it from attack, many of them stationed in Queensland, where the general was soon ordered to organise the country's defence. Before the onset of the Pacific War, Brisbane had been a sleepy city isolated from the outside world. By the middle of 1942, the influx of American military personnel had almost doubled the population, and the city became used to the navy-blue uniforms of countless American sailors. In the suburb of New Farm alone, roughly eight hundred American servicemen were stationed at Capricorn Wharf, from where sometimes as many as eight American submarines were visible. Concrete air-raid shelters lined the Brisbane River.

While in Brisbane, Douglas MacArthur found the man he wanted to accompany him wherever he went and to meet his needs from early in the morning until late at night. This was Francisco Salveron, a 31-year-old Filipino sergeant now serving with the US Army. He had previously worked for many years as a purser on a luxury liner sailing between the Philippines and Australia. When Manila fell to the Japanese, he lost contact with his wife and two daughters and had good reason to believe that they were dead.

With the onset of war, he was conscripted into the American Army and assigned to a supply ship, the *Don Isidro*, which transported medical supplies to Allied forces. When the Japanese sunk the ship, Salveron was among the one-third of the ship's company to survive. Despite his injuries, he got ashore and rescued several men who had lost arms and legs, covering them with sand so that the scent of their blood would not attract crocodiles. He was hospitalised in Brisbane with a shoulder wound when Douglas MacArthur came to visit the wounded and talked with him about recent events in the Philippines.

MacArthur considered himself an honorary Filipino. As Salveron told him about the recent events in his life, a strong rapport developed between the two men. MacArthur saw that Salveron was a good soldier, brave, resourceful, adaptable and likely to be totally loyal. He invited him to be his aide-de-camp.

From that time on, Salveron went wherever MacArthur went, staying by his side to take care of his everyday needs. He started work at four in the morning, when he woke MacArthur, cooked him his bacon and eggs, laid out his uniform with belt, shoes, dark glasses and the cane which the general felt brought him good luck. He carried the general's gun as well as extra tobacco for his pipe. As time passed, Salveron began to regard MacArthur as a father-figure.

Though Douglas MacArthur was delighted to meet Francisco Salveron in Australia, he was less pleased to meet another of his compatriots, whom he suspected to be a political commissioner sent to tell him what to do. The young American in question, Congressman Lieutenant Commander Lyndon Baines Johnson, had a letter of introduction to MacArthur from a mutual friend in Honolulu. Johnson had persuaded his hero and mentor, Roosevelt, to make him an observer of events in the Pacific War. Johnson was a Democratic Congressman who represented a constituency in southern Texas and was itching to go further. Roosevelt felt he had the ability and drive to go all the way to the top: 'With any luck, if the chips go right and he hangs onto the friends he makes, this boy Lyndon Johnson can wind up being President of the United States. He's got it.'

Johnson was an imposing six foot three but seemed even taller in his navy, gold-braided uniform. He was still quite slender. He was admirably suited to political life; as a communicator he was peerless and his warmth worked magic on many he encountered. He still showed characteristics of the teacher he had been before entering politics, for he counselled, cajoled, chivvied. He had enjoyed teaching, but it offered too small a platform for a man of his drive and ambition.

Though he was in a foreign land, he fitted in almost seamlessly. Wherever he found himself, at home or abroad, he took the measure of his surroundings with remarkable acuteness and made himself the centre of them. Like a fox, he was constantly scrutinising his world, on the lookout for whatever opportunities might come his way.

MacArthur's Number Two, General Willoughby, wanted Johnson to meet prominent Australians. Among them were Norman and Mabel Brookes, whom he met at *Kurneh*. Mabel sensed that Johnson's mind was often ahead of those of his interlocutors as he tried to anticipate their next words. Before long, he had found a favourite chair in the Brookes' sitting room and made it his own, enjoying a few hours rest and a good deal of talk.

At *Kurneh*, the young American congressman was introduced to Holt. As they related the stories of their lives to date, they discovered that they had been born just twenty-two days apart. They shared warm personalities, an enormous capacity for work and for enjoyment, and were both brimming with ideas about what they wanted to do in their respective countries.

After leaving Melbourne, Johnson did not forget the Brookes, who had become like family to him. Nor did he forget his new political friend, Holt. Who knew what future circumstances might bring them together, when each could be of assistance to the other?

Douglas MacArthur was soon sent further north to Townsville, as was Lyndon Johnson, who stayed for a time at Buchanans Hotel, a fine, old filigree-style building dating from the early years of the century, embellished with elaborate cast-iron panels.

Johnson's exposure to the war was limited, his only direct experience of it coming as an observer with an American Air Force crew on an operation close to New Guinea. But with his future political career in mind, he made the most of this and sought to ingratiate himself with MacArthur. The general obliged him by recognising his part in the mission with the award of the Silver Star.

While confined to the home front, Holt had now encountered one of the most famous of all Americans, as well as another who aspired to join that group. He now saw the US as a source of help to a beleaguered world, a force for good, willing to flex its muscles when necessary. And as he considered the threat to Australia arising to the north of Queensland, the idea that his country was a part of Asia began to take shape in his mind.

* * *

As well as finding a job in Australia, Francisco Salveron found love. One day he was walking beside the Brisbane River, the warships and boats reminding him of his life thousands of miles away, and of his arrival on the *Don Isidro* to Australia. As he walked, he encountered a mother walking with her teenage daughter. He initiated a conversation with the woman and learned that she was Clarissa Gray, who had come to the river with her daughter Lorraine to show her the warships. Clarissa was divorced and lived with Lorraine in inner-city Brisbane. She was six years older than Salveron.

He suggested that they all go into the city together for lunch. They did so, and began to share their life stories. Over the next weeks and months, they began to see each other frequently; before long their friendship turned romantic. In 1943, Clarissa discovered she was pregnant and early the following year she gave birth to a girl she named Frances. Although Clarissa was not married to Francisco, she had her and Frances's surnames changed to Salveron.

In the world beyond Australia, the Japanese armies were being pushed back across South-East Asia. The time was coming for Douglas MacArthur to redeem his pledge to return to the Philippines. Francisco returned with him, but not before he learned that Clarissa was pregnant again, her baby due the following February.

Francisco Salveron returned to the Philippines with MacArthur on 20 October 1944, when they splashed ashore at Leyte Gulf. *Life* magazine's Carl Mydans preserved the moment in a photograph that became well known across the world. By February 1945, when Manila was liberated from occupation, Francisco had not heard from his family in almost three years.

Meanwhile, in Brisbane, on 17 February, Clarissa gave birth to her first and only son, whom she named Douglas, in honour of Douglas MacArthur. For his other given name she chose Javing, his father's middle name.

The situation in Manila was dire when Francisco returned, but it was the happiest moment of his life to find his wife and children, ailing but still alive. MacArthur arranged for the family to migrate to the US, where they settled in Bladensburg, Maryland, just outside Washington, DC, and Salveron joined the US Air Force. The welfare of his Filipino family was now his immediate concern, but he must have sometimes wondered about his distant Australian family, the children of his exile.

10

Married and
Back in Government

*A lively and agreeable man has not only the merit of liveliness
and agreeableness, but that also of awakening them in others.*

—Sir Fulke Greville

B Y THE END OF THE WAR, HOLT'S PERSONAL LIFE WAS
beginning to take a definite shape. For the first time in
his life he was part of a nurturing and cohesive family,
and he and Zara finally contemplated formalising their de facto
relationship. Whenever Harold returned from Canberra to Melbourne, he visited her and her three young sons at 50 Washington Street, Toorak. They went out on weekend picnics with the boys and spent time together at home. Holt carefully nurtured his bonds with Zara's growing brood. He and the boys had started out as friends, but now the bonds of paternity had strengthened. Harry, as they called him, was the nearest to a father they had ever known.

On 9 October 1945, Holt learned that his father had died at a private hospital in Melbourne, aged only fifty-nine. Still in her early thirties, Lola Holt was now a widow with a young daughter, Frances. For many years Tom Holt had been in poor health and had retired early. He died almost broke, a sad end to a colourful and productive life. Now both of Holt's parents had died prematurely and only Cliff was left from his birth family.

But professionally, Holt was on the rise. A reporter from the Sydney *Sun* wrote that 'his counsel carries a lot of weight with his colleagues. He is considered a certain successor to Robert Gordon Menzies and a potential prime minister.'

Menzies' first term as prime minister had ended in tears, as he bemoaned his party's betrayal of him and lamented that he had been 'done'. He decided to allow himself a period of wound licking, declaring: 'I'll lie down and bleed awhile.' But he soon stood up again. During the war he had stayed in the public eye with weekly radio broadcasts, emulating Roosevelt's 'fireside chats'. After the United Australia Party collapsed at the 1943 elections, he set out to reinvent himself by forming a new party, the Liberal Party, which would govern in coalition with the Country Party.

Holt must have been looking forward to the new year of 1946, with the war over at last and marriage with Zara to contemplate. The ground had shifted under his feet when they had separated, but now he stood on firmer ground, all the more so with the addition of the boys.

Shortly after the birth of the twins, Zara took a job with her father, redesigning, packaging, and doing advertising for his grocery stores. As it was wartime, she also secured work rolling Red Cross bandages and growing 'victory gardens' – a feature of the 'Dig For Victory' publicity campaign launched by Curtin. This campaign encouraged householders to grow their own vegetables as a contribution to the war effort. Some people formed gardening collectives to raise funds for this effort. Meanwhile, Zara watched every penny.

The house in Washington Street finally became available for purchase, so this would become the family's permanent home. When Harold found out that the house would have to be furnished and equipped with sheets and blankets and linen and cutlery, he said with genuine surprise: 'I thought every house came with all those things.'

Perhaps his unawareness of domestic realities resulted from spending so much time living in hotels and boarding houses.

But now, at last, he was going to be established as a permanent resident of a private house, instead of as the longest-ever resident of the Hotel Canberra.

Unlike most middle-class children, Nicky, Sam and Andy Fell had two working parents. Mary Edith Lawless, known as 'Tiny' because of her physical stature, lived with the family at Washington Street and worked both as housekeeper and surrogate parent.

Harold and Zara had to wait until after the federal election to be held on 28 September before they could marry. Zara's divorce was on the way to being finalised and James Fell was planning to remarry, too. Enough time had elapsed for Harold not to be implicated in the dissolution of the marriage. For a politician in the 1940s, marriage to a divorced woman was far from ideal.

Harold repeated to Zara his usual caveat: politics was the centre of his world and she would have to accommodate herself to that. She must do nothing to interfere with his career. When he brought to her the legal document confirming that she was officially divorced, she began to cry. Though it was what she had wanted, she hated the idea of divorce because it broke the sense of wholeness which she valued. Perhaps she also felt a sense of failure and the social embarrassment which often accompanied divorce in those days.

Harold did not propose until the next day. She told Nicky that she and Harry wanted to get married; this would be good for everyone. What did he think? He was silent for a moment, then announced that it was a good idea. When he told the twins the news, Andy was pleased: 'Oh, that's good. That means we'll have a car.'

As expected, the Chifley government was re-elected on 28 September, the first time that Labor had won two successive elections. In its first electoral test, the new Liberal and Country Party coalition was convincingly defeated, but they took six seats from Labor. Holt was comfortably returned in his electorate. Interviewed before his impending wedding, he said, 'It goes without saying that I count myself extremely fortunate. Two big wins within a couple of days is good going, don't you think?'

Zara and Harold married on 8 October 1946, almost exactly a year to the day after his father's death. Like Tom Holt's second wedding, it was a quiet affair. The ceremony took place at the Dickins' house in St Georges Road, Toorak, where Sydney Dickins 'gave away' his daughter, who was dressed in a smoky-blue woollen suit with a flared skirt and high-necked jacket, with a matching felt hat. Robert Menzies gave her a congratulatory kiss, which was snapped and featured on the front page of the next morning's Melbourne *Sun*.

The buffet luncheon that followed the wedding was a larger affair for 120 guests, held at the Hotel Australia in Melbourne. According to one report, there were 'unstinted libations of bubbly' and 'representatives from such disparate strata of our society as the crème of Canberra (or how do you view the Opposition?) and a flock of perennial good-timers from the Portsea beach scene'.

Nicky, Sam and Andy farewelled their parents at the aerodrome, from where the newlyweds left for Sydney. After a long-delayed flight, they arrived, exhausted, at 3.30 a.m. There were no taxis around, so they pushed their suitcases to the Hotel Australia in Castlereagh Street. Zara had never seen the city before and had had only a cursory look at the harbour. Now she was enchanted by it and by the beaches. It was a nostalgic journey for Harold, back in the city of his early years. But so much had entered his life since then that those early years must have seemed to him to have been lifted from a different life.

He was still thinking of politics, of course, during this rare interlude away. With a little luck and some false steps by the Chifley government, he might soon be a minister again.

By 1949, when the next federal election was due, the government was on the ropes. When Holt heard Chifley announce his plan to nationalise the banks, he felt certain that Menzies would win the election. Holt believed that to many of Chifley's supporters, bank nationalisation would be construed as a needless intrusion into their lives, and would prompt enough of a rebellion to defeat the government.

On election night, 10 December 1949, the Holts and the Dickins assembled at Chattanooga, Sidney and Violet Dickins' house in Sorrento, to listen to the results on the radio. Everyone was jubilant, including the boys, who were now old enough to understand the concept of an election.

It wasn't often that you got a second chance, as Holt knew. Robert Menzies had a new start at the head of a new party. The memory of his failures in his first term as prime minister was erased by his victory, leaving him with a clean canvas on which to paint a new story.

Holt easily won the new seat of Higgins, which adjoined his old electorate of Fawkner, and took in the comfortable Melbourne suburbs of Malvern, Armadale, Caulfield and Darling. He almost doubled his opponent's share of the vote in what *The Age* called 'a full tide of public favour'. A 'new chapter in political history' was declared. Menzies had forgiven Holt for his betrayal in 1941, and Holt had been reassigned to his former portfolio of Labour and National Service, to which the role of Minister of Immigration was added.

One new member of parliament for the Liberal Party was a childhood friend of Holt's, William 'Billy' McMahon. He had built a successful career as a solicitor and an image of a dapper man about town. He had lost nothing of his penchant for self-promotion. To some he was like an annoying blowfly, to others a man of energy and purpose. Still unmarried at forty-one, he was known as a generous host at his Sydney home. His thinning hair further highlighted his oversized ears. Partial deafness had helped to create the sing-song cadence of his voice, with its surprising glissandos and tremolos. But nothing was going to thwart his strong ambitions – he hoped to secure a ministry in the government.

As the new government's first term progressed, Prime Minister Menzies began to look impregnable. His double-breasted suits fortified him; his expressive eyebrows swept aside opposition. With a few devastating words he could deflect criticism or score a direct hit on an adversary. His voice was a mellifluous legato as he reassured the electorate in tones that seemed to rise above the troubles of earth and iron out its tangles. As well as a politician he was a convincing actor, and now he had a stage large enough to display his talents.

He alerted his listeners to the perils of the world, both domestic and foreign, while assuring them that they would all be secure if they put their trust in him. After the end of World War Two, a period of 'cold war' between the US and the Soviet Union had begun. Menzies drummed up fear of the communist menace abroad and at home within the trade union movement.

Since June 1950, Allied troops – American, British, Australian and others – had been fighting in Korea to stop communist North Korea from overrunning the Western-backed South Korea. In 1951, Menzies addressed the American Congress, speaking on behalf of a world which he felt needed 'every scrap of democratic sentiment'. Before long, he placed before the Australian parliament the Communist Party Dissolution Bill – an effort to outlaw the Communist Party in Australia. This move raised the question: how liberal really was the Liberal Party?

The High Court of Australia thwarted the prime minister's plans by declaring the bill to be unconstitutional. Menzies was disappointed but not deterred, and soon he initiated a referendum seeking public approval to ban the Australian Communist Party. Though the proposal was narrowly defeated, he vowed to continue the fight.

*　*　*

Even during the days of the Pacific War, Curtin's government had given thought to building Australia's population. He told his cabinet that at war's end there would have to be a Ministry of Immigration, for Australia needed more people to develop and defend it. For Australia, the threat of invasion had been very real.

In July 1945, Arthur Calwell was appointed Australia's first Minister for Immigration. A few weeks later, he argued in parliament that the 'lesson' to be learned from the Pacific War was that 'we cannot continue to hold our island continent for ourselves and our descendants unless we greatly increase our numbers'.

Both the government and the Opposition agreed that Australia needed rapidly to increase its population, still currently at just seven million. The US, after all, had much the same land area as Australia but twenty times its population. Australia would have to 'populate or perish'. Since the war, industry was being redirected from production of armaments to economic growth, and there were far more jobs available than people to do them.

As Chifley's Minister for Immigration, Arthur Calwell had overseen the early phase of postwar immigration to Australia. He made a promise to prospective immigrants from those countries he considered suitable: 'The door to Australia will always be open within limits of our existing legislation to the people from the various dominions, United States of America and from European continental countries.'

Immediately after the war, the Chifley government introduced the Assisted Passage Migration Scheme, which encouraged residents from the British Isles to migrate to Australia for the sum of £10, the cost of processing fees. These immigrants were widely known as 'Ten Pound Poms'. Residents from British colonies such as Malta and Cyprus were also included in the scheme.

Under the terms of the government's White Australia policy, immigration from Asian countries was prohibited. Calwell presided over the deportation of many Malayan, South-East Asian and Chinese refugees, invoking the *Wartime Refugees Removal Act* of 1949. This was a bipartisan policy that soon came under scrutiny.

Probably neither Holt nor Calwell had ever heard of Francisco Salveron, but the name of Lorenzo Gamboa – another Filipino – soon became well known to them both. Like Salveron, Gamboa had come to Australia during the war years and found love. Born on the last day of the First World War, he had, like Salveron, served with the US army during the Second. His personal war was remarkably similar to Salveron's – he was evacuated to Australia after the Japanese conquest of the Philippines and was later attached as an orderly to General MacArthur's headquarters in Brisbane.

Gamboa was at first stationed in Melbourne, where he met a young woman named Joyce Cain, who lived in the inner suburb of Brunswick. With the blessing of her parents, the two were married in October 1943. In November of the following year, while her husband was stationed in the Philippines, Joyce gave birth to their son Raymond. Gamboa was later stationed in Japan, and while he was there, in January 1947, Joyce gave birth to Julie, their second child.

In November 1945, Gamboa had returned to his wife and family in Melbourne, but the next year his presence came to the attention of the Department of Immigration. He was ordered to leave, as were other 'Asiatics' who had come to Australia during the war. He went to the United States, rejoined its army and became an American citizen, mistakenly believing that this was how he could obtain an Australian visa. In 1948, while on MacArthur's staff, he applied unsuccessfully for a permit to enter Australia. After MacArthur had intervened on his behalf to no avail, Gamboa turned to sympathetic newspaper editors to fight the immigration department and its minister. 'Why did they let me marry an Australian girl if they wouldn't let me into the country to see her?' he asked.

But Calwell was adamant – Gamboa would not be granted permanent residency in Australia. The White Australia policy was in force. Although Arthur Calwell had many friends in Melbourne's Chinese community, he felt he had a clear responsibility to keep Australia white for generations to come. Since the recent war, when the Japanese had posed a direct threat to Australia, the idea of hordes of Asians pouring down from the north had for many Australians taken on an aspect of almost mystical horror. Calwell preyed on those fears:

> We can have a white Australia, we can have a black Australia, but a mongrel Australia is impossible, and I shall not take the first steps to establish the precedents which will allow the floodgates to open.

Holt and Calwell disagreed over whether Gamboa should be allowed to stay. Calwell insisted that he had to use his head in such matters.

As Opposition Spokesman for Immigration, Holt discussed the case with Calwell. When dealing with his opponents in parliament, Calwell was intransigent, but in private he was more accommodating. He told Holt that he understood his concern for Gamboa and his Australian family, but explained that he had a job to do. He had to stick to the rules: 'If I used my heart in these matters I would not interfere with these Asiatics, but, after all, as a responsible minister, I have to use my head.'

But Holt felt there were wider issues. Gamboa was a stranger in our midst and during the war he had fought on our side. He assured Calwell that Gamboa was a good man and would be a good citizen. Besides, he disliked the idea of splitting up families.

Holt seldom shared his innermost thoughts with others, unless he felt a pressing need to do so. The Gamboa case had touched something deep within him, perhaps because the central narrative of his early life had been one of uphill struggle to find a secure place in the world. Gamboa had found his place in the world, and that was Australia; the government should help him stay there.

The case was widely publicised in the Philippines and the fallout was damaging Australia's relations with that country. One Australian diplomat found that 'all Filipinos from Manila to the most distant hinterlands know of Gamboa and the White Australia policy'. For some Filipinos those two items represented their only knowledge of Australia, where 'the Gamboa case' was now an issue in the 1949 election, as Arthur Calwell made clear to his audience at Brunswick Town Hall: 'I am sure we don't want half-castes running over our country. If we let in any US citizen, we will have to admit US negroes. I don't think mothers and fathers would want to see that.'

Earlier in the year, two Filipino golfers had arrived in Sydney to play in a tournament. Holt accused the government of hypocrisy:

It is incredible that Filipino golfers are on a golfing tour of Australia while the Minister for Immigration is keeping out one of their own countrymen who wants to discuss the future with his wife.

Before long, Holt had replaced Calwell as Minister of Immigration. Gamboa's future was now in his hands. Within months, he opened the gate to him.

* * *

Many of Holt's colleagues and opponents alike felt that his best quality was his abilty to see and sympathise with points of view other than his own. Albert Monk, president of the Australian Council of Trade Unions, shared that quality and appreciated it in others. Over time, the two men built a warm personal and professional relationship. Shortly after the election of 1949, Monk phoned Menzies to persuade him to give Holt the labour portfolio, as well as the portfolio of immigration.

Menzies knew that Holt's emollience would work to the government's advantage when it came to the labour portfolio. There was no one more suitable for the job, he thought. Ever since his days at Queen's College, when he had handled negotiations between the student body and the administration, Holt had shown the ability to help resolve disputes. Knowing this, Menzies took Monk's advice and brought together the labour and immigration portfolios under Holt's aegis. Thereafter, Holt and Monk worked together on the problems of immigration and industrial disputes.

When Holt became Minister for Labour in 1949, Albert Monk was middle-aged, with a scholarly appearance created by the black-rimmed glasses he wore over his striking brown eyes. He was thoughtful and intelligent, and though he was slightly frail in physique, this was offset by the fighting qualities which his earlier life had forced him to develop. He had started life in Australia as a migrant, arriving from England at the age of ten with his parents. Having suffered from bullying by both his school teacher and peers as a child, he was particularly sympathetic to the problems of migrants coming to a new country.

Monk's trials at school became so bad that he played truant for months, taking to the bush, smoking tea – perhaps he could not afford tobacco – and exploring riverbanks. Eventually he went back to school and satisfied his intellectual inclinations by assiduously collecting the works of his favourite author, Leo Tolstoy.

Those who knew Monk described him as almost pathologically shy, but Holt's disarming manner must have helped him feel more comfortable. The two men shared the capacity to understand the feelings and ideas of others. The press reported that Monk had Holt's blessing on all his overseas trips: 'They have been so often abroad,' quipped one journalist, 'that they probably exchange postcards.'

The minister and the trade union leader got along so well that there was talk of a 'Holt–Monk Axis'. Some of those who saw them working together felt that they shared 'twin souls'. Both men knew that you could become fond of an opponent, provided that certain core values were shared and the argument avoided dogmatism.

During the Great Depression, Monk had been the organising secretary of the central unemployed committee in Victoria. The Communist Party ran a rival unemployment movement and played rough. For Monk, it was a replay of his schooldays – he was shadowed through the streets, followed onto trams, threatened, jostled, sometimes even stoned. Once, a communist-led mob cornered him in the Trades Hall, knocked him down and put their boots into his head. He buried the hatchet with the men who did this, practising his philosophy: 'You can't sing hymns of hate in this game all your life.'

Now Holt and Monk were singing from the same songsheet as they reasoned together. Despite their philosophical differences, each held a strong belief in the brotherhood of man and in the healing power of goodwill. Monk was known as a quiet backroom operator who, like Holt, relied on private agreements between gentlemen.

Both favoured reason over histrionics; both tried to limit the human suffering caused through industrial confrontations.

But it was not always easy. 'Big Jim' Healy, the general secretary of the Waterside Workers' Federation of Australia, was an adversary of a quite different stripe. He was the most powerful figure on the Australian waterfront, which was front and centre of industrial trouble in the country, and he was known as one of the gruffest and most formidable communists in the country. During World War Two he had initiated a series of strikes; by refusing duty during wartime, especially in 1943, his wharfies had often delayed essential cargoes. Prime Minister Curtin denounced this as treachery.

Almost every day during Holt's tenure as Minister for Labour, newspapers ran reports of strikes or disputes between the government and the stevedores. Yet despite his militancy, Healy had a more amenable side. With his ruddy, smiling face, his lower lip supporting a curved pipe, he looked like a popular country publican. He was a good host, with friends of various professions, including doctors, architects, lawyers, shipowners and clergymen, and also Harold Holt, whom he considered 'a good bloke'. Given the philosophical and political differences separating them, relations between these two men were a model of cordiality. Newspapers reported that losses caused by strikes had been halved during the course of the year 1951.

There were still bitter battles between Holt and Healy, and Holt's experience with the waterside workers kept his hostility to communism alive. He provoked bitter criticism when he used troops to take control of cargo facilties during a waterside dispute in Bowen, Queensland, in September 1953.

But overall, he had earned a reputation for tolerance, restraint and willingness to compromise. This helped to explain why he had friends on both sides of politics, as well as friends of a different political persuasion, such as Brian Fitzpatrick, a civil libertarian, journalist and socialist whom Robert Menzies had named as one of communism's 'fellow travellers'. Fitzpatrick's support of individual cases of injustice won the respect of Holt, who often acted on his advice.

Employers and unionists alike knew Holt as a peacemaker, and eventually his reputation spread beyond Australia. In the US, General Motors offered him the job of head of the organisation and tried to lure him with a huge salary. Zara was upset that he didn't even consider it, but why should he have? He had found a secure place in the national life of his own country, where he was widely respected for his work. This was worth more than a big pay cheque and not even the most lavish salary could compensate for uprooting a family and leaving the land you loved.

11

Childe Harold's Pilgrimages

It had all the flavour of a nineteenth century Grand Tour –
The Hague, Vienna, Rome, Malta, Naples, Milan, Venice,
Geneva, Frankfurt, Cologne, Bonn, Berlin, Paris, Stockholm,
Amsterdam, London and the Isle of Capri.

—Alan Reid on Harold Holt's 1952 overseas trip,
Sydney *Sun*, 21 July 1953

ALTHOUGH THE MENZIES GOVERNMENT HELD A COM-
fortable majority in the House of Representatives, the
Labor Party held a four-seat majority in the Senate. In 1950
it used this majority to reject the Commonwealth Bank Bill, through
which the government aimed to establish a Commonwealth Bank
Board – a board it believed would only represent private banking
interests. Thus, Menzies found an excuse to call a double dissolution
election for 28 April 1951, in which the government lost five House
of Representative seats to Labor, but gained control of the Senate. As
expected, Holt held his seat of Higgins very comfortably.

In June 1951, little more than a month after the election, Australia was saddened by the news that Labor leader and former prime
minister Ben Chifley had died suddenly in his room at the Kurrajong Hotel in Canberra, at the age of sixty-five. Like many of his
compatriots, Holt had admired the kindly, pipe-puffing Chifley and
respected his homespun commonsense and humane approach to

his job. With her husband's death in mind, Chifley's widow warned Menzies to watch his health: 'Politics are a hard and bitter business. Politics sap your life blood.'

But Menzies had not worked his way to the top only to relinquish his place there. He remained committed and full of energy, and 'Young Harold' was prepared to wait patiently for as long as his boss wanted to keep his job. And while Holt had turned down a lucrative offer to work overseas, his present job was bringing more and more opportunities to engage with the wider world.

In July 1952, accompanied by Zara Holt and Noel Flanagan, his private secretary, he travelled on official business to Europe and the US. The trip was scheduled to last more than three months, during which time Tiny Lawless would look after the boys at Washington Street. Holt would consult with a wide range of his counterparts in the areas of immigration and industrial relations. A steady stream of more relaxed social interactions had also been arranged for him. He planned to keep a detailed daily record of the trip, including vignettes of the places he visited and sketches of the people he met.

He got off to a nauseous start, acquiring a case of 'Karachi tummy' during his stopover there on the way to Rome. Plane sickness was followed by more vomiting due to a hot and bumpy car ride from Rome airport, his Panama hat pressed into service to contain the mess. He explained in his diary that he had included these 'unsavoury details . . . to give a more balanced picture of official international travel'. It was 'not all wine, roses, and *joie de vivre*'. His continuing illness ensured that his visit with the Pope at Castel Gandolfo, while naturally memorable, was not entirely pleasurable.

After recovering from his illness, he met with the Italian Minister for Labor, Leopoldo Rubinnoci, to discuss the issue of Italian migration to Australia; bathed in the Lido at Venice; and in two Venetian churches inspected paintings by Old Masters – Tintoretto, Titian, Veronese and Bellini.

In London, he made a short call on Prime Minister Churchill. He was scheduled to see him at 3.15 in the afternoon, and his cabinet was scheduled to meet at 3.30. While he was waiting to be ushered in, 'the old boy' walked out with Keith Holyoake, the deputy prime minister of New Zealand. Holt and Churchill went into his room together, where the Australian found he had to 'make the running' with conversation, although the Englishman's eyes twinked with mischief while he made droll asides. He puffed away at the inevitable cigar and toyed with what looked like after-dinner whisky and soda:

> I had expected to find him looking much older, and in a saggy physical shape. He looked extremely well, with firm pink cheeks, and fixed me with a clear blue appraising eye . . . There wasn't much time for talk going beyond the pleasantries, but I was able to say something about the value I placed on the work of the [Commonwealth Parliamentary] Association in binding the Commonwealth together, and how important I thought it that the occasion of the Coronation should be fully exploited for its symbolic significance to the Commonwealth countries.

Though pessimistic about England and Europe, Holt saw a bright future for Australia:

> England did little on this short visit to weaken the belief, which has been steadily growing in my mind, that the civilisation of Europe is moribund, and that if there is to be a real revival or more glorious future it is to be found in the younger countries such as Canada and Australia, which having inherited a European culture and tradition, still have their greatest development ahead of them.

Next, he and Zara set off for the US. Their first stop was New York, where he was to attend the American Federation of Labor Convention. Here, the Holts found time for sampling popular culture and entertainment, such as television, not yet available in Australia. They did not become fans, however, with Holt concluding that 'it could be a voracious time consumer, if you let yourself drift along with it'.

But for a politician, it was a fascinating time to be in America, with campaigning well underway for the presidential election in November. Governor Adlai Stevenson of Illinois was the Democratic candidate, running against Dwight Eisenhower – with the slogan 'I Like Ike' – for the Republicans.

Eisenhower's running mate, Richard Nixon, turned to television to refute accusations of impropriety associated with financial support he was receiving from a special fund set up by a select group of wealthy Californians. The Nixon Fund Crisis had come to dominate the election, and Nixon's speech – known as the Checkers speech, named for the little black-and-white-spotted spaniel given to Nixon's young daughters by a Texas campaign supporter – was broadcast to an audience of sixty million. Nixon sought to elicit the sympathy of the audience, declaring that he wasn't a rich man: 'My wife doesn't have a mink coat, but she does have a respectable Republican cloth coat, and I always tell her she'd look good in anything.' Pat Nixon looked on, almost cringing. Holt himself thought the performance 'hammy'.

For Harold Holt, the star candidate of the election was Adlai Stevenson, who on 22 September was the keynote speaker at the American Federation of Labor conference, on the subject of 'The Role of Labor'. Holt considered Stevenson a brilliant candidate and wrote that he was the kind of man he would very much like to have as a close personal friend. He described his speech as 'a well-delivered blend of wit and shrewd politics, studded with statesman-like passages, displaying, at times, a true nobility of mind'. The Democrats had been in power for twenty years and the electorate was in the mood for change. Stevenson was relatively unknown, Holt observed, 'whereas Ike is known to everyone and of world stature'. Regardless of the election result, which was still unclear, Holt was sure that Stevenson was going to be a big figure in American politics for a long time to come.

Stevenson held similar beliefs to Holt. He argued that 'only human freedoms are basic and that economic power must be exercised so as not to curtail them' and that 'the power of government must be restricted to the point that government stands never as master and always as servant'. Stevenson's speech remained in Holt's mind for a long time, as did his later meeting with the man himself.

In his capacity as labour minister, Holt would have endorsed Stevenson's statement in support of free enterprise, whereby 'employees can prosper only as their employers do, and that irresponsible demands are only self-defeating'. He also would have approved of the way Stevenson applauded his audience for its anti-communism: 'Your effective fight against communism goes clear back to the time it was called bolshevism. You have licked it in your own houses, and you have gone after the roots from which it grows.'

If Holt had been American and had the influence of a friend like Stevenson, he may very well have been a liberal Democrat. He endorsed Stevenson's commitment to humane and liberal principles and his belief in the use of government to enhance people's opportunities, without attempting to dominate or control them. He judged Stevenson to be urbane and refined, somewhat European in nature, representing the best that America had to offer. He also liked his honesty and self-deprecating humour.

Each night, after his days of meetings and discussions in New York, Holt attended the theatre with Zara. They saw *The King and I*, which enchanted them. They saw Edith Piaf sing at the Versailles restaurant. In his diary, Holt noted:

> I didn't like the look of the place much, smoky, over-crowded with a minute dance floor, but there is only one Edith Piaf so we decided to chance it. She is short, rather solid, with bobbed auburn hair, and every inch the artiste chanteuse. She sang about ten songs with that haunting appeal that is uniquely her own.

Next, the couple travelled by train to Washington, DC. In the capital, they found that 'impressive architecture, wide well-made roads, ample park space, and general attractiveness all reflected the planning of enterprising and cultivated minds typical of what is best in America'. Not surprisingly, Georgetown was full of charming

Georgian houses. There, Holt met Sue Dickerson, an old friend from Australia, who took him for a drive beside the Potomac River and on to the Lincoln Memorial, 'where I stood by old Abe, seated larger than life size in his big chair, and read the Gettysburg Address'. When it came time to leave Washington, Holt declared it 'one of the loveliest cities we'd seen, and we'd only had time to scratch the surface of all the interesting things to be found there'.

During his travels he found himself in close proximity to his favourite element. At Pearl Harbor he saw the memorial to the battleship *Arizona* and was moved by the knowledge that still inside were the remains of one thousand drowned sailors. On the way home to Australia, he and Zara made a stop in the southern province of China, Canton (today Guangdong). They visited a small circular tropical atoll enclosing a lagoon, where Holt had a paddle in the water and with Zara walked along a little pier. They lost a day crossing the International Date Line: 'The only way I can see of getting even is to make another trip round the world going the other way. I must do that little thing.'

Then it was back home to Washington Street, to Tiny Lawless and the boys. Holt presented Andy with his special request, a large 'I Like Ike' badge, the slogan emblazoned on a white background, sandwiched between broad red and blue stripes. Holt liked Stevenson, but it was now looking as if the American electorate preferred Ike and would elect him.

The next year, the Holts travelled again. In his capacity of chairman of the Commonwealth Parliamentary Association, Holt was going to host various related functions and, most memorable for him, attend the coronation of Queen Elizabeth and later to be installed as a Companion of Honour.

At St James Court he caught up with his aunt Vera, his last living connection to his late mother. After a gap during the war years, she had returned to filmmaking, mostly comedies, such as *One Wild Oat*, in which she starred opposite Stanley Holloway. She still worked on the London stage in musicals and pantomimes.

In the course of their travels, the Holts found time to take in some art works in Europe. In the Museum of Modern Art in Rome they saw a special Picasso exhibition, which impressed Holt powerfully:

> Most of them utterly baffled understanding by me, and even Zara acknowledged defeat, but their graphic power and violent colouring made a terrific impact. We felt dizzy and exhausted after a few rooms of them, and turned to the other exhibits as to water after strong wine.

He found the oil painting of Lord Byron which hung in the Greek Embassy in Washington intoxicating in a more agreeable way. From the evidence of the portrait, he concluded that Byron 'was certainly a strikingly handsome man, with a dark sensitive face of great beauty'.

The poet, lover and adventurer had been a hero to the Greeks, and was still remembered for his role in their War of Independence, in which they sought to free themselves from the Ottoman Empire. He died of a fever contracted after participating in the first and second sieges of Missolonghi, leaving much of his personal fortune to the Greeks to support their cause. They had revered him ever since, and he was still a national hero.

Holt was inspired by the human form and the ideal of youth and beauty of both body and mind, which the portrait of Byron embodied. The poet's life story resonated with him – the story of a man who had died young, still ravishingly handsome, having crowded many lifetimes into only thirty-six years. In some respects, Byron resembled Sir Walter Raleigh, one of Holt's personal heroes, whom he admired for the mixture of adventurousness, sensitivity and gallantry which he embodied.

Byron and Holt shared a love of the sea. Between 1809 and 1811, the poet made his own Grand Tour, as was customary for a young nobleman. With his friend and travel companion John Hobhouse, he cadged a ride from Smyrna to Constantinople on the ship HMAS

Salsette. On 3 May 1810, while the ship was anchored awaiting Otto-man permission to dock at the city, Byron and Lieutenant Ekenhead of *Salsette*'s marines, swam the Hellespont, the strait separating Europe from Asia at the Dardenelles. Byron considered this feat superior to all his poetry.

According to the legend, the Hellespont was the body of water which claimed the life of Leander as he was crossing from Abydos, where he lived on one side of the strait, to reach his beloved Hero at Sestos on the other side. Every night he swam across the Hellespont to be with her, guided by the lamp she lit at the top of the tower where she lived. One stormy winter night, the strong wind extinguished the lamp and Leander lost his way and drowned. When Hero saw his dead body she threw herself over the edge of her tower to join him. Their bodies washed up on shore together in an embrace and were buried there in a lovers' tomb.

Perhaps Holt thought back to English classes at school, and the study of Byron's long poem 'Childe Harold's Pilgrimage'. When he entered parliament aged only twenty-seven, his fellow members called him 'Childe Harold' – sometimes they still called him that. He may have reflected that Byron had died prematurely, his physi-cal beauty preserved forever in memory. Perhaps he knew the poet's words about the sea, the eternal giver and taker of life:

> Roll on, thou deep and dark blue Ocean – roll!
> Ten thousand fleets sweep over thee in vain.
> Man marks the earth with ruin – his control
> Stops with the shore; – upon the watery plain
> The wrecks are all thy deed, nor doth remain
> A shadow of man's ravage, save his own,
> When, for a moment, like a drop of rain,
> He sinks into thy depths with bubbling groan,
> Without a grave, unknell'd, uncoffin'd, and unknown.

*   *   *

As the 1950s drew on, the Holts made many more excursions into the wider world. Zara treasured the moments during long flights when her husband relaxed and graced those around him with the good cheer which showed in sometimes surprising ways. On a flight between Singapore and Karachi, for example, he composed a short ditty which he sang to a prudent Dutch steward who expressed concern over the effects of eating more than was strictly necessary:

> If you're more relaxed, and fitter
> It really doesn't matter
> If you eat another fritter
> And become a little fatter.

Wherever Zara travelled, she seemed to notice everything. The artist in her sought out patterns beneath the surfaces of things, especially in nature. Once when she and Harold were being driven around in Bangkok, she sat 'just consuming' the coral trees lining the road, until remarking:

> These are large spreading trees just the way I most admire them –
> lovely, twisted, mottled trunks and branches making beautiful
> patterns, and not too much old vegetation, so you can see the shape
> it grows.

Little had changed since the days of her childhood, when her father would stop his car so she could alight and inspect more closely something she had seen along the way.

The Holts also enjoyed the human works of art they witnessed. In London, they saw *Summer of the Seventeenth Doll*, a new Australian play by Ray Lawler. Harold expected the worst, but in the end he and Zara were thrilled by the play:

> Weeping, both of us, through most of the first act – proud of the
> Australian author, proud of the all-Australian cast, and proud of

the country which had produced the types in the play and the types who played them.

Afterwards, they met the actors from this initial production, including June Jago, the female lead. This was a high point of the trip for theatre lovers, and they returned exhilarated to their room at the Savoy.

* * *

When the Holts were seated together on a plane, Zara could savour the physical proximity which was missing during Harold's long absences. Often she heard rumours of his private behaviour during those absences. He was becoming known as a philanderer.

While in Canberra he was often away from her; sometimes he travelled overseas or interstate without her. News of his public life in Canberra often reached her through radio or print news, but there was a secret life, too. It was as Benjamin Disraeli, nineteenth-century British prime minister, had said: 'The world is governed by very different personages from what is imagined by those who are not behind the scenes.'

Zara enjoyed the life her marriage gave her; it was like a cherished piece of material that she hated to imagine being cut up. She had made her choice – it was preferable to stay with an imperfect husband, keeping his infidelities hidden. Her pride was wounded, and she felt that her husband was 'quite a dangerous chap to have around'. Yet she would not confront him; she would see, but not see. She had already been through one divorce, and she knew that bringing up three sons on her own would be hard. And now they had all taken the name Holt.

The inconsistencies of both nations and individuals puzzled her. When she travelled to Japan with Harold, she struggled to reconcile the grace of the people she met with their savagery during World War Two. She was philosophical about this contradiction, and perhaps was thinking of her husband when she wrote in her diary:

> I suppose, to be fair, we are all inclined to be different people under different circumstances, and only a nation of philosophers could truly say they always acted correctly – and if they said that they wouldn't be philosophers.

Her career was now thriving, as was her husband's. With Harold away in Canberra much of the time and her sons at school, she took the opportunity to pick up the threads of her earlier life. Holt had always thought of his wife as a frustrated painter. He explained that she had great artistic ability and had always wanted to paint, and she had found her outlet for this in interior decoration and fashion designing, emphasising cut and bold use of colour.

She discussed with her husband the idea of opening a new dress shop: would it cause any problems for him if she did? She had done it as a teenager and it worked all right while it lasted, but it had eventually exhausted her. But now she was older and wiser, with much more business and fashion acumen, and with considerable skill at managing people. Harold agreed to her plan, so long as it wouldn't interfere with his political career: 'If you have to come abroad with me you have to come, and you'll just have to leave your business.'

Zara's new boutique was situated in Toorak Road, South Yarra, not far from the family home. Betty James – now Betty Grounds – partnered Zara once again in this new venture. They named the shop Magg, after an old bookshop which Zara had once noticed in London's Berkeley Square. The name was etched stylishly on the shop's plate-glass windows, in letters so small they were scarcely noticeable.

Inside, the main room was furnished with two identical sofas in rich mauve and purple striped material, covered with scatter cushions in red, bottle green, dark brown and black. Mustard-coloured wall-to-wall carpet covered the floors. Two light beige wardrobes were covered with Thai silk. Behind these stood three dressing-rooms, each designed to look like a miniature Japanese tearoom. Each dressing room was furnished with a full-length mirror surrounded by huge light bulbs, as if in the dressing room of a theatrical star. Harold's influence was also on show, as two oyster shells which he had fished out of the sea stood on one of the side walls, adding a maritime touch, even here.

In a large room at the back of the shop, seamstresses in white coats worked to bring Zara's designs to life. Wedding dresses were one of Magg's specialties. As time passed, many of the shop's customers came from families known to Harold in his political life, such as Kitty Howson, wife of his friend Peter Howson, whose electorate adjoined his own.

Zara was also able to use her talents in the service of ballet, an art form for which she and Harold shared a passion. Margaret Scott, who had formerly danced with the Rambert Ballet in London, worked near Zara in Toorak and opened a ballet school there in 1955. In 1957 the two women staged a dance performance at the Toorak Village Theatre. Zara looked after the fashion elements while Margaret managed the staging with help from her friends, the choreographer Rex Reid and the designer Ann Church.

Zara was now becoming something of a celebrity, featured in newspaper articles and popular magazines. Alongside her enjoyment of publicity was a strong sense of privacy in thought and feeling. That contradiction was visible in photos of her in which she looked directly at the world beyond her as if giving it her full attention, yet with a slight suggestion that part of her remained in her private world.

Over the years, while attending political meetings, she had mastered the skill of 'designing away in my head'. She sat on the stage or the front row with a quite intelligent and even rapt expression on her face, as if she were taking in what was being said. The words sailed past her, but she laughed and clapped at the right times, while inwardly designing another dress or embroidery. This was Zara's equivalent to her husband's ability to zone out and hold his breath during dull periods in parliament.

Since her childhood, when she had diligently cut the tulips from her mother's new bedspread and pasted them on her bedroom wall, she had possessed a powerful feeling for beauty. She loved painting, and for her, fashion design was a sort of painting. Clothing could create beauty that was more than skin-deep; it could make a spiritual statement. When she handled a piece of material in the shop, she could feel and see the artistry behind it, the skill and the technique. Sometimes she would keep it because she couldn't stand to sell it or cut it up.

She was self-deprecating about why she liked fashion design – 'because I've got an impossible figure'. She liked to design and wear loose-fitting clothing 'to hide the bumps, because I'm fat'. But she also favoured kaftans and tent-style dresses because she hated the material to be 'interrupted'. She didn't want to 'cut it up into darts and carry on with it'; she just wanted it to flow. Wholeness was the point for her. When an idea for a design came to her, she could see the whole dress completely finished inside her head.

She could not sew a stitch, but she could see possibilities for designs, ways of creating wholeness out of fragments, sometimes in unexpected circumstances and places. One such moment of revelation she never forgot. She and Harold were flying from Melbourne to Canberra, when it started to rain. The wind kept pushing the rain about on the plane windows, and every so often, rhythmically, the moving raindrops shattered but then came together again to form a ribbon. As she watched the patterns of the raindrops unfold, an image began to form in her mind. She used it as the design for the strands of one of her favourite embroideries.

12

A Lucky Escape

*The Minister for Labour and National Service, Mr H.E. Holt,
received injuries to the head, back, and lacerations to the face
when a car in which he was travelling crashed into a brick wall
of the Masonic Hall at North Sydney at 1.30 a.m. today.*
— The Sydney Morning Herald, 22 November 1955

ON 29 MAY 1954, THE MENZIES GOVERNMENT WAS returned to power despite losing the two-party preferred vote to Labor, then led by H.V. Evatt. This was the first federal election in which a party had received a clear majority of the votes but was unable to form a government.

Late in the following year, Menzies called an early election to take place on 10 December, hoping to exploit recent developments in domestic politics. His government had benefited from a major split in the Labor Party. A faction which felt that communist influence was taking over the party and the trade unions allied to it had split off and formed a new party. With their strongest influence in Victoria, they announced that they would direct their preferences to the Liberal Party.

In the same year, 1955, Harold Holt celebrated his twentieth year as a parliamentarian. In the leadup to the election, and in his capacity as Minister for Immigration, he welcomed to Australia its one millionth postwar migrant, Barbara Porritt, who had arrived in Melbourne on the ship *Oronsay*. Her husband, Dennis, an electrician contracted to work for the State Electricity Commission of Victoria, accompanied her. At a press conference held on *Oronsay* after it docked, Mr Holt greeted Mrs Porritt: 'Mrs Porritt, Australia salutes you as the representative of our million post-war migrants. Now we are looking forward to our second million.'

Robert Menzies may have considered 10 December an auspicious date, for his government had first come to power on that date six years earlier. However, 22 November 1955 was a very inauspicious date for Harold Holt. During the election campaign, he was travelling around Australia to support Liberal Party candidates in marginal seats, as his own seat was safe. On 21 November he was chauffeured from Sydney to an election meeting in Newcastle, about 150 kilometres north. He and his driver, Gustav Heilster, arrived there at around 6.30 in the evening and set out to return to Sydney at around ten.

They travelled in a Humber Pullman car, which Holt favoured because it allowed him to work on ministerial papers in the back seat. He was weary after the long day. He swapped his coat for a cashmere sweater, raised the dicky seat, put his feet up, covered his eyes with a mask, and tried to sleep.

He dozed fitfully, waking several times between Newcastle and Gosford, the nearest large town. He noticed that Heilster was driving steadily and well. They passed through patches of fog and Heilster stopped to clean the windscreen. Holt awoke the next time he felt the car stop.

'Where are we?' he asked.

'Gosford. I've done a cylinder head gasket,' replied the driver.

They stopped for a few minutes. In between snatches of sleep, Holt realised that his driver was changing gears more often than seemed necessary. He concluded that for some reason Heilster must have been nursing the car.

Holt checked his watch – 12.50 a.m., on what was now Tuesday, 22 November. He removed his eyepad, dozed off again, then awoke and noticed that they were passing Sydney's Mater Misericordiae Hospital. The next thing he remembered was waking up there.

He had a severe concussion – his head was swathed in a bandage and the right side of his face was heavily bruised. He was very sore, but his injuries were not life-threatening. The doctors examined him for a possible fracture of the skull and treated him for severe shock.

The local police established that the driver had failed to negotiate a bend, crashed into a telegraph post, bounced off it and travelled another twenty feet before crashing into the brick fence of the local Masonic Hall. The force of the impact uprooted about forty feet of the fence. The back offside door of the car was ripped off and both front doors were crushed back against the bodywork. Pieces of the car lay scattered over an area of about thirty feet.

Holt's thoughts turned to the driver of the car.

'How is Mr Heilster?' he asked the doctor.

'I'm afraid he's dead.'

'Was he married?'

'He was, with two young children, a girl and a boy.'

Holt was distressed, hearing this news. He asked that the family's welfare be attended to. If they were renting accommodation, could arrangements be made to help with the payments? 'I am a very lucky man,' he concluded, adding that 'all my feeling is for the Heilsters'.

During his convalescence, his ministerial activities continued. A Cypriot immigrant named Kemal Asilturk was also in the hospital. He was in the process of writing to Holt to ask for help in bringing his family to Australia to escape riot conditions in their homeland.

Holt asked to see him. Asilturk was wheeled into his flower-filled room.

'I knew fate was on my side when I heard you had come,' he told Holt.

'It's only the riot conditions in Cyprus that are slowing things down. You can stop worrying now. We'll hurry it up for you,' Holt assured him.

Holt spent two weeks in hospital. He was still groggy when he was released, but still smiling, He had been spared a sudden death.

His schooldays sobriquet, 'Cat', seemed apt; a good measure of luck had attended him.

His campaign for re-election came to a sudden halt with a period of enforced rest, but a few weeks later he was returned for another three years as the Member for Higgins with a swing towards him of over 10 per cent; his Labor Party opponent, A.A. Hughes, scored barely a third of Holt's share of the vote.

The Menzies government was back with an increased majority, seventy-five seats to Labor's forty-seven. The split in the Labor Party had badly damaged it; its vote in Victoria dropped by 13 per cent. Seeking a less negative image, Anti-Communist Labor soon renamed itself the Democratic Labor Party, or DLP. This party secured a high percentage of the Roman Catholic vote, and with almost all DLP preferences in the more marginal seats, the future of the Menzies government seemed assured, at least into the near future. Meanwhile, Holt's political future appeared more promising than ever.

So did his personal life. His family had moved to a new house at 112 St Georges Road, Toorak. The house had wide windows, almost all of them overlooking the Yarra River. The terraced garden, with its fringe of wattles and other native trees, swept down to the river. The house was brick, painted 'dead' brown – a kind of greenish chocolate with white paintwork with black trimmings. The living room had wide windows. On the mantelpiece Zara placed a statue of the Eight Chinese Virtues in glazed white china, and around the house she scattered some of her collection of Nubian slave figurines.

The year following his car accident was a very good one for Holt. He was appointed deputy leader of the Liberal Party, which automatically made him leader of the House of Representatives. The latter position was a fitting reward for a man who had always valued the institution of parliament highly, thinking it the greatest instrument man had so far devised for the organisation of a free society. As a parliamentarian, he had been praised for 'his charm and frankness of manner, for the ease with which laughter came to him, for his impeccable dressing and for the assured grace with which he manages business in the House'.

Though his black hair had gone grey, he still looked youthful and seemed to have his best years ahead of him. His public profile had grown greatly throughout the 1950s; he was widely known overseas and had been given the responsibility to oversee Australia's role in hosting the 1956 Olympic Games in Melbourne.

'The spear-fishing lawyer could be Australia's next Prime Minister,' editorialised Melbourne's *The Argus* on 27 September. The editorial continued:

> He has three great ideals: the cake is big enough to share; we must continue to strengthen ties between British Commonwealth countries (he is chairman of the Commonwealth Parliamentary Association); we must build up a big, virile population . . . Long considered the up-and-coming man in the Liberal Party, Harold Holt now has no rivals as 'heir apparent' to Mr Menzies. It's been a long battle for the debonair, urbane solicitor who became Australia's youngest Federal Minister at the age of 32.

13

Another Jolt

THE HEAT IS ON HANDSOME HAROLD
> —Editorial headline, *The Observer*, 17 May 1958

MANY POLITICAL OBSERVERS CONSIDERED HOLT the best industrial relations minister the country had ever had. They admired his skill in defusing conflicts and bringing opponents together. They noted that during his tenure from 1949 to 1958, the number of working hours lost to strikes had dropped from over two million to 439,000. They praised his work in the Ministry of Immigration, where he oversaw the rapid post-war expansion of the program, while showing his usual concern for solving human problems.

Despite a major global downturn early in 1958, the Menzies government was again returned to power. There was an even further swing against the Labor Party, largely due to increased support for the DLP. As Holt's name was increasingly mentioned as a successor to Menzies, it became clear that he would need a more prominent portfolio. His personal preference was Minister for External Affairs, which he felt would allow him to make direct use of his social and negotiating skills and to attend directly to the needs of people.

But it was in the treasury that a vacancy first appeared with the retirement of Treasurer Arthur Fadden in 1958. It was tradition for the deputy prime minister – the leader of the Country Party – to be treasurer but, in this case, John 'Black Jack' McEwen preferred to retain the trade portfolio. This left the position open to Holt, who realised that if one of his Liberal Party colleagues were to become treasurer instead of him, that colleague would be better placed to threaten his own prime ministerial ambitions. Holt assumed the position in 1958; it was prestigious, but not wholly suited to his natural abilities.

As treasurer, he was on foreign ground. While his advisers in treasury blinded him with science and economic jargon, he got bogged down in econometric technicalities. Every day, Zara wore a bracelet with the gold medal given to him when he was elected Queen's College Orator of 1930. Since then, his diction had changed for the worse: the lucid debater of his university and earlier parliamentary days became mired in a swamp of longwinded explanations expressed by means of legalistic qualifying phrases and clauses. As a result, the verbs of his sentences often ended up a long way from their subjects. He was so worried about making a mistake that he abandoned simplicity for circumlocution; the less sure of himself he felt, the more he felt compelled to explain himself.

Since becoming treasurer, he had created the ritual of travelling to North Queensland in early August with Zara, shortly before presenting the budget in the House on the third Tuesday of that month. As his birthday fell at that time, he could celebrate it in a holiday setting, no matter how much work he had to do. He would 'go into smoke' at Mission Beach, near Innisfail on the Cassowary Coast.

Nearby at Bingil Bay his old friend Johnnie Busst lived with his wife, Alison, who had long been a close friend of Zara. Johnnie had moved north from Melbourne to Bedarra Island with his sister Phyllis. Later, they had purchased almost the whole island. After Phyllis returned to Melbourne, Johnnie married Alison, who joined him on the island. The Holts often visited the Bussts there. To them, Bedarra was a paradise, which Harold felt rivalled the beauty of the Mediterranean. When he visited Greece in 1953 he had reflected that 'the dry warmth, clear blue skies, and islands sparkling in the sunlit sea of Greece was the closest we'd come to Johnnie and Ali's private paradise'.

The Bussts moved to Bingil Bay in 1957, the year before Holt became treasurer. There, Johnnie enjoyed his involvement with his strongest interests: art, architecture, and later, advocacy on behalf of conservation of the nearby Great Barrier Reef. He had built on a block that included extensive areas of tropical rainforest and the rocky headland known as Ninney Point, so the Bussts named the new house Ninney Rise. Behind it was rainforest; in front were the waters of the Coral Sea and the Great Barrier Reef.

Johnnie Busst built Ninney Rise as a fortress to outlast the cyclones which periodically smashed into the coast. On the outside, he used bricks and reinforced concrete; on the inside, he used bamboo to make ceiling features, architraves and fittings throughout the house. He was building for posterity, just as he had been during the construction of Montsalvat many years earlier, for he was 'not interested in making anything that won't last for a thousand years'.

Holt, too, was building for posterity, helping to secure his country's economic future. But Holt had shorter-term goals than Busst, since constant fluctuation was built into economic reality. From year to year, from budget to budget, he had to negotiate the vagaries of the economy.

On the evening of 11 August 1959, the new treasurer brought down his first budget in the House of Representatives. On budget day, snippets of his pre-budget activities kept trickling through to the press. He had a slight cold, the effects of which he was treating with throat lozenges. The previous night he had indulged his enthusiasm for his favourite art form, relaxing at Canberra's only performance of the Bolshoi Ballet at the Albert Hall. Speculation arose about how he had managed to secure a seat when the performance had been booked out for weeks beforehand. 'When the box office did open, the rush was so great that it closed in a matter of minutes,' reported *The Age*, whose writer went on to ask: 'But if a Treasurer about to bring down his first budget cannot get a seat at the ballet, who can?'

The treasurer's first budget aroused neither alarm nor enthusiasm. But the following year, things went wrong. Just after his arrival at Innisfail, strained and overworked, he collapsed from nervous exhaustion.

The date was 5 August 1960, his fifty-second birthday. He had been more sleep-deprived than usual and now he was required to rest. He usually tried to get by on four hours of sleep a night, working on ministerial business while his colleagues were resting. The goal of never wasting a second, of filling the unforgiving minute, was damaging his health. This time of illness at Mission Beach was a bad omen. There was trouble afoot for the national economy, and thus for the government, too.

But by the time he presented the budget on the night of 17 August, he had recovered and felt more at ease, speaking in a clear, steady voice. But he could not escape reminders of his recent illness; at his first mention of taxation increases, a voice called out from the Opposition benches, 'No wonder it made you sick.'

The treasurer explained during his speech that 'the pace of expansion has become a little too fast and we have to ease it off a little'. As a result, the government decided to introduce a credit squeeze. *The Age* editorial of the following day foresaw few significant problems with Holt's budget: 'The year's Budget, with its modest increase in taxation, its general restraints and its urgently needed concessions to pensioners of all classes is not going to hurt anyone much.'

Other national newspapers disagreed, and hit the treasurer with a fusillade of criticism. In a cartoon in the Sydney *Sun* the economy was depicted as a shackled kangaroo protesting: 'Don't Tie Me Kangaroo Down, Sport!' Similarly, Sydney newspaper *The Daily Mirror* lamented: 'We are sorry for Harold Holt. He is such a nice chap. As a Treasurer, however, he has proved a miserable failure.'

The fallout from the budget continued into the following year. The car industry was hit when sales taxes on new cars were set at 40 per cent. The errors of the budget would have to be rectified, so the treasurer introduced a mini budget in February of 1961 to try to patch up the problems. This became known as 'Holt's Jolt'.

Then the prime minister unilaterally decided that the sales tax on new cars needed to be cut. Menzies had not consulted his treasurer before asking cabinet to reverse its policy on the tax. Rather, the prime minister told cabinet of his decision, gave the still virtually uninformed treasurer a statement to distribute to the nation, and boarded a plane for the United States. One editorialist considered Menzies' decision not to consult his treasurer a 'snub' of Holt. There were rumblings behind the scenes that the treasurer might even lose preselection as the member for Higgins. George E. Knox, insurance company chief and Liberal Party member, threatened to oppose him in the seat as an unendorsed Liberal candidate, asserting that the treasurer had been 'a disaster for Australia, and a great embarrassment to Mr Menzies'.

Mr Knox finally withdrew 'for family reasons', but the damage was done and Holt was blamed for the reverse the Menzies government suffered at the end-of-year election, in which it lost many seats, especially in Queensland, where the economic effect of government policies had been most strongly felt. For a time it seemed that the government might be defeated; when the counting of votes eventually ended, its majority had been cut to only two.

There were moves afoot in Higgins to withdraw Holt's endorsement for the next election. When Zara won a fashion award from the clothing industry for designing the 'Gown of the Year' in 1961, the deputy leader of the Opposition, Gough Whitlam, drew attention to the treasurer's failings: 'It is Australia's tragedy that the husband of our best designer is our worst planner.'

If Menzies had been defeated, Holt would have been consigned to the Opposition benches with him and probably stripped of any hope of becoming prime minister. It was another life for 'Cat' Holt.

Soon he and Zara had a new house of their own at Bingil Bay, only two miles away from the Bussts'. Zara had found the land for the house, the way she found everything – 'by my usual habit of looking, looking, looking at everything that's around me'.

The house started as a one-room weekend fishing shack, almost hidden by thick tropical jungle. It was unremarkable, but what staggered Zara was the view: seven rows of mountains running away into the distance on the left-hand side of the house; behind and on the right-hand side a garden, and then solid jungle. In front of the house were beaches, and the islands of the Great Barrier Reef.

They kept the original house, but added to it so that it could accommodate six people. There, in a bright, bamboo-lined room overlooking the Pacific, Holt prepared his budgets for the rest of his tenure as treasurer, working at night by yellow kerosene lamps. According to neighbours, he kept a low profile: 'That's the quiet bloke, goes spear-fishing a lot. I think he's a Member of Parliament.' To some of the locals he was known as 'Holtie'.

North Queensland was a different Australia from the one the Holts were used to in the south. It was a tropical world of jungles, vines, creepers and huge trees with twisted roots and branches. There were birds of every conceivable colour, announcing their presence with strange, strident cries, and the plopping sounds of crabs in the rivers.

The Holts were 3000 kilometres away from Canberra and even further from Melbourne, and the distance was psychological as well as physical. Harold and Zara felt different when they were in the north. For Harold, the difference was embodied in aspects of his clothing, such as his cane-cutter's hat, the sarong he sometimes wore when dining with the Bussts, and the necklace of shiny white shells which Zara made for him. For Zara, North Queensland meant a change of name. In Melbourne, Harold had long called her by her middle name, Kate, but up north everyone called her that.

The Holts now had a hideaway in two ends of the country, southern Victoria and northern Queensland, the sea nearby in both places. Here the treasurer enjoyed views of the ocean while he prepared his budgets, and when he had time he swam and snorkelled with Johnnie.

The building of the new house at Bingil Bay coincided with a more secure period for Holt. After the reverses of 1960 and 1961, the waters eventually calmed and the course of domestic politics helped Menzies strengthen his position. The treasurer prepared his 1963 budget under much happier circumstances than had attended the one three years earlier, confident that this budget would not frighten the voters. The economic problems of 1961 had diminished; unemployment was negligible and inflation was low. It was 'an even-keel budget', which suggested that no storms were on the horizon in the coming year, and no early election either. It was an unremarkable budget, notable only for some modest tax concessions and pension increases, and a lifting of the immigration target to 135,000.

By 1963, the Labor Party was in trouble on a number of fronts. The party was sharply divided over the issue of federal aid to non-government schools. Its federal executive strongly opposed funding private schools and this policy was harming the party, especially among its Roman Catholic supporters, some of whom were still defecting to the DLP. Some Catholic priests were preaching against what they regarded as the sinfulness of voting Labor.

To exploit these circumstances, the prime minister pulled off a masterstroke. He entered the field of direct state aid with promises to provide science blocks and other facilities for independent schools – promises lifted from those made by the New South Wales branch of the ALP, but rejected by the party's federal executive.

Education policy began to take a backseat as foreign affairs began to dominate – especially in South-East Asia, where South Vietnam was contending with a communist insurgency. The dominant perception in the electorate was that the Menzies government could be trusted to keep Australia secure in an unstable world. It had forged strong defence alliances, and the electorate was uncertain whether a Labor government would maintain them – especially when Labor's policy on matters such as defence was being determined by the unelected members of the party's federal executive, known as 'the thirty-six faceless men', a disparaging label coined by the veteran Canberra journalist Alan Reid.

On the evening of 21 March 1963, Alan Reid engineered a journalistic coup when he saw the Labor leader, Arthur Calwell, and his deputy, Gough Whitlam, waiting in the dark late at night outside the Kingston Hotel in Canberra. Inside the hotel, the 'thirty-six faceless men' were determining party policy on the government's proposal to allow the United States to set up a defence communications base in Western Australia. Calwell and Whitlam were trying to find out what was happening inside the hotel from delegates who had absented themselves from the meeting.

No press photographers were present, but Reid tracked down a scientific photographer at the Australian National University named Vladimir Paarl, who happened to be at the Kingston Hotel. Reid asked him to drive home and to return as soon as possible with a camera with a flashlight, which he did. He snapped a highly unflattering photograph of Calwell and Whitlam waiting outside the hotel for instructions. In the darkness, Calwell's face was ghostly white.

Later in the year, the prime minister decided to capitalise on the difficulties of the ALP by calling an election for the last day of November, a full year ahead of the appointed time. Menzies argued that Calwell was unfit to be prime minister, as he was a pawn of the thirty-six faceless men, and *The Sydney Morning Herald* repeated the line.

Only one week before the election, President Kennedy was assassinated in Dallas, Texas. 'We've lost!' Calwell exclaimed. The assassination certainly did not help Labor's cause, creating alarm and a sense of insecurity throughout the world. In uncertain times, Australian electors clung to Menzies as a child to its father's leg.

But the Kennedy assassination was not the most important factor in the Labor Party's defeat. Enough voters had already turned against the party for it to be defeated, and the death of the American president only added to the government's favour. Gaining ten seats, the government's narrow majority widened; Holt increased his own majority in Higgins, reversing the adverse swing of two years earlier.

There was talk now that this election might be the last that Menzies would contest. There was still more change in the air. By 1964 the treasurer was engaged in preparations for Australia's transition to decimal currency. The new money – dollars and cents – was designed to be simpler for use and calculation than the prevailing system of pounds, shillings and pence. The treasurer made a short film to introduce the new coins and the native fauna that would be depicted on them. The size of the animals corresponded to the value of the coin. The kangaroo and emu from Australia's coat of arms would decorate the fifty-cent piece; the platypus the twenty; the lyrebird the ten; the echidna the five; while the smallest of the animals, the frill-necked lizard and the feathertail glider, were chosen for the two and one cent coins respectively.

* * *

As the date chosen for the currency changeover – 14 February 1966 – drew nearer, Holt was frequently in the public eye, but still unencumbered by the heavier burdens carried by a prime minister. He cherished his freedom to come and go as he pleased. When he disappeared to go snorkelling or spearfishing, he shed his public responsibilities, losing himself in his favourite places, especially Cheviot Beach.

Often he went there alone. One day, around Christmas 1964, he made a small slip which drew the attention of others to the risks he was running. He had been spearfishing at Cheviot Beach from early in the morning, and on returning to his car to drive home for rest and food, he found he had locked his keys in the boot.

Cold and hungry, he waited in the front seat. It was early afternoon before another car appeared near his, above the beach. When he heard the car, he wriggled back into his wetsuit and got out to greet the occupants.

They were a family from Melbourne, Mr and Mrs Griffiths and their two young sons, who were on their annual holiday at Sorrento. Mr Griffiths was a public servant at the government aircraft factory and he applied each year for a pass that allowed him to enter the grounds of the Portsea quarantine station, inside of which was Cheviot Beach. Recognising the famous face, Mr and Mrs Griffiths exclaimed: 'Good God! It's the treasurer!'

Mr Holt was a little sheepish as he explained his predicament and asked if Mr Griffiths could drive him the four or five miles back to his house to get another set of keys. When he arrived home with the Griffiths family, he appeared not to have been missed. His wife and son seemed unperturbed by his long absence, skindiving alone at one of Victoria's most dangerous beaches.

After a while he returned from the house to his rescuers, dressed and munching ravenously on a sandwich while jiggling a huge bunch of keys. He told Mr and Mrs Griffiths that his son would drive him back to his car, and invited the family into his home.

Wishing not to impose, Mr and Mrs Griffiths declined his invitation. Instead, they drove back out to Point Nepean. They had recently read a new book about Liberal Party politics which contained a picture of Holt, considered the logical successor to Menzies, dressed in his skindiving gear and holding up a fish for the camera. The caption read: 'Holt – fishing in deep waters.' On the drive back through the quarantine gates and out along the headland, Mr and Mrs Griffiths talked with animation. They were incredulous that anyone, let alone the federal treasurer, would dive alone along such a dangerous stretch of coastline.

Back at Cheviot Beach, Mr Griffiths stood on the cliff with his sons and pointed towards the sea. He drew their attention to the rocks, explaining that together they formed three gutters that sucked water off the beach into huge holes just offshore. These holes were filled with bull kelp – enormous seaweed that could trap a swimmer. The beach was also known for its dangerous rips and undertows. He feared for Mr Holt.

14

Unleashing the Furies

Anyone who counsels our getting into a ground war on the
continent of Asia should have his head examined.
— Douglas MacArthur, quoted in *Many Battles*,
US Senator Ernest Gruening's autobiography

THE MENZIES GOVERNMENT WAS TAKING AUSTRALIA into deep waters of another kind. Next to *The Age*'s front-page report of Harold Holt's 1963 budget was a headline reporting the latest of a series of self-immolations by Buddhist monks in South Vietnam. These suicides by fire had been staged in protest against the repressive policies of President Ngo Dinh Diem. He had declared martial law, imposed a strict curfew, ordered the arrests of Opposition leaders and more than one thousand Buddhists, and directed his soldiers to attack pagodas in Saigon and Hue. Photographs of barbed wire around the entrances to these pagodas symbolised the state of affairs in South Vietnam.

In the US, President Kennedy rebuked the South Vietnamese government; the Australian government expressed concern. Thus far, very few Australians had been directly affected by the situation, as their country had only a handful of military advisers in Vietnam, assisting South Vietnamese troops in their struggle against the Viet Cong guerillas. A small article in *The Age* on 3 June that year noted the accidental death of one of these advisers, William Hacking from Melbourne, the first Australian to die in the guerrilla war.

South Vietnam was not the only country in South-East Asia to trouble the Menzies government. It was very worried by Indonesian president Sukarno's policy of *konfrontasi*, or confrontation, with the newly created Federation of Malaysia. Sukarno saw the creation of the new Malaysian state as a neo-colonial ploy by Britain to retain some of its dwindling power in South-East Asia, and he threatened to 'gobble Malaysia raw'. By September 1963, while the Buddhists were rioting in South Vietnam, Indonesia was practising subversion in Singapore and Malaysia.

As immigration minister, Holt had expressed concern about the 'Asiatics' to the north of Australia, worried that they might see the country as a rich prize in years to come. He referred to Asia as 'the great threat' to Australia, albeit in twenty to fifty years' time – 'when Asiatics will look on Australia as a ripe plum ready for the plucking'.

The Australian government saw the hand of China behind the growing instability in South-East Asia and wanted American troops stationed there as a bulwark between Australia and China. Now living in an apartment at the Waldorf Astoria Hotel in New York, Douglas MacArthur had reached his own conclusions about the war in South Vietnam: 'Anyone who counsels our getting into a ground war on the continent of Asia should have his head examined.'

In 1963, Arthur Calwell visited the United States and met with the two Americans whom he felt Australians most admired – General MacArthur and President Kennedy. The leader of the Opposition was proud of his American ancestry. His paternal grandfather, Davis Calwell, had been born in Pennsylvania and had come to Ballarat, Victoria, for the Gold Rush. Arthur Calwell felt that his grandfather's American origins had encouraged his own keen personal interest in American history, politics and literature. Although Calwell was kindly disposed to the United States, he had deep misgivings about the growing American role in Vietnam. But he was loathe to do or say anything which might endanger the Australian–American alliance. He and his party would have to walk a tightrope, opposing the American role in Vietnam without opposing the US.

President Kennedy and his successor, President Johnson, had also met with the octogenarian general. MacArthur had withered away rather than faded away, as he said old soldiers did. In civilian clothes, with much of his body weight gone, he was hardly recognisable as the man known to the world during his years of military command. He had not much longer to live.

His body had shrunk, but his wisdom had expanded. After the Pacific War, he had commanded the allied forces in Korea for more than a year in a war which had ended in a draw after years of stalemate. Now he implored Kennedy and Johnson to avoid entanglement in another war on the Asian mainland.

Francisco Salveron, still one of the general's greatest admirers, was by now a long-established member of the expatriate Filipino community near Washington, DC. His Filipino family had grown with the addition of three more children, but he had no knowledge of the activities of his family left behind in Australia. He had continued his military career in the US by enlisting in the Air Force, reaching the rank of master sergeant. He had been assigned to Eisenhower's flight crew, and later served as a flight steward to Truman as well as a number of secretaries of state.

After MacArthur's death in April 1964, Salveron strove to keep his legend alive, founding the General Douglas MacArthur post of the Veterans of Foreign Wars. Memories of World War Two surrounded him in his house, where the walls were lined with photographs of former secretaries of state and secretaries of war and, of course, of MacArthur.

Clarissa Salveron had struggled for years to bring up her children without the help of their father. In age they were barely more than a year apart, and very close to each other. Frances had been kept back a year at school so that she and Douglas could be together in the same class. Clarissa could not afford to support the children unaided, so after second form they had to leave school to go to work. Douglas found a job as an office boy at the shipping firm of Abel, Lemon and Company, where he worked his way up to the position of office manager. The company had its office in the custom house beside the Brisbane River, near where his parents had first met in 1942. This job suited him, but he contemplated investing some money in a block of flats or a cafe or restaurant.

Early in August 1964, President Johnson announced that North Vietnamese PT boats had attacked two American destroyers, the *Maddox* and the *C. Turner Joy*, on the high seas off North Vietnam in the Gulf of Tonkin. He ordered retaliatory bombing raids on bases in North Vietnam and assured the public that the American response would be 'limited and fitting'. In Canberra, his action won bipartisan approval. In supporting the president's action, Arthur Calwell declared that 'the gravity of the situation could hardly be exaggerated'.

At Syracuse University in New York, where he had gone on 5 August to dedicate a new Communications Centre, President Johnson put aside the speech he had planned and spoke instead of the recent events in Vietnam. Facing a huge banner which read 'Syracuse Loves LBJ', he claimed that the attacks on the American ships had been 'deliberate' and 'unprovoked', a claim which was later strongly disputed. Within days, both houses of the American Congress passed the 'Tonkin Gulf Resolution', designed to allow the president to take any steps he believed necessary to promote the maintenance of peace and security in South-East Asia. He now had a blank cheque to conduct war in Vietnam.

On 3 November, Johnson was elected to a full term as president in a landslide win. Much of the world was relieved that he had beaten Senator Barry Goldwater, whose aggressive stance on Vietnam had enabled Johnson to run as a 'peace' candidate. But he was not about to pull America out of the war. Both the American and Australian governments saw the war as part of a larger struggle against communism. The Australian government felt that the whole of South-East Asia and ultimately Australia itself would be endangered if South Vietnam could not maintain its independence.

With employment levels in Australia very high, army recruitment was difficult. So on 10 November, Menzies announced the introduction of conscription, to be known as 'national service'. A ballot would be held twice a year, with marbles coded to match birthdates. All twenty-year-old males were required by law to register, and those whose birth dates corresponded with the numbers on the marbles would be considered for service in the Army and would also be liable for overseas service.

Each year there would be two registration periods, the first for twenty-year-olds with birthdays in the first half of the year, the second for those with birthdays in the second half. All the men in the 1965 ballots had been born during the year of 1945: the children born at the end of one war would now be liable to serve in another. Douglas Salveron's birthday, 17 February, was one of the dates drawn in the first ballot.

The introduction of compulsory military service raised a familiar question: how liberal really was the Liberal Party? It was difficult to see how this policy was consistent with the party's avowed commitment to a maximum of personal freedom, especially when Australia was not facing a direct threat to its security.

On 8 March 1965 a battalion of combat-ready American marines splashed ashore on the beaches of Da Nang. Their arrival marked a new escalation of the conflict. Two days later, the first national service ballot was conducted at the Department of Labor and National Service in Swanston Street, Melbourne, and the first marbles were drawn, representing the 4200 new recruits required for the June and September intakes.

Outside the building, about twelve young people demonstrated against the compulsory call-up, marching in an orderly single file in circles on the footpath. A girl carried a placard that read 'We Oppose The Call-Up'; a young man carried one that read 'We Don't Want to Kill.' But overt protest was limited. When it came to obeying the law and accepting the decisions of their elders, most of Australia's youth were compliant.

On 29 April, a half-empty House of Representatives heard the news that Australia was to send a battalion of regular soldiers to

South Vietnam as a supplement to the military advisers who were already there. There was a possibility that, as well as regulars, conscripts would be sent.

It was an article of faith on the part of the government that the country's most solid insurance policy was its alliance with the United States. At the end of April, in his capacity as treasurer, Holt went to Washington as a supplicant to negotiate the lifting of American trade restrictions against Australia. In talks with Secretary of State Dean Rusk and Secretary of Treasury Henry Fowler, he drew attention to Australia's current defence efforts.

With the pun undoubtedly intended, *The Age* headlined the story 'AMERICANS SEE NO HALT TO CAPITAL':

WASHINGTON, May 2. – The Treasurer (Mr. Holt) said on Friday American Cabinet members had told him they foresaw 'no interruption' in capital funds for Australia. Mr. Holt said there was a 'strong desire' on the part of the United States to help Australia meet any difficulties arising from America's foreign investment restrictions. Without directly saying so, he left the impression at the press conference that Australia had all but secured an unwritten exception from the curbs on private capital outflow which President Johnson introduced in February. Australian investment in the United States would be allowed to continue at the current level. Mr. Holt referred to the United States' willingness to help Australia in the context of Australia's general economic development and its commitments in South East Asia – including the decision to send combat troops to Vietnam.

The Labor Party began to use the slogan 'Diggers for Dollars' to describe the government's motives. Sending troops to Vietnam was the down payment on Australia's insurance policy with America, and Harold Holt would soon be responsible for defending the Australian commitment.

PART TWO

THE NEW
PRIME MINISTER

15

A Death and
a New Beginning

Vera Pearce, actress and aunt of Harold E. Holt, new Prime Minister of Australia, died on Tuesday at St Thomas Hospital, it was learned today.

—*The New York Times*, 21 January 1966

IN MARCH 1965, HOLT RECEIVED THE NEWS THAT HIS much-loved aunt, Vera Pearce, was seriously ill in St Thomas' Hospital in London and was not expected to survive. He immediately wrote about her to his friend Alick Downer at the Australian High Commission in London:

I would like to feel that she is receiving every care and comfort. My late mother's half sister has always been close to my brother and myself and I am saddened that, at a time when she may be so much in need of us, we are so remote from her.

Throughout 1965 he must have often thought of his aunt and worried about her, but there were other matters claiming his attention during that year. It was finally clear that the prime ministership of 'old man Menzies', as Johnson affectionately called him, was drawing to a close. He would be seventy-two by the time of the next election and was reluctant to put himself through the rigours of another campaign.

Contentious matters rarely fazed Menzies, but once in 1965 when a group of angry anti–Vietnam War protestors assailed him at close quarters, he recoiled in shock, hands shielding his face. Perhaps he no longer had the energy to wage a spirited defence of the war, especially amidst the tensions of a general election.

By the mid-1960s, the name Menzies seemed almost synonymous with 'prime minister'. The treasurer would have been reluctant to challenge his leader, even if he had decided to remain in office until he was eighty, though it had long been accepted that Holt would replace Menzies when he finally retired. Profiles of the treasurer and his family became commonplace as 1965 drew to a close. He had bided his time patiently, like an incoming batsman waiting for a teammate to declare his long innings closed.

Holt suspected that the 1965 budget would be his last, coinciding with the thirtieth anniversary of his election to parliament. He found it 'rather a solemn thought to have spent half a lifetime in this odd occupation'. He would have to be replaced as treasurer, a portfolio that was one of the stepping-stones for prime ministerial aspirants. No one doubted Billy McMahon's ambitions in that direction, and the smart money was that he would take Holt's place, promoted from his ministry of Labour and National Service. His career path would be closely following Holt's.

Menzies was relieved that in retirement he would be rid of McMahon. He could not wave away this man or eyebrow him out of his life. He sometimes discussed his McMahon problem with his intimates, reproaching himself: 'I should have done something about that dreadful little squirt.' Others in the government shared Menzies' contempt for McMahon, especially John McEwen, the Country Party leader and deputy prime minister. The journalist Alan Reid noted that in the early stages of their association, McEwen had shown towards McMahon 'the tolerance of indifference':

A man who at 19 had made his start on a rabbit-ravaged, eighty-acre returned soldiers' farming block at Stanhope with capital

assets of a horse, gig, health and 50 shillings in cash – an unprom-
ising block similar to those on which almost an entire generation
of soldier settlers worked themselves despairingly into bankruptcy,
but now the heart of one of the show farms of Victoria – McEwen
was not likely to be impressed by McMahon's inherited wealth and
close connections with Sydney socialite society.

As time passed, indifference had turned to a mutual loathing
which threatened to become a fault line under the coalition. Both
men were highly ambitious, combative and reluctant to compromise. McEwen did not trust McMahon, who, he felt, told stories to
the media with a slant, and leaked secrets from cabinet. McMahon
was no friend of the Country Party, resenting that party's power
within the coalition. He would have preferred the Liberal Party to
govern alone.

Holt had already had his own trouble with McMahon. At least
once, during the first parliamentary session of 1964, McMahon
had shaken Holt's equanimity. Ignoring the protocol of consult-
ing Holt, the leader of the House, McMahon sought to change the
order of speakers. On his way to Menzies' office to report this infrac-
tion, Holt encountered McMahon in a corridor, grabbed him by
the shoulders, picked him up, whisked him around the corner and
warned: 'McMahon, if you interfere in my side of the house any
more I'll have you right out of parliament.'

Holt was not easily roused to anger, but when he was, he would
not resile. At such times, 'Puss' Holt quickly became 'Tiger' Holt.

Robert Menzies wished McMahon well, with some fatherly
advice: 'Well, my boy, if you want to be PM, you're going to need a
wife and kids, you know.' McMahon took this advice. During 1965,
he established contact with Sonia Hopkins, a Sydney socialite who
worked as an occupational therapist, courted her and married her a
fortnight before Christmas. She was elegant and statuesque and, at
thirty-three, still young enough to have children. To many observers,
McMahon's marriage was a clear indication of his future intentions.

Twenty days into the following year, the septuagenarian prime minister called a press conference and announced his retirement:

> I went to Government House and told the Governor General that I was resigning. I produced the document in such English as I could command and advised him to send for Mr Holt, which, as I know, he did.

The new prime minister had almost the whole of 1966 to establish himself before the federal election due before the end of the year. There was only one cloud over his happy news: the death of his aunt Vera in London on 18 January. He received the news on the same day he learned he had become prime minister. He had the task of presiding over the formalities that marked the ending of her life. To her close friend John Andrews, he wrote:

> The years ahead seemed so difficult for her, and those of us who have love for her would not want to see her live out indefinitely an invalid's existence. You can look to me for whatever provision or arrangement you find necessary.

Vera Pearce's funeral was held at Golders Green crematorium on 27 January 1966. Her nephew, unable to attend, sent a wreath. Cliff Holt later wrote to his brother, informing him of the memorabilia which he and his wife had recovered:

> We did bring home with us a case full of old snaps and dozens of large and medium-sized photos of A.V. but no oils . . . You figure in a number of old snaps, and we're both in one with Mum – it must have been about the last taken with her as we appear to be in our mid-teens.

On Australia Day in 1966, the incoming prime minister spoke warmly and suggested the way in which he intended to carry out

Harold in 1921, posing in football jumper.

Reginald John David 'Spot' Turnbull and Harold Holt: photo taken 1922.

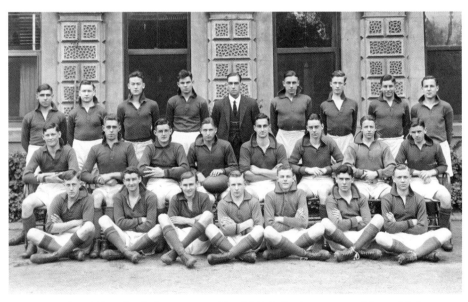

Wesley College football team, 1926: Harold Holt (back row, second from right); Spot Turnbull (middle row, fifth from left).

Young Harold Holt [c 1930s].

Holt as Minister for Immigration, greeting two girls with wife Zara.

Holt at home in August 1960, preparing for the federal budget as treasurer.

Harold and Zara Holt, on the day Harold became prime minister of Australia.

Harold with his daughters-in-law
at the beach.

Harold and Zara with their
grandson Christopher.

The Age

34.541 MELBOURNE, MONDAY, JANUARY 24, 1966 20 PAGES PRICE 4d. (AIR 6d.)

Mr. Holt will refer referendum to Cabinet

THE Prime Minister-designate (Mr. Holt) declined last night to say whether his Government would proceed with a referendum designed to increase the size of the House of Representatives.

"We haven't even formed a Government yet, so I am not going to try to imagine what sort of view we will take as a Government," he said.

"There are obvious problems in whatever course is pursued.

"The new Cabinet has not been formed and there has been no opportunity therefore for discussions on the matter.

PM's lot . . .

Australia's Prime Minister-designate (Mr. Holt) had yesterday a taste of the privileges — and the sacrifices — that are the lot of a national leader.

Mr. Stewart will urge U.S. to continue pause

From Herbert Michael

LONDON, January 23.— The British Foreign Secretary (Mr. Stewart) is to visit Washington this week armed with authority to urge the United States to continue the present bombing pause in Vietnam until after Mr. Wilson's visit to Moscow on February 21.

Cents only on private buses

Pressure

STOP PRESS

Reports of N-bomb finding

A candid snap of Harold's daughters-in-law bringing him a cup of tea at Portsea,
as seen on the front page of *The Age*, 24 January 1966.

Sir Robert Menzies and Harold Holt [c 1950s].

Harold Holt and Lyndon Baines Johnson, president of the United States.

John and Alison Busst: photo taken 1968.

Holt at Cheviot Beach.

Marjorie Gillespie and policeman looking at where Holt went missing.

Four witnesses on beach. Left to right: Marjorie Gillespie,
Vyner Gillespie, Alan Stewart, Martin Simpson.

The front page of *The Age*, 18 December 1967, reporting the disappearance and assumed death of the prime minister.

Map of where Harold Holt went missing.

his duties: 'Here is a country to be greatly enjoyed with all its beauty and infinite variety. Here is a country to be loved, to be served with devotion.'

Part of Holt's personal myth was that he had always been 'uphill'. His early years had been afflicted by loneliness and family dysfunction. During the years of the Depression he had struggled to find work as a solicitor. Certainly he had enjoyed social advantages which had helped him on his upward climb, but still he saw his life in terms of struggle. Few people considered him brilliant, but most respected him for his conscientious and dedicated service to his country.

He could look back from the top of the hill to a distinguished career as an outstanding parliamentarian and a highly successful minister in the portfolios of Immigration, and Labour and National Service. He considered his greatest achievements to date the implementation of the immigration program, the creation of industrial peace and the productivity and soundness of the national economy. Though his record as treasurer had been mixed, he had survived some torrid times and emerged with his reputation as an administrator largely intact. In the course of his travels he had become more widely known abroad than any Australian politician other than Menzies, and at home he continued to enjoy the respect and even the admiration of both colleagues and opponents.

Arthur Calwell, though, did not expect that his new counterpart would enjoy a long tenure as the new national leader. Ever since Calwell had entered parliament in 1940, he had respected Holt. But now that Holt was to be his direct counterpart, he was less than complimentary when he assessed his chances as prime minister: 'I do not think Mr Holt will have much success in managing dissident elements in the party because he has not got and never will have the status of Sir Robert Menzies.'

Calwell felt that the Country Party leader, John McEwen, would be allowed to exert far greater influence as junior leader in the coalition than he had been allowed to do under Menzies. Certainly, the

new prime minister's personality was much softer than his predecessor's. Now his fellow Australians would see if he could succeed in
a role which required a good deal of toughness.

16

Early Days as Prime Minister

Mr Holt is not expected to dominate his Cabinet and party as Sir Robert Menzies did, nor is he likely to attempt to do so. But his even temperament and easy manner will serve him well.
—*The Age*, 22 January, 1966

Win any way as long as you can get away with it.
Nice guys finish last.
—Leo Durocher, American baseball player, manager and coach

THE HOUSE KNOWN AS THE LODGE, IN THE CANBERRA suburb of Yarralumla, was completed in 1927 – ready for the opening of the new national capital. Built in the style of Australian Georgian revival, with American colonial interior, it was not initially intended to be used as a permanent official residence for prime ministers, several of whom lived elsewhere while in office. James Scullin, prime minister from 1929 to 1932, objected to the cost of running the Lodge, and so lived instead at the nearby Hotel Canberra. When he began his term as prime minister in 1945, Ben Chifley moved into the Kurrajong Hotel. When Robert Menzies and his family first occupied the Lodge in the late 1930s, it was still surrounded by grassland filled with grazing sheep.

Shortly after Harold and Zara Holt took up residence in the Lodge early in 1966, the new prime minister answered the front doorbell to greet Tony Eggleton, his newly appointed press secretary. Having become used to the ways of Menzies, Eggleton was surprised to be greeted by a prime minister dressed only in his underpants.

After moving in, Holt intensified his usual working habits. In the bedroom on the top floor of the house, he allowed only four hours for sleep, which he called 'a little death'. His briefcase was his constant companion at his bedside and he rarely slept more than two hours at a stretch before awakening for more work. No later than six in the morning he sprang out of bed, greeting each new day as if it represented a new life. Breakfast, often consisting of his favourite stewed apple and rhubarb, was at 6.30. He and Zara ate in silence, absorbed in the national newspapers.

Usually he seemed none the worse for skimping on sleep. Sometimes his good cheer switched on instantly, such as on Saturday mornings, when Zara was sometimes woken by his voice, singing, 'Saturday is the best night of the week.'

At the Lodge, Zara quickly started renovating the house, making the task sound like a military offensive: 'The house was so dark that I hit it much harder than I normally would hit a house.' She had the main bedroom repainted in shocking pink, and the dark wood panelling in other parts of the house reclothed in bright white. In an offbeat touch, she had two shiny brass euphoniums attached to a wall. Her makeover was described as one of 'cheerful almost impudent' 1960s style. To journalists, she was known as 'Zany Zara', a term of endearment to match 'Handsome Harold'.

When he visited the Lodge after his retirement, Sir Robert Menzies was less than impressed by Zara's makeover:

The psychedelic hand of Zara Holt is heavy on the house. The guest rooms are painted in what I am told is a shocking pink, and the colour certainly shocked me. I am sorry for any guest who is not feeling well when he first encounters the blow.

As the wife of Australia's new prime minister, Zara still maintained her outside interests. As well as the Toorak Road business, she had set up another Magg boutique in the Sydney suburb of Double Bay. She enjoyed sharing her acumen in fashion design with her daughters-in-law. While she was in Canberra, she employed Nick's wife, Caroline, to manage the Melbourne store, and she gave Andrew's wife, Paulette, informal training in the study of shape and form in clothing. Paulette felt that her mother-in-law was the first person to teach her to look critically at these matters.

But her number-one priority was still Mr Holt, as she sometimes referred to him in public. 'Harold's a nice man,' she assured the public when he became prime minister. 'Truly he is.' Leo Durocher's philosophy – 'nice guys finish last' – seemed wrong. For once, a nice guy had finished first. What pleased Holt himself most was that he had reached the position 'without stepping over any dead bodies'. He was going to be himself, a leader with a more genial and accommodating personality than his predecessor. Sir Robert Menzies sent him on his way with a paternal pat on the head, waving his other hand in front of himself, as if to say to his successor: *The job's all yours now. Off you go and make a success of it.*

The new prime minister was photographed at Portsea, stretched out on a chaise longue on the front lawn, with tea-trees and Port Phillip Bay in front of him. His daughters-in-law, Amanda and Caroline, were serving him tea, looking proud as he smiled up at them.

But it was another image that made the biggest splash, both at home and abroad: a photo of a wetsuited Holt standing in the shallows of the beach at Portsea with his three bikini-clad daughters-in-law, Caroline, Amanda and Paulette. It was a close family group, and Holt looked pleased to play the role of paterfamilias. Though his hair was white, his face still showed traces of youth. White-toothed and tanned, he stood with the sea stretching out behind him as he beamed into the future, an older man reaching out to youth. *You know me as a politician,* he seemed to be saying, *but this, too, is me, as much at home in a wetsuit as in a business suit*. His skin shone with salt water and wellbeing, like that of a genial seal.

That photo, as it came to be known, was bound to attract attention. In Britain, Holt had already been called 007, for in his black wetsuit he reminded people of Sean Connery in the latest James Bond film, *Thunderball*. He and his family quickly became the subject of good-natured joshing. *The Mavis Bramston Show* parodied them as 'The Five Hilarious Holts'. The prime minister was cast as a dashing figure in wetsuit and flippers, his daughters-in-law came on and off the stage in bikinis, and his wife looked like a whale in a tent-style dress.

It was a long way from the image cast by Menzies. His habitual air of grandeur was beyond mockery. It was hard to imagine him in casual clothes, much less in a wetsuit. With his stolidness of body and stateliness of bearing, Sir Robert had seemed an immovable mountain. If he had not voluntarily relinquished his office, it would have been almost impossible to dislodge him, just as it had been to stir him into vigorous physical movement. 'If I ever feel the urge to take exercise,' he boasted, 'I lie down until the feeling passes.'

Despite his advancing years, Holt, by contrast, was determined to maintain his fitness. He was proud to be in good physical condition. He drank sparingly, and the moderate smoking in which he indulged seemed not to have reduced his remarkable lung power. While he usually avoided being photographed smoking, a packet of Rothmans filters often lay on his office desk. It seemed he could be spurred into motion at the drop of a hat, and he was starting to urge his compatriots to concentrate on their physical welfare: 'Australia doesn't have enough people,' he complained. 'All the more reason for us to be fit people.' Indeed, one of the first visitors Holt invited to Portsea after becoming prime minister-designate was Percy Cerutty, the volatile fitness fanatic whose book title – owned by the prime minister – issued a dire warning: *Be Fit or Be Damned*.

Soon, Holt's penchant for vigorous action became one of his defining traits in the media. In one cartoon by Jeff Hook he was portrayed as a cheerful, goofy figure in half-a-dozen different guises: straining to touch his toes; sweating through a bout of push-ups; swiping at a tennis ball; swinging a golf club on the ninth hole of the green; spreading his arms and legs, in the midst of star jumps. But it was his enthusiasm for aquatic pursuits that was front and centre, with Holt depicted as wetsuited, masked and flippered.

That was the public view. What was Holt's view of himself in his new role? Menzies had been the benign dictator, but Holt was going to be the captain of the team, the chairman of the board. He hoped to be 'fair, firm, forthright and friendly'. The cabinet and the government backbenchers relaxed, looking forward to working with a more easygoing boss. For many years they had been used to a leader who kept them in line with a wave of his hand or a few withering words.

A journalist put it to Holt that a former British head of state had argued that all prime ministers fell into one of two categories – quietist or activist. Asked to which category he himself belonged, Holt was unequivocal in declaring himself an activist. 'If you've had any other impression it could be because for many years I was lieutenant to a very strong captain,' he said. 'It would not have been in the party interest to be active publicly in trying to command a fitting share of public recognition.' He favoured 'a leadership which can lead but at the same time be close enough to the team to be part of it and be on the basis of friendly co-operation'.

For Harold Holt the public man, 1966 had started brightly. But for Harold Holt the private citizen, the news was darker. Not long after he learned that Aunt Vera had died, he received news from Sydney that Cliff, his only sibling and close companion since childhood, had been diagnosed with pancreatic cancer.

*   *   *

The new prime minister and the leader of the Opposition were silk and sandpaper, smoothness and scratchiness. Holt's voice was mild and pleasant, while Arthur Calwell's had never recovered from a bout of childhood diphtheria. Perhaps this was why he was known as 'cocky', for his voice had an element of a cockatoo's stridency and his face an element of its slightly comical appearance.

The camera was unkind to Calwell; in some photos he looked almost like a character from a Boris Karloff film. Although only twelve years Holt's senior, he seemed to belong to a different generation. He looked grey all over, and his face showed more and more the marks of decades of torrid battles within his party and within the parliament. His uniform of dusty grey suit and hat, with a black tie, symbolised eternal mourning for his beloved son, Arthur, who had died from a childhood illness.

Arthur Calwell Senior began his working life in Melbourne as a clerk for the Victorian state government. He had become involved in the labour movement as an office holder in a public-sector trade union, and had trained himself in public speaking on the banks of the Yarra River during the 1916 and 1917 debates over the federal government's campaigns to introduce conscription for overseas service, of which he was a fierce opponent.

Later, he held various positions in the ALP's organisational wing, serving terms as state president and as a member of the federal executive. In 1940 he entered federal parliament as member for the safe Labor seat of Melbourne. After the election of 1943, he joined the cabinet of John Curtin's government as Minister for Information, overseeing government censorship and propaganda during World War Two. After that, he made his most lasting mark as Australia's first Minister for Immigration. He was an honest and truthful man, respected by both colleagues and opponents, and especially generous toward people in financial need.

When they were outside the bear pit of parliament, Calwell and Menzies enjoyed each other's company. In her role as president of the Queen Victoria Memorial Hospital, Mabel Brookes knew Calwell, as his electorate included this hospital; she had often gone to him seeking funds when he was a government minister. She found him to be easy and pleasant, but when he was in the House and roused, he could be 'a tiger'.

By the time Holt became head of his party, Labor had already lost two elections under Calwell's leadership. The first loss was narrow, but the second substantial. Calwell seemed destined to remain the permanent leader of the Opposition in a country on its way to becoming, in effect, a one-party state. He resisted all pressure, informal or otherwise, to step aside. Menzies and Holt both knew that it was in their party's best interests for Calwell to continue as Labor leader. 'Look after Arthur,' Menzies counselled his successor. 'As long as he leads the Labor Party you have nothing to fear.'

After a career of three decades in parliament, Holt was by no means inexperienced, but beside Calwell he seemed fresh. If Calwell was grey, Holt was silver, like his hair. So much productive life still seemed ahead of him. Perhaps he was thinking of himself when in his first days as prime minister he predicted that his party's best days were still ahead of it.

As he settled into his predecessor's office, he remembered his advice to 'look after Arthur'. The Labor Party was caught up in internal leadership wrangles. Calwell and his deputy, Gough Whitlam, were now permanently at loggerheads. Whitlam was twenty years younger than Calwell and was itching to take the party back into government. The conflict between the two men was front-page news through the early months of 1966, and there were moves afoot to expel or at least suspend Whitlam from the party. He was accused of showing gross disloyalty to his leader after claiming he could defeat Mr Holt in the end-of-year elections. But the optimists in the party predicted that ten Labor members would lose their seats in the elections; the pessimists said twenty.

The new prime minister was getting an easy run. He had been blessed by the good fortune of coming to office with the Labor Party deeply divided. He wished Calwell very good health so that he could continue to lead the Opposition indefinitely. Holt may have had a preference for Calwell over Whitlam as Opposition leader, but

Whitlam quipped that it was Holt who 'would make a better Opposition Leader than either Mr Calwell or myself'. Calwell was more disparaging:

> The best that can be said for Mr Holt is that he is the best available in the Liberal Party. And that is no compliment to the Liberal Party. Sir Robert Menzies *was* the Liberal Party. Mr Harold Holt was never anything more than the office boy.

'Office boy' was unkind, but Calwell had some reason to predict that Holt would have trouble managing dissident elements of the party, arguing that 'he has not got and never will have the stature of Sir Robert Menzies'. Indeed, Menzies had been happy to have Holt as his deputy for so long precisely *because* he did not have his stature and thus would never pose a threat to him.

But Holt had never aspired to match the stature of his predecessor, nor, as it turned out, had he needed to. He seemed happy as he played host to distinguished overseas visitors such as US vice president Hubert Humphrey, whom Johnson had sent to enlist further support for the American role in Vietnam. Holt was beguiled by Humphrey's speech in Canberra and praised it as 'the greatest speech I have ever heard in my years of public life'. He wished that 'what the Vice President has so movingly and compellingly put to us today could reach every household in every free country and into the darkest recesses of the Communist world'.

In one of his first press conferences, Holt had denied that the number of Australian troops sent to Vietnam would be increased. But at a news conference following his weekend discussions with Humphrey, he admitted that the government was considering the dispatch of more Australian troops.

In the month after Humphrey's visit, two American astronauts, Colonel Frank Borman and Captain Walter Schirra, made a 22-hour stopover in Melbourne as part of an eight-week goodwill tour of Australia and Asia. These men were the command pilots of Gemini

6 and Gemini 7, which had made a rendezvous in space the previous December. They visited the Holt family home at St Georges Road, met members of the family and let the prime minister's six-year-old grandson, Christopher, try on a space helmet.

From Thailand, for his first visit to Australia, came Field Marshal Thanom Kittikachorn. In his first weeks as prime minister, Holt had signalled that a major focus of Australia's attention in foreign affairs would be the countries of Asia. 'We are in the most critical upheaval in the affairs of mankind,' he explained. 'It is registering itself mostly in the countries of Asia.'

He had long endorsed the idea that Australia was part of Asia and could not separate itself from events there. He stressed Australia's commitment to economic development in the region through the Colombo Plan and the Asian Development Bank.

Within three weeks of taking office, Holt and his cabinet had re-examined laws pertaining to Asian immigration that Menzies had rejected two years earlier. Provisions were adopted to allow a number of 'temporary resident' non-Europeans to become permanent residents after five rather than fifteen years, thus creating parity with the policy for European migrants.

Everything seemed new and fresh, even the money, as new coins and banknotes poured out of the mint in preparation for 'C Day' – the day when the country would make the change to decimal currency. Television stations constantly played the jaunty jingle heralding the changeover, set to the tune of the Australian folk song 'Click Go the Shears':

In come the dollars and in come the cents
To replace the pounds and the shillings and the pence,
Be prepared, folks, when the coins begin to mix
On the fourteenth of February, Nineteen Sixty-six.

C Day went off smoothly. Meanwhile, Whitlam intensified his battle with the party's federal executive, whom he branded 'the twelve witless men'. The key issue of contention was the continuation of the party's electorally unpopular policy of opposition to state aid to non-government schools. The policy was linked to the intransigence of the party's autocratic organisational structure, which made it particularly resistant to change. Whitlam complained that the party was 'controlled by people who want to use it for their own prejudice and vengeance'. Arthur Calwell, who had described Whitlam as 'that elongated bastard', pushed for his suspension from the party.

In the midst of the battle, Whitlam engaged himself fully in his party's campaign for the rural Queensland electorate of Dawson, which was due for a by-election in February. Working tirelessly in tandem with the Labor candidate, Rex Patterson, he helped bring off a stunning victory. In what was described as 'the biggest political upset since Federation', the Labor Party captured the seat from the Country Party.

The Queensland delegates to Labor's federal conference were instructed to show their gratitude for Whitlam's efforts by voting against his suspension. Whitlam was saved, and thus so too was his hope of one day taking the leadership from Calwell. A potential leader from whom Holt had much more to fear than from Calwell was waiting in the wings.

*   *   *

Holt made his debut as prime minister when the parliament's autumn sitting opened on 8 March 1966. For the first time in thirty-two years, Menzies was absent from an opening session; for the first time in sixteen years, a new prime minister was presiding. For the first time in many years, Australia had a female minister in government – Senator Annabelle Rankin – who was given the housing portfolio. The Labor Party's new member for Dawson, Rex Patterson, was welcomed to the house with ambiguous words from Holt: 'Congratulations, I hope it will not be a long stay, but anyhow . . .'

Calwell described the occasion as 'most auspicious' for Holt, and congratulated him on his 'great achievement' in becoming Australia's seventeenth prime minister. 'Today we come to praise the new Caesar,' he told the parliament, 'not to bury him.' He went on to remind his audience that Mr Holt had 'served his party for many years and was loyal to his leader for seventeen years'.

In his reply, Holt explained that while he and Mr Calwell did not often agree, on all matters affecting the wellbeing of Australia they were in complete agreement. He hoped that 'our daily confrontations in this parliament' would 'be marked with that recognition he has always given to the national interest'. Moreover, he shared Calwell's regard for the institution of parliament:

> It is as a servant that I shall report faithfully from time to time what the government proposes to do. It is in the friendly co-operation in the conduct of the affairs of a representative democracy, whatever the differences in matter of policy, that the true expression of democracy is found.

The major area of difference between the government and the Opposition soon emerged. Holt used his first speech to parliament as prime minister to announce that his government had decided to treble Australia's commitment of troops to Vietnam and to send conscripts there. By the middle of the year, he announced, there would be 4500 Australians serving in South Vietnam, about one-third of them national servicemen. Australia had a responsibility to support its loyal ally, the United States, in the war: 'We cannot leave it solely to our allies – and their national servicemen – to defend in the region the rights of countries to their independence and the peaceful pursuit of their national way of life.'

This was no civil war, he argued, but part of the downward sweep of aggressive Chinese communism bent on the conquest of all of South-East Asia. He assured the public that the search for peace would go on, but warned them that there was the prospect of a long period of fighting ahead.

Calwell's opposition to Australia's involvement in Vietnam had deepened when he learned that conscripts were going to the war. He had honed his oratorical skills during World War One, arguing for a No vote in the two successive government referenda seeking to introduce conscription for overseas service, a policy which he had vehemently opposed ever since. Now he railed against conscription for Vietnam.

Further, he argued, the prime minister's assessment of the war as part of China's design to conquer South-East Asia was wrong. The war in South Vietnam was, according to him, 'a cruel, unwinnable civil war aided and abetted by the North Vietnamese government, but neither created nor principally maintained by it'.

Although by 1966, Australia had held military personnel in South Vietnam for four years, most Australians were still untroubled by the conflict. Both psychologically and geographically, it seemed very distant. Calwell was largely right when he claimed that the only Australians interested in the war were those who had relatives engaged in it. But now that small country, shaped like a snake slithering southwards, was about to engage more and more of those relatives. Public awareness was slowly building, in the manner in which one becomes aware of a dripping tap or a gradually worsening cough.

In the midst of the debate over Vietnam, a by-election had to be held in Kooyong – one of the government's safest Victorian seats – to replace the outgoing prime minister. Andrew Peacock, a young and glamorous candidate, had been chosen to replace the Liberal Party's father-figure. He was only twenty-seven, Holt's age when he had first been elected to parliament, and he was being groomed for a long tenure in the seat. On the Monday before the by-election, Holt went to Kew Town Hall to make the opening speech of the campaign.

Protesters had gathered outside the hall holding signs that read 'Don't Give 007 Holt A Licence To Kill'. Inside were more signs. This was not like the usual party meeting from Menzies' time. A large portion of the audience were opponents of conscription voicing their displeasure.

NO VOTE
NO VOICE
NO CHOICE
NO LIKE IT
NO CONSCRIPTS FOR VIETNAM

As Holt reached the stage, he felt a series of small blows against his legs. They were caused by marbles, symbolising the government's conscription lottery. Under fire from the anti-conscriptionists, he spoke for fifty-five minutes. His audience slow hand-clapped, booed and taunted him with Nazi salutes. He had worked out his strategy for meetings like this: keep talking, no matter what. If you stopped, you might never get started again. If you kept talking, you may at least be able to get in a few words during a lull. The meeting over, he ran the gauntlet from the town hall to his car. All the tyres were flat.

The next day, an editorial in *The Age* commenting on the uproar at the meeting encouraged Australians to refrain from dissent and to rally in support of the troops in Vietnam. But parts of the article were more nuanced:

So far as can be gauged by tests of public opinion, a majority of Australians supports our commitment in Vietnam, and does not dispute selective national service. But few accept without serious reservations the despatch of national servicemen to Vietnam.

Holt's son Andrew listened in to a broadcast of the by-election meeting over the Melbourne radio station 3XY, which his grandfather had once managed and of which the Liberal Party now held the licence. He wrote to his 'Dear Pop' the next day to try to cheer him up with his estimates of the numbers of listeners who might have tuned in to hear him, assuring him that, despite the uproar, he had got across the most important parts of his message.

Pop got through the meeting and, despite the customary by-election swing, his government held the seat. But it had not been like the good-humoured meetings of his past. For a number of days afterwards he remained shaken by his experience, and he now felt more reluctant to speak at public meetings.

17

At Home and Abroad

CANBERRA, TUESDAY: Mr Holt admitted in the House of Representatives today that he had based an answer to a question on an anonymous letter – and veteran parliamentarians said later they could not remember a Prime Minister having made a greater blunder. Ministers and government backbenchers sat stern-faced and obviously most unhappy with Mr Holt's disclosure.

—The Sydney Morning Herald, 21 April 1966

VIETNAM CONTINUED TO BE A CONTENTIOUS ISSUE IN Australian political life. Now that conscripts were about to be sent there, Holt seemed compelled to continue defending the policy. His predecessor would have waved away his critics or eyebrowed them into submission – if he had acknowledged them at all. But for Holt, Vietnam was a scab that he could not leave alone.

On the night of 19 April, while the first Australian conscripts were leaving Sydney for Vietnam, a dispute arose in parliament after Calwell asked Holt if he had received a letter from the editor of the Brisbane *Sunday Truth* advising him of a state-wide poll the paper had conducted on the sending of conscripts to Vietnam. The results had allegedly shown that about 90 per cent of respondents were opposed to the policy.

Holt replied that he had just seen the letter and explained:

Attached to this letter is another one in which reference is made to – for 'your information as you see fit' – several left-wing organisations in Brisbane which organised their own vote by buying copies of the paper in great quantities.

Calwell moved that Holt table the letter. The acting Speaker, Mr Lucock, ruled that it was up to the prime minister whether he did so.

Holt could have ended the matter then and there, simply by refusing to table the letter. Instead, he went on to say that he was willing to show the letter personally to Calwell, but he could not table it because the names of certain individuals were involved. Lucock ruled that Holt had given reasons why it could not be tabled, and within the standing orders of the House, it was the province of the prime minister whether it was tabled.

Calwell moved dissent from the ruling, claiming that 'the prime minister has not even made the claim that [the letter] is confidential. He put it in such a way as to suggest and insinuate that it came from the editor of the *Truth*.'

Holt replied that the second letter contained reasons for not accepting at face value the voting strength of the poll. 'To me,' he explained, 'it is only a confidential document if it contains the names of several people.'

The government then gagged the debate, and the Opposition lost the vote on the 'gag' along party lines. But Opposition members persisted. Holt, flushed and obviously rattled, revealed that the letter ended with the words, 'For obvious reasons, I am unable to append my own signature to this.'

Holt's colleagues were aghast as they took in his words. Opposition members broke into an uproar and took over the House. 'An anonymous letter! From how far can you fall?' asked Labor backbencher Bert James.

Holt's smile was gone and his colleagues were frowning and muttering as he left the chamber later that night. Many of them had long known him as a master of parliamentary protocol. But now they saw him becoming rattled under pressure and compounding one error – quoting from an anonymous letter – with another. He had not known when to stop and had persisted instead of leaving well enough alone.

*   *   *

A few days later, Holt embarked on his first overseas trip as prime minister. There was symbolic meaning in his decision to make South-East Asia his destination, given that he had already announced his intention to strengthen Australia's ties with the countries of Asia. Now he was going there 'to make Australia and its policies better known'.

One of his stops was Vietnam, where he met the troops, the military leaders and the members of the Australian surgical team. On Anzac Day he stood at a ceremony, immaculate in a pearl grey suit. It cheered him to see the troops in the war zone, including some of the first national servicemen to be sent there. 'You are right to be here, and we are right to be with you,' he told the troops. This war was 'the most important issue of this generation'.

Seeing them there cemented his belief in the rightness of the war. It was one thing to know that Australian troops were there, another to see them and move among them. As leader, he had to give them every support and encouragement. He was emotionally and intellectually committed to Australia's role in the war.

From Saigon he flew on to Thailand. On arrival in Bangkok, Prime Minister Kittikachorn garlanded him with traditional Thai flowers of welcome. Holt had passed through Asia on overseas trips during the previous decade, but usually on the way to somewhere else. Now he was tying Australia more tightly to Asia.

He liked to travel and feel part of the wider world. After being prime minister, he said, he would like to be external affairs minister. Already he was starting to feel imprisoned in his new job, looking back nostalgically to his previous ministry, regretting that:

The Head of the Commonwealth of Australia has less freedom than the Federal Treasurer. It seems a mystery to me how Sir Robert Menzies stuck it out for sixteen years. Let me give a public assurance that I am not aspiring to break his record.

Shortly after returning from South-East Asia, he was chief guest at the centenary celebrations of Wesley College at the Melbourne Town Hall. Speaking in front of an audience of 800, he seemed nervous. He was introduced by his old school friend Judge Trevor Rapke, who included in his speech a long list of Holt's awards while at the school. Among them was one for dancing, which the prime minister acknowledged in his speech: 'I never learnt the Charleston, but many people have said that I quickly learnt to twist.'

He made the notes for his speech on his menu card – a speech filled with fond memories of his beloved headmaster, L.A. Adamson, whom he described as a man who had passed on an immortality of influence, because his precepts had become his own present-day standards and his own public life was enhanced whenever he reflected on Adamson's clear perceptions. In the course of his speech, he also recalled his nervous singing in 1926 of 'The Leaving Song', with its poignant line: 'You've still your corner in my heart'.

While he was there, the Town Hall was surrounded by police. Fears of disruption from anti-conscription protesters turned out to be groundless; a mere sixteen were present and they disbanded when they saw that they were greatly outnumbered by police. The prime minister left the building with unalloyed pleasure at his return to his old school community and with its warm good wishes.

18

Turnbull Returns

The news today of the internal fighting in Vietnam should open
the eyes of all doubters in Australia to the fact that the masquer-
ade of our government that we are fighting in Vietnam to contain
Communism is too absurd to continue.
                    —Senator Reg Turnbull, quoted in *The Age*, 16 May 1966.

N OT ALL OF HAROLD HOLT'S OLD WESLEY FRIENDS
were happy with him. In early 1966, Reginald 'Spot' Turnbull was using his seat in the Senate as an independent
to voice his opposition to the Holt government's Vietnam policies.

After leaving school, Turnbull had married in secret, as his wife
was under-age. He qualified as a doctor and, in search of a suitable
medical practice, moved first to Brisbane, then to Launceston in Tasmania. Medicine and politics were his twin passions; he thought of
medicine as his wife and politics as his mistress. He especially loved
obstetrics, feeling a thrill whenever he helped a mother give birth.

His interest in politics had grown from his advocacy for compulsory screening for tuberculosis. He sought support from the United
Australia Party, but when it declared itself opposed to the policy, he
joined Labor instead.

After war service, he won a seat for the Labor Party in the Tas-
manian parliament, and became the health minister. He introduced
anti-cancer clinics and mandatory screening for tuberculosis, putting
Tasmania at the forefront of preventative medicine.

Like Holt, he was suave and impeccably groomed; he reminded
some people of the actor David Niven. Yet he was also blunt and

often disagreed publicly with the government's policies and criticised his fellow ministers, for he had little time for the political conventions of collective responsibility. As if in recognition of the spot on his forehead, he had maintained his reputation as an individualist. Eventually he made so many enemies that he was forced from the cabinet and, after refusing to resign, had to be dismissed by the state governor. This was not the end of him, however, for he successfully contested his seat as an independent.

Growing tired of the life of a backbencher in state parliament, he contested the 1961 Senate election and won a seat, again as an independent. Along with the senators from the Democratic Labor Party, he often held the balance of power when votes were taken.

Senator Turnbull and the DLP senators were strange bedfellows. He mocked their tendency to see communists 'behind every tree', but he sometimes voted with them. He managed to work alongside the two highest-profile DLP senators: Vincent Gair, erstwhile premier of Queensland, the roly-poly, whisky-drinking party leader; and Frank McManus, a former school teacher whose voice quivered with foreboding as he warned of the threat of communism.

Turnbull was destined to be an independent, for he refused to subject his own will to that of any party and, unlike most politicians, said exactly what he thought. Because of the way he embraced controversy, he was known as 'the stormy petrel'. Now he shaped up to oppose the policies of his old school friend, speaking out against Australia's involvement in Vietnam.

In early 1966 the conflict between the Buddhists and the government of South Vietnam was turning as violent as it had been three years earlier. The Buddhists were as unhappy with the regime of Air Vice Marshal Nguyen Cao Ky in 1966 as they had been with that of Ngo Dinh Diem in 1963. The saffron-robed monks were being attacked with tear gas, clubs and even bullets in Saigon, and to the north in Da Nang and Hue. In what was becoming a civil war within a civil war, rival factions of the South Vietnamese Army were shooting at each other.

Against this background, Turnbull declared his opposition to Australia's role in the war. He referred to Paul Hasluck, the Minister for External Affairs, as 'Mr Paul Rusk', implying that Hasluck was the mouthpiece of Dean Rusk, the American Secretary of State. The senator repeated the 'diggers for dollars' charge, arguing that sending troops to Vietnam had been 'an extraordinary piece of horse trading' with the Americans.

Early on 16 May, the prime minister read the senator's words of challenge to him:

> I call on the Prime Minister to tell Australia the truth. We have had enough of the misleading, inaccurate – if not deliberately untruthful – statements from the Minister for External Affairs, who already on two occasions has deliberately echoed his master's voice – that of Mr Dean Rusk. In fact, as far as Vietnam is concerned we may as well let Mr Rusk be our Minister for External Affairs. The sooner the Americans and our own boys get out of Vietnam the better for that country.

Hasluck's 'master' had his own problems. Johnson's erstwhile friend Senator William Fulbright was questioning the administration's policies in Vietnam and had convened televised hearings on the war. Impassively, the secretary of state fronted Fulbright and his fellow senators behind his black-rimmed glasses, sucking on a cigarette while answering their questions.

Sometimes Holt would have to answer questions from the press about his troubles with the pesky independent. They got along all right together and understood each other well enough, he replied. After all, they had shared a dormitory at school once. But for all that, the prime minister still felt twinges of hurt from his schooldays and perhaps they resurfaced when Turnbull gave him trouble now. 'You were Captain of the School. I was only Acting Captain,' Holt complained to Turnbull. 'But you're prime minister, Harold. And I'm not,' Turnbull reminded him.

19

One Dead –
How Many More?

This day brings you your birth, and brings you death.
—Sophocles, *Oedipus Rex*

I N APRIL 1966 THE FIRST AUSTRALIAN CONSCRIPTS WENT
to Vietnam to help the regular soldiers perform their Sisyphean
task. To minimise exposure to protests, the troops were flown
out and back in at night.

In the second half of May, Holt flew north to Queensland to take
part in the campaign leading up to the state election on 28 May.
On the 19th he spoke at the Theatre Royal in Brisbane and also in
Ipswich, where anti-conscription protesters heckled him with con-
tinuous chants of '*Holt, Holt – no conscription!*' He tried to make the
significance of events in South-East Asia resonate with his audience
in Queensland, reminding them that 'it should be remembered that
Saigon is closer to Australia than Brisbane is to Perth.'

He flew up to Townsville for a weekend that month. Johnnie Busst
was there to meet him and drive him to Bingil Bay. While there, the
two friends sometimes sold coconuts and pineapples near the hotel
in the neighboring town of El Arish, where they greeted members of
the Portsea entourage who were visiting northern Queensland and
had stopped to soak up the atmosphere of this local pub.

Busst found Holt in excellent form and wrote to him after he
returned to Melbourne, looking forward to his next proposed visit

around the time of his birthday, and promising to protect him from any intrusions from members of the press. In his letter, Busst expressed concern at Cliff Holt's current condition:

> I sincerely hope that Cliff is as comfortable as can be. There isn't much one can put into words except perhaps to quote John Donne – 'No man is an island, entire unto itself. Every man is a piece of the continent, a part of the main; if a clod be washed away by the sea Europe is the less . . . any man's death diminishes me.'

While Holt was in Queensland, Calwell was the main speaker at a meeting of about two thousand people in Melbourne protesting against Vietnam and conscription. Folk singer Glen Tomasetti stirred the audience with her performance of anti-war songs, the audience joining her in singing 'We Shall Overcome'.

A few days later, it was announced across the country that Errol Noack from Adelaide had become the first Australian conscript to die in Vietnam. This was a watershed, and the lottery which had contributed to the young man's death was henceforth more often described as 'the Lottery of Death'.

Noack had worked with his father as a tuna fisher. He liked the sea, swimming and spearfishing, and while in Vietnam he was looking forward to swimming in the South China Sea. He was also a committed Lutheran, who entertained thoughts of becoming a minister of religion. He considered applying for conscientious-objector status and sought the advice of Clyde Cameron, his local member of parliament. Citing his religious beliefs, Cameron advised him to register as a conscientious objector but Noack ultimately declined and went to Vietnam.

Noack's athletics coach from his Adelaide high school learned of his former student's death when he read the headline outside his local newsagency. He sat on the nature strip and cried. Holt cried, too. A boundary had been crossed. Now the 'Godfather of a million children' was becoming responsible for the deaths of some of them.

Nothing could have been more alien to his true nature than sending men off to war to be killed and wounded, but he believed it was necessary and braced himself to stand by the commitment.

Zara Holt was troubled that conscripts were being sent to the war zone. She felt sick when she heard the news of Australian casualties, as well as when she saw film footage depicting the suffering of the Vietnamese. It was similar to the feeling that overtook her when she saw other images of suffering, such as red foam coming from the nostrils of racehorses. Her own sons were not under threat, all having reached the designated age for call up before the end of the previous decade. But she sympathised with those who had to part with their conscripted sons. 'I'll march in the streets against you,' she told her husband.

Other middle-class Australian women shared her concern, many of them loyal Liberal Party voters like her. In the previous year, Jean McLean, a thirty-year-old mother and housewife from the Melbourne bayside suburb of Beaumaris, had been discussing the war and the draft with women friends, some of them anxious that their sons would be conscripted. 'Why don't we do something about it?' she asked.

At her instigation, they held their first meeting on 18 August 1965. They called the group Save Our Sons, following in the footsteps of a similar group in Sydney. The number of women on the SOS mailing list soon grew to 480, many of whom, according to McLean, had always been Liberal voters. Two days after Noack's death, the group staged its first vigil. McLean was one of twenty-eight white-sashed women who silently stood outside Melbourne Town Hall with their heads bowed. Later they handed out leaflets advertising a protest. The Melbourne *Sun* reported that a young man burned one of the leaflets, but that a national serviceman bought a bunch of chrysanthemums at a nearby stall and gave it to Mrs McLean.

On 8 June 1966, the first battalion, recently returned from Vietnam, was given a tickertape homecoming parade in the streets of Sydney. It went smoothly, until a young woman named Nadine

Jensen broke out from the crowd, approached Lieutenant Colonel Alex Preece, who was marching at the head of the line of his troops, and smeared his shirt with blood-red paint.

That night more conscripts were flown out from Brisbane on the way to Vietnam, among them Douglas Salveron. He had completed basic training at Kapooka in New South Wales and jungle training at Canungra in his home state. His prowess in shooting was recognised with a special plaque; he seemed to be following successfully in the military tradition of both his father and the man whose first name he shared.

His fellow soldiers called him 'Mr Smooth', as he was always impeccably dressed, with not a hair out of place. His physique was slender, and he disliked the baggy look of his uniform so much that he got his girlfriend to alter it to fit the contours of his body.

He and his fellow Queenslanders were going into exile in a country where there was little besides the tropical heat and the sight and scent of frangipani, the flower that the Vietnamese believed had healing properties, to remind them of their home state.

Their battalion passed through the Philippines during the flight, briefly stopping to refuel in Manila before the westward flight across the South China Sea to Vietnam. For the first time, Douglas set foot in his father's country of birth. The Philippines was the site of two of the largest American military bases in South-East Asia, Clark Air Base and Subic Bay. Every day, Americans wounded in Vietnam arrived there for treatment in military hospitals.

20

A Shot in the Dark

The Leader of the Federal Opposition (Mr Calwell) returned
to Melbourne last night wearing a suit with a bullet hole in the
left coat lapel.

—*The Age*, 23 June 1966

I T WAS 21 JUNE 1966, THE NIGHT OF THE WINTER SOLSTICE
in Australia. In Vietnam, Thich Tri Quang, a Buddhist activist imprisoned by Marshal Ky, was steadily weakening on the
twelfth day of a hunger strike. Holt was due to leave for the United
Kingdom and the United States the following week.

At the Town Hall in the Sydney harbourside suburb of Mosman,
Arthur Calwell was speaking at a rowdy public meeting opposing
the war. Communism in Vietnam shouldn't be fought by way of war,
he argued. 'You can't defeat an ideal with a bullet. We want to pre-
serve humanity, not destroy it. We stand for peace.'

Following his speech, and accompanied by his colleague Senator Douglas McClelland, he returned to his car. In the darkness he
made out the figure of a youth standing near the car door. The youth
appeared to be hiding something.

The bang that followed sounded like a firecracker. The car window absorbed most of the force of the bullet, but glass splinters stung
Calwell's face and chin. He was stretchered into the back of an ambu-
lance, his face as white as the blanket covering him.

Apart from shock and minor injuries, he escaped unscathed. His
chin was spattered with small fragments of glass and the bullet had

torn a hole in his coat lapel and stained his black tie with blood. He was released from hospital the next morning and was back home in Melbourne by the afternoon. He was an old soldier wounded in action, his chin pock-marked, but his jaw jutting out defiantly.

Peter Kocan, the would-be assassin, was a lonely youth, isolated and fatherless, who disapproved of Calwell's views on Vietnam. He was hoping for fame in killing the Opposition leader, but Calwell promptly forgave him – 'poor fellow, mentally ill, I think' – and later wrote to him in the mental hospital where he was confined.

The first shooting of a political leader in Australia's history to date shocked the prime minister, but about his own safety he seemed unperturbed. Not long before, he had found a bullet hole in the window of his Parliament House office, in a direct line with his work desk. Commonwealth police took into custody a young Yugoslav, Nedeljko Gajic, who reported that he had wanted to kill Australia's 'top man'.

Holt remained philosophical about any dangers he may have been facing. If someone was going to kill him, nothing could stop them. Whether on land or in water, he remained calm in the face of danger. Though he was the most senior of Australia's politicians, he objected to the provision of more stringent security – especially when he was at Portsea or Bingil Bay.

21

A Sharp, Compelling Cry

Lyndon Johnson felt he was in need of a friend, and he had found one. The newspapers were black with the headlines of the bombing of Hanoi and Haiphong . . . [He] was feeling the loneliness of power and responsibility.

—The Age, 1 July 1966

IN THE WEEK AFTER THE ATTEMPT ON ARTHUR CALWELL'S life, Harold and Zara Holt set out on another overseas journey, this time to the US and Britain. The main purpose of the trip, the prime minister explained, was to establish closer ties with President Johnson and Prime Minister Harold Wilson.

The Holts were excited to be returning to Washington, DC, a city which had charmed them in the past. As they approached Dulles Airport, they spotted on the ground below the Washington, Lincoln and Jefferson monuments and the Reflecting Pool. The summer sun shone on the Potomac River as their plane prepared to land.

Holt addressed the National Press Club in Washington, warming up with some anecdotes told against himself. In San Francisco, he explained, he was greeted as 'Mr Ambassador', and later he was presented with a bottle of whisky after being introduced as 'the Canadian prime minister'. In Washington, the captain of his aircraft approached him, saying that he was looking for the Australian prime minister but didn't know his name. Holt concluded that 'my ego needed recharging on arrival'. His audience warmed to his humility.

The Holts stayed at Blair House, the vice president's residence, across the road from the White House. Zara was taken with the wallpaper in one of the drawing rooms, which consisted of an image of a wildly exotic pattern of trees and brightly plumaged birds on a background of brilliant green. She decided that this was exactly the paper her dining room needed, so off went the cables to Canberra to stop the hanging of the paper she had previously chosen.

Twenty-four years had passed since the president and the prime minister had met in Melbourne for the first time. Now, in 1966, both were late-middle age, and Johnson needed Holt's friendship and support more than he could have possibly imagined in 1942.

Despite their differences, they had much in common: an enormous capacity for work; a desire to waste not a minute of their waking hours; an enjoyment in the company of others; and an irreverent sense of humour and fun, which they revealed far more often in private than in public. Johnson, for example, often froze in front of the public cameras, but away from them he could be very charming and entertaining, delighting his audiences with off-colour jokes and pitch-perfect mimicry of his political colleagues and rivals.

They shared similar attitudes to politics: Holt was fond of saying that 'politics are all I have'; Johnson that 'I seldom think of politics more than eighteen hours a day'. They felt a common concern for people and their problems and believed in using their power to help solve them. They believed in the power of reason in settling disputes. The president's favourite biblical scripture was from the Book of Isaiah: 'Come now, and let us reason together.' That injunction had been his guide from his earliest days in Congress three decades earlier. Harold Holt had adhered to the same basic principle as he worked to settle disputes, especially in the ministries of Labour and Immigration.

As the war in Vietnam expanded, the two leaders shared a belief in the importance of maintaining their commitment there, asserting that their two countries could help provide a shield beneath which South Vietnam could eventually become secure and prosperous. But in both the US and Australia, more and more of their constituents were beginning to doubt the wisdom of that view – especially in the US, where the cost and extent of the commitment to the struggle were proportionately much greater than Australia's.

The two men kept remarkably similar working hours, each allowing themselves to sleep only between the hours of two and six a.m. The president's period of sleep was often delayed by his night reading; the prime minister interspersed sleep with work, waking after two hours' sleep for more work. The president often took an afternoon nap, getting into pyjamas and sleeping for an hour. In this way, he felt he could pack two days' work into one.

Yet they differed, too. Holt had interests beyond politics – in ballet, cinema, theatre and art. For Johnson, by contrast, it seemed politics was all he had, for he concentrated on them to the exclusion of everything else. If he attended a baseball game, he gave it not the scantest attention. His eyes were all over the crowd, waving to this one, calling out to that one, for here was an opportunity to cultivate his constituents.

Johnson and Holt were both the firstborn in their families, though their birthplaces could hardly have been more different – the largest city in the Antipodes, and the hill country of south Texas. Johnson's mother, Rebekah Baines Johnson, had written a family history, which was published in the early days of her son's presidency. The lyrical description of her son's birth showed traces of the mystical awe woven into the birth narratives of Messianic religious figures:

> Light came in from the east, bringing a deep stillness, a stillness so profound and so pervasive that it seemed as if the earth itself were listening . . . And then came a sharp, compelling cry.

Popular biographies of the time sometimes included a photo of Lyndon, aged about five, dressed in overalls and broadbrimmed hat, hands folded, eyes squinting at the camera. Already you could see the man in the boy as he sized up the world, his eyes seeming to take in everything. Already he seemed prepared to impose his will upon his environment, to request its attention with that sharp, compelling cry. The intense concentration on the face of Lyndon the boy still marked the face of Johnson the president as he took the measure of his surroundings.

There were other early photos from his childhood. In one, he was snapped at age thirteen, towering over his four siblings in his first pair of long pants. In another, dressed in a suit and hat at the age of sixteen, he looked more like a man in his twenties than a boy. He was itching to leave behind the powerlessness of childhood and adolescence, and to exercise the power of the adult world.

When he succeeded at school, his mother's love and praise came in floods; when he failed, the praise dried up completely. Sometimes she would not even speak to him. Perhaps she only wanted to see him always at his best, but it was hard when a mother's love was conditioned on success. The lesson was that he had to succeed in order to be loved, and in politics he could make the world love him.

Johnson had to be at the centre of things. Unlike Holt, who was happy playing second fiddle to Menzies, Johnson was utterly miserable as vice president, relegated to the performance of purely ceremonial tasks. He found it unbearable to be on the outside, straining to look in.

His initials were not just a means of identification – they were the distillation of a force of nature, stamped on all in his orbit. From the beginning of his career in politics, Lyndon Baines Johnson had set out to become universally known as LBJ, just as Franklin Delano Roosevelt became universally known as FDR. By the time Johnson had become president, LBJ denoted not only him, but his wife, Lady Bird, and his daughters, Lynda Bird and Luci Baines. In addition, one of his dogs was named Little Beagle Johnson.

Some observers considered him the greatest parliamentarian in the Western world. With sheer will he pushed through legislation that his predecessors had found impossible to enact. He wheedled, entreated and shoved both allies and adversaries. Some of his legislation on behalf of the poor and other disadvantaged groups in society could have been described as socialist in nature, but that word was taboo in mainstream American political circles.

The story of Johnson's life showed in his face. It was a ploughed field, the furrows deepening year by year with the daily harvest of worry, arm-twisting and conflict from both within and without – a face now even more marked than it had been less than two years before while he was happily barnstorming, a shoo-in against his opponent, Barry Goldwater.

Johnson was a strange man, for he was riddled with contradiction. He could be both sensitive and savage; he could be both kind and cruel; mean and magnanimous; prosaic and poetic. He was the repository of many virtues and many vices and he could recognise and exploit them in others. His press secretary Bill Moyers poetically described Johnson's complexity: 'Better to try to drain the Atlantic Ocean into a bathtub than to try and take one sentence to describe this President.'

Johnson was particularly skilled when it came to understanding the needs and motivations of others, even those they kept hidden. He was no intellectual and often mocked those who were, but he was highly intelligent, with a laser-like psychological acuteness. He could make even his opponents feel close to him. How much more, then, could he endear himself to those in awe of him.

As Senate majority leader, he had undertaken the most searching studies of every member of that legislative body. He knew some of them more deeply even than their intimates did – their habits, their preferences, their deepest needs. Now, he instinctively felt Holt's need for attention and approval. These he gave unstintingly, binding his new friend tightly into his world.

Not long before Holt visited Lyndon Johnson in Washington, the British journalist Michael Davie had met the president and found him thoroughly beguiling, reporting that

He is one of the most extraordinary human beings ever to become President of the United States. He is more interesting, because infinitely more complex, than Kennedy. To meet him is to be awed and excited.

Now it was Holt's turn to be 'awed and excited'. The seduction began when Holt felt the voltage of Johnson's huge right hand shoot through his own. Johnson's practice was to lean in to his interlocutor as if trying to impart some of his personal power, to look him in the eye as if he were the only person in the world who mattered.

Johnson took the measure of his counterpart with the acuteness of a tracker dog, sensing his need for approval. He listened intently, his right hand poised thoughtfully on his cheek, his head tilted like that of a canine, attentive to the most subtle verbal cue. Back in 1942, Mabel Brookes had felt that his mind often seemed to be working ahead of the mind of whoever was speaking to him, anticipating what was coming next. He spoke intimately, his voice low enough to penetrate any defences, winning the hearts of many. He assured the prime minister that he still had the warmest memories of Australia: 'The Aussies have been my brothers since 1942. You're our kind of folks.' In the aftermath of his first meeting with the president, and still lit up with the warm glow of his company, Holt reported to his wife that 'I've never met a nicer, warmer, straighter or better fellow in my life.'

For his part, Johnson now knew that Holt would support him unequivocally. He would be where he said he would be, would do what he said he would do. Once he had given his word, that was that.

Johnson had many virtues. but few people who viewed him with a modicum of objectivity would have considered him 'straighter or better' than most others. Certainly not 'straighter', as he had a reputation for duplicity that was second to none. It was no surprise that the cartoonists exaggerated his long, sloping nose and showed it growing like Pinocchio's. That was not the only feature of his anatomy which cartoonists parodied. In October the previous year, he had been admitted to hospital to have gallstones removed. While recovering at his ranch, he lifted his shirt to show reporters his scars. The cartoonist David Levine drew them in the shape of a map of Vietnam.

The president had agonised over what to do about the war he had inherited. 'It's just the biggest damn mess you ever saw,' he told advisers. For a long time he was indecisive, but by the middle of 1965 he could no longer vacillate. As if willing the problem to disappear, he took to his bed and pulled the bedclothes over his head. Then he made the decision to escalate the war and there was no turning back. He told a delegation of senators that the war would last for six or seven years.

He set aside his doubts and committed to the war. 'We're not going to shimmy and we're not going to yield,' he insisted. He listened only to those who told him what he wanted to hear; he wanted allies – more flags, as he put it. Now the Stars and Stripes and the Australian flag were flying together on the South Lawn of the White House.

On the day before Johnson and Holt met, American bombs hit the oil storage plants in Hanoi. The photo of a huge plume of black smoke snaking upwards appeared on front pages across the world, an emblem of the pall which the war was casting over Johnson's presidency. The president was so anxious about the bombings that he went to pray with his daughter Luci at her Catholic church in Washington. He feared the opprobrium that might descend on him due to this new extension of the war. He later called it 'the night of the little priests', who scurried around, both flattered and alarmed by the presence of their famous visitors.

Johnson's need for spiritual comfort arose in part from the loneliness of his office. Two years earlier, journalist Mario Rossi had heard him make his speech about Vietnam at Syracuse University and sensed that loneliness more keenly than anything else:

Every second, every minute, he was absolutely alone. He was a human apart from others. Though he might communicate easily among others – both the individuals and the multitudes – he was constantly a man unto himself, a man whose burden imprisoned him in a sphere of loneliness.

Now the loneliness had deepened, as discontent with his war policies grew in Washington – especially within his own party, where prominent senators were speaking out publicly. They saw the attempt to bomb Hanoi as counterproductive and morally objectionable. There was also widespread opposition abroad: Canada 'regretted' the bombings, France was strongly opposed. While Britain publicly supported the American presence in Vietnam, British foreign secretary Michael Stewart announced that 'we regret the difference of opinion with Australia and with America over this bombing'.

The president welcomed his guest on the South Lawn of the White House, the large expanse framed by trees, with a view over the Ellipse to the Washington Monument and the Jefferson Memorial. Snapped together there, they made a symmetrical pairing, with both heads in profile and bent slightly forward. They both had silver-grey hair; they both wore white shirts and dark suits; both were smiling. The president was much taller and the extra height showed, but with their faces hidden that seemed the only difference, so much in sync they were.

Johnson felt that the welcome being prepared for Holt was not demonstrative enough. He instructed his head of protocol to see that the prime minister was greeted with sufficient fanfare: 'Let's do more. We must look after our Australian friends. They fight for us.'

Holt was ultimately greeted with an honour guard and seventeen-gun salute. The ceremonial was dramatic and colourful. Later, the press reported a scene of

scarlet tunics, vivid flags, red carpet and the lush green of Washington in summer, with drifting smoke from the saluting cannonades, all orchestrated by 'Hail to the Chief', ruffles from side drummers, flourishes from trumpeters and national anthems from the marine band.

Holt smiled bountifully, the smile of a man who had at last come into his own, accepted into the power centre of the world. He was basking in the present moment. Johnson's face was more calculating, always on the *qui vive.*

Johnson introduced Holt as 'a brave leader, a long-time and very loyal friend, and a wise statesman'. Then it was Holt's turn. Thinking of Johnson as a friend as much as the president, he took to the microphone:

> You mentioned, Mr President, your time in Australia twenty-five years ago. A new Australia has arisen since then. When can we see you there again? And this time I hope with Mrs Johnson, and perhaps the whole family.

As he reached his conclusion, perhaps he thought of the *The Leaving Song*, which he had sung in his own loneliness, all those years ago at school. The song spoke of the 'corner of my heart' which held memories of the places and people who might assuage that loneliness: 'And so, sir, in the lonelier and more disheartening moments which come to any national leader, I hope there will be a corner in your heart which takes cheer from the fact that you have an admiring friend, a staunch friend, that will be' – and now he turned and smiled at the president – 'all the way with LBJ'. Johnson was pleased, but his political instincts told him that this phrase might rebound against his friend in Australia.

Holt later admitted to Tony Eggleton that the inclusion of 'All the Way with LBJ' had been improvised. Thinking on his feet and being courteous was part of Holt's charm. But sometimes courtesy was just a step away from sycophancy. He needed affirmation so much that he would ingratiate himself with the powerful without counting the cost.

As part of his efforts to 'do more' for his Australian friends, President Johnson arranged a lavish state luncheon with one hundred guests. Before it, in the East Room, he introduced the Holts to his cabinet ministers and the Congressmen and Congresswomen who were present, including senators Fulbright and Mansfield, who had both criticised the bombings of Hanoi. Among the other guests were the astronauts Walter Schirra and Frank Borman, whom Holt had met at his home in February.

Holt was visibly moved by the welcome he had been given. When he spoke at the luncheon, he described his feelings:

> This is a memorable moment that no man who is not completely insensitive to human affairs could either forget or erase as a recollection moving to himself and an occasion which will be received with pride by my own country.

His visit to Washington was as brief as it was memorable. He soon left for meetings with Wilson and others in London. But he was still under Lyndon Johnson's spell as he strove to extend support for what he saw as 'the world struggle' in Vietnam. On 8 July, *The Age* reported on the prime minister's concern about Europe's lack of aid for the war in Vietnam.

According to the story, Holt had trenchantly criticised Western European countries, especially France, for their reluctance to support the war effort. The struggle there, he argued, was the same as the struggle for Berlin in the late 1940s. France had taken a 'hostile' attitude to the American effort, calling for the US to withdraw its troops and seek a political settlement. The prime minister was puzzled: 'I don't know by what process of Gallic logic this has been decided.'

As far as Vietnam was concerned, the 'Gallic logic' which advocated non-involvement made good sense. The French still had bitter memories of their attempt to reclaim Vietnam following World War Two, especially of the climactic siege of Dien Bien Phu, where the garrison of their expeditionary force had been overrun by the Viet Minh, the forerunners of the Viet Cong. General de Gaulle, the French president, and politicians of every stripe in that country, were well aware that Vietnam was a trap in which Western countries and their soldiers could easily be caught. Holt prudently excluded Britain from criticism, but noted that it was 'a matter for regret' that Australia did not have British troops at its side in Vietnam.

Johnson pressed Holt to return for more talks after he had finished his business in Britain. One of the president's planes met him in New York to fly him down to Washington. This time he was treated to an evening on the Potomac River on the presidential yacht *Sequoia*. The new friendship was now firmly stitched into place. Holt was entirely satisfied; the trip was 'mission accomplished'. He had made his mark in Asia, in the US and in Britain, all within six months of taking office.

After returning home, he had one more thing to do before taking rest. Within ten hours of returning to Canberra he indulged one of his greatest passions by attending a performance of the Ballet Folklorico of Mexico. The director of the ballet, Madam Amalia Hernández, had flown in from Mexico to meet Australia's ballet-loving prime minister.

At his first press conference the next day, Holt insisted that by saying he was 'all the way with LBJ' he was not implying Australia would follow the US blindly; Australia did not lack independence of mind.

As his wife had noted, he always did everything with his whole heart, and this was no exception. In his powerful friend he saw security, both for himself and for his country. But in allowing himself to be seduced, there was, of course, the threat of having to go all the way.

Holt could look back now on a series of meetings with distinguished American leaders. He had been so taken with Adlai Stevenson that he wished for a close personal friendship with him. He had met Eisenhower and observed an array of admirable qualities – 'vigorous, alert, incisive, well-informed and intelligent, with a warm friendliness of manner'. While in Washington as treasurer, he had met Johnson's urbane predecessor, Kennedy. But having encountered Johnson, he heard the call of a sharper, more compelling voice. He thought of Johnson as 'the greatest man I have ever met and known'.

22

August 1966, Bingil Bay

Certainly we have crocodiles, but you don't go to those sorts of rivers to swim. Harry did, of course. He worried us dreadfully up there. He was completely fearless.

—Zara Holt, *My Life and Harry*

IN EARLY AUGUST, THE HOLTS TOOK A SHORT BREAK IN North Queensland. This time there was no budget to prepare, but Holt was glad to take the opportunity to recover from the strains of weeks of overseas travel and the domestic concerns to which he returned. Johnnie Busst hoped that the few days would give him a quiet rest, but this was unlikely as, like Johnson, Holt rested from one activity by engaging in another.

All the better, too, if it contained an element of danger, and in that respect the area around Bingil Bay excelled. Holt insisted on spearfishing in local rivers known for their assortment of lethal creatures like sharks, crocodiles and twenty-foot-long gropers, all of them ready to attack intrepid humans. Danger beckoned, so he followed.

Things were far from restful for Zara, Johnnie and Alison. Harry's penchant for taking risks obviously taunted their nerves far more than his. He was determined to fish in the dark, muddy water. Johnnie acted as a self-appointed sentinel – standing on the rocks, watching for sharks. Zara fruitlessly warned her husband of crocodiles but Holt replied that, 'I don't care. I'm going to get a fish for our breakfast.' Another time she saw a fin cutting the water around him:

'Shark! Shark! Get out, get out,' she cried. 'I know. Go away, you're disturbing the fish.'

Two months later, Johnnie wrote to his friend. In his letters he often asked him to support his efforts to protect the Great Barrier Reef from the threats of mining companies. Ellison Reef, which lay next to Beaver Cay, the prime minister's favourite spearfishing location, was also threatened. But in this letter Johnnie addressed another cause – persuading his friend to halt his recklessness. He tried to scare him:

> Listen, cock, stop being so bloody brave. Must you insist on making yourself natural assassin bait? We really don't want to lose you, either as Prime Minister – or as you. Just think of it this way. Every cow in North Queensland that follows the same daily cattle pad to drink at the river is sooner or later taken by a crocodile.
>
> Do you get the message?
> Love to all Holts, and Tiny,
> Very affectionately,
> Johnnie

23

August 1966, South Vietnam

Why should mothers bear sons in a world that believes in war?
I live in fear that before my son has the chance to become a man,
the government will conscript him – teach him to kill, to obey
orders without question, contrary to all that I teach him.
　　　　　　　—Letter from Jean McLean, *The Age*, 27 August 1966

ON 11 AUGUST, SHORTLY AFTER HIS RETURN FROM Bingil Bay, the prime minister announced that the federal election due before the end of the year would be held on 26 November. As usual, domestic policies would be matters for decision, but the most important issues this time would be defence and foreign policy.

In the week following this announcement, most Australian news was bad. On 13 August, twenty-nine men perished in a fire at a Salvation Army home in Melbourne. In Vietnam, in the early hours of the morning of the 17th, fifteen Australians were wounded, some seriously, when their base at Nui Dat was mortared by the Viet Cong. This signalled that more danger was close and was later interpreted as a sign that North Vietnam was seeking to turn Australian public opinion against the war by inflicting massive casualties on Australian soldiers.

The only good news amid these stories of death and injury was the saving of a suicidal young man in Melbourne who had threatened to jump 200 feet from scaffolding on the partly finished western tower of Princes Gate overhanging Flinders Street. After almost two hours, he finally changed his mind, when Robert Dann, an Anglican Archdeacon, told him: 'You have a right to die, and you can jump if you want.'

The next Thursday, 18 August, almost one million Chinese college and high-school students gathered in Tiananmen Square to pledge themselves to the Red Guards movement and to hear Chairman Mao encourage the crowd to fight against the 'Four Olds': old customs, old culture, old habits and old ideas. This marked the beginning of the period known as The Cultural Revolution. The Australian government was worried about Chinese influence in Vietnam, but so too were they worried about domestic politics in China.

In Vietnam, in the late morning of the same day, D Company, 6th Battalion, The Royal Australian Regiment, set out to find the recent attackers of their base. On their way, they crossed the Suoi Da Bang River – it was then in flood, so they had to use toggle ropes to get across, as they were carrying full packs. They passed two platoons of Bravo Company who were returning to their base after having been out overnight. One passing soldier warned a soldier from D Company to be careful: 'There's something funny out there.'

They slogged through lush plantations, old and new rubber trees cut up by belts of thick jungle, old paddy fields and chunks of spiky bamboo. At 3.40 p.m. they reached the Long Tan rubber plantation, where one of the platoons spotted a small number of enemy soldiers. The Australians fired a few shots and took off after them, spreading out in extended line. Soon they came to a barbed-wire fence. Two hundred yards behind it was an old house which they assumed contained Viet Cong, so they called in artillery. Finding nobody in the house after the bombardment, they kept going in hot pursuit. Then at 4.08 p.m. they suddenly came under enormous fire from their left flank and immediately suffered casualties.

Meanwhile, in Canberra, two hours ahead of Vietnamese time, the House of Representatives was debating Australian policy with regard to the war. Minister for External Affairs Paul Hasluck was arguing for the necessity of the commitment, and concluded that 'unfortunately we must recognise that the present outlook is for a long and hard struggle'. Allan Fraser, Labor member from New South Wales, warned that,

> Australian families are now to be conditioned to read casualty lists as a newspaper feature. We are facing an ever lengthening struggle, a continual build up of forces, and a continuing series of casualty lists of young Australians lost in the jungles of Vietnam.

While the debate wore on, three platoons from D Company were pinned down in the rubber plantation in a battle which was inflicting the heaviest Australian casualties of the war to date; most of one platoon were already dead or wounded. In blinding tropical rain, the survivors were fighting for their lives against a full battalion of North Vietnamese regulars who outnumbered them at least twenty to one. Thin rubber trees were the only cover for the Australians as they mowed down lines of Vietnamese advancing in human waves, charging over piles of their own dead to continue the attack.

In Canberra, at 11.44 p.m., when parliament finally ended for the night, the battle in Vietnam had also ended. Four Australian soldiers had been confirmed dead and fifteen others were missing. Two of them, Queenslanders from the Brisbane suburbs of St Lucia and New Farm, were still alive on the battlefield, immobilised by their wounds.

The following afternoon, the news that Australian soldiers had been involved in a major battle began to reach Australia. To quell rumours that the casualties had been enormous, the Minister for Defence announced the figures – seventeen had been killed and twenty-six wounded – causing anxiety to all Australians with relatives fighting in Vietnam.

On the same afternoon, the Australian survivors of the battle returned to collect their dead and wounded from the plantation, now a graveyard of mud, blood, shattered bodies and rubber trees bleeding latex. Among others, they wrapped up the body of Douglas

Salveron, 11 Platoon's forward scout, who had been killed early in the battle. His mother had once forbidden him to play rugby because it was 'too violent'.

In the US, Francisco Salveron was following the progress of his country's war. Most likely he heard about the battle, but he did not know that one of the children of his Australian exile had died, relatively close to his own birthplace.

Until then, the war for the Australians had consisted of a series of skirmishes, one or two dead and a number wounded here and there. Now, for the first time, Australians from almost every state had been killed in a battle in Vietnam. Eleven were conscripts, one of whom had inscribed the motto 'Save Our Sons' on his Army hat.

The following night at Paddington Town Hall in Sydney, hundreds of members of the Hungarian community received the prime minister as a guest at their St Stephen's Day celebrations. 'The brave men fighting in Vietnam are helping to build the greater Australia of the years ahead,' he assured them.

When he compared the Hungarian fight for freedom with the Australian war effort in Vietnam, the audience stood to applaud. Communism anywhere was anathema to them; they still remembered the Russian invasion of their homeland ten years before and the Russian–Hungarian water polo match at the Melbourne Olympic Games in which blood had been spilt.

The reception buoyed the prime minister. But the next morning he saw the faces of some of the Australian dead displayed on the front page of a Sydney newspaper. One face was that of Douglas Salveron, his Asian features differentiating him from the faces of his fallen comrades. Frankie O'Leary, his sister, was living with her husband in Townsville when the news came through in a telegram from her mother's landlord in the Brisbane suburb of Coorparoo. She was pregnant. *I don't want it to be a boy*, she thought to herself. *Otherwise he'll be sent to a war and get killed.*

It took two weeks before the dead, along with some of the wounded, were flown back from Vietnam. Clarissa and Frankie went to see Douglas's body, his head covered with a bandage. Because she couldn't see his face, his sister felt he was still alive, just missing. 'We'll remember him as he was,' their mother counselled.

* * *

Several days later in parliament, Gordon Bryant, a Labor MP from Melbourne, reported on his recent trip to South Vietnam. The South Vietnamese were far from fully mobilised for war; everywhere he looked he saw young men engaged in a multitude of civilian tasks. Of the Australians fighting on their behalf, he felt that 'every one of them is more precious than the cause for which they are fighting at the moment'.

On the evening of 27 August, the prime minister put the war to the back of his mind while he attended the premier of the new Australian film *They're a Weird Mob*, promoted as a film made in Australia about Australians, with mainly Australian actors. This gave him hope that an Australian film industry might finally get underway. Perhaps he also felt the link to his old ministry of Immigration, for the central character was an Italian immigrant who quickly adapted to his new country and found love and happiness there.

The same day, one of the wounded from the Long Tan battle died, taking the number of dead to eighteen. That morning, a letter filled with dismay had appeared in Melbourne's *The Age*. It had likely been inspired by recent events in Vietnam, and its author was Jean McLean, of the Save Our Sons movement.

24

The Return of LBJ

If ever I am banished, I am going to Australia.
  —Lyndon B. Johnson, quoted in *The Age*, 17 October 1966

IT WAS LIKE WATCHING A MOVIE IN WHICH THE FIRST appearance of the star is delayed to heighten the suspense. In the lead up to Thursday 20 October, Australian newspapers continually headlined the impending arrival of President Lyndon B. Johnson and his wife, Lady Bird. The president had accepted Holt's invitation and would be the first serving American president ever to visit Australia; he would be the most important American visitor since Douglas MacArthur in 1942. After his four days in Australia, he would go to Manila for a conference of the Vietnam allies.

The president's youthful press secretary, fellow Texan Bill Moyers, reached Australia ten days early to prepare the logistics of the visit and to brief the press. He had been by Johnson's side since he was eighteen, when he applied for a job with then Senator Johnson. After starting by addressing envelopes, he was promoted to answering letters from the senator's constituents. When he heard the news that Kennedy had been assassinated, he went straight from Austin to Dallas, to the plane on which Johnson was being sworn in as the new president. He had a note for him: 'I'm here if you need me.'

Johnson did need him. Sometimes he thought of him as the son he did not have. There was no Lyndon Baines Johnson Junior, but there was Billy Don Moyers, the former divinity school student and Baptist pastor, looking studious in his black-rimmed glasses, impeccably groomed, his boss's idea of what a young American man should be. Their connection was so close that Moyers said they were joined by an umbilical cord, suggesting that Johnson was a mother as well as a father to him. But Moyers managed, when necessary, to resist the pull of Johnson's often overpowering world. 'I work for him despite his faults,' he explained, 'and he lets me work for him despite my deficiencies.'

He had the reputation of being the only man who could say 'no' to the president or put him in his place, such as when he was saying grace before a meal and the president demanded that he 'speak up' – 'I wasn't addressing you, Mr President,' he replied. Moyers had recently been troubled by the war in Vietnam, and this was becoming a source of tension between the two men. At last the moment came when the Johnsons arrived on Australian soil. 'They're really here,' the prime minister excitedly told his wife. Johnson was 'the biggest fish I ever caught'.

A rainbow was arching across the darkening sky as the president stepped out of his plane and strode towards Holt and the rest of the reception committee. He knew he would get a better reception in Australia than almost anywhere in his own country. Two years earlier, he had barnstormed the country campaigning for re-election, greeted everywhere by enthusiastic crowds.

Since then, as the war in Vietnam intensified, his popularity had slumped. Mid-term elections were approaching in America, but he decided to leave the campaigning to others and instead play the statesman overseas. On the other side of the world, he could be of some help to his friend Holt, who had his own election to win. To Australians, Johnson held an office that still retained some residual glamour from the Kennedy years, and, like MacArthur, the president was coming in a time of war, the iron chain that linked America with Australia.

He reframed Holt's promise to be 'all the way with LBJ' so as to make it sound more temperate:

When your prime minister symbolically said in Washington, in speaking of the crisis that faced our men on a faraway battlefront at the moment, that he would go all the way with LBJ, there wasn't a single American that felt that was new information.

But Holt continued to repeat this slogan, a mantra that seemed to make him feel more secure. It was as if he had conflated his sense of his own security with Australia's.

The next day at Parliament House, Johnson spoke at a luncheon held in his honour; Holt listened with head bowed deferentially. Every so often he applauded, politely but enthusiastically, especially when the president, smacking his huge hands together after every major phrase, declared that,

> There's not a boy that wears the uniform yonder today who hasn't always known that when freedom is at stake, and when honourable men stand in battle shoulder to shoulder, that Australians will go all the way, as Americans will go all the way, not part of the way, not three-fourths of the way, but all the way, until liberty and freedom have won.

Calwell, by contrast, was less deferential. Johnson was moved by Calwell's words expressing affection for the United States, but visibly annoyed by his claim that there was no real difference between the Democrats and the Republicans. The two parties, he said, were like 'empty bottles with different labels'.

For Johnson, this was a sentimental return to Australia that reminded him of a simpler time during a war that attracted almost universal support. He planned to revisit the people and places that remained in his affections, such as Melbourne and Norman and Mabel Brookes, and Townsville and Buchanans Hotel.

Later that afternoon, his first motorcade took him along Swanston Street in the middle of Melbourne's central business district. He pointed to the man sitting beside him in the car and shouted to the crowd: 'Here's your prime minister!'

Holt, for his part, looked happy, a man who had finally come home to himself and to his place in the wider world. He had initiated this visit and was shining in reflected light. Even the Melbourne Town Hall seemed to acknowledge Johnson's presence, for behind him was the foundation stone that had been laid on the very day of his birth – 27 August 1908 – as if his influence had impregnated the building itself. That was also the birthday of Sir Donald Bradman, one of Australia's most revered sportsmen. But today belonged to Johnson, as he shouted through his megaphone, 'Australia, I love ya!'

The president then made a visit to see Norman and Mabel Brookes at Elm Tree House, their South Yarra home which had been extensively remodelled since Johnson's visit in 1942. The Johnsons, Holts and Brookes posed for the cameras, the prime minister smiling unselfconsciously. Dame Mabel was arrayed in satin and pearls. Lady Bird Johnson, in a bright red suit, with Norman Brookes' hand around her right arm, smiled straight into the camera.

A gathering crowd outside raised a roar to bring out Johnson, which the president could not resist. With them went Rufus Youngblood, the bodyguard who had shielded him with his own body on the day of Kennedy's assassination, and who had become a fixture by the president's side.

The crowd was in awe of Johnson. 'Touch my baby!' screamed one woman, dragging the child from its pram and holding it over four or five rows of heads. Johnson's long arm flashed out and patted the infant.

Two brothers, aged eighteen and twenty-one, came with a different purpose. Johnson was already inside his car when he saw the paint spatter it, along with four bodyguards and some bystanders, with the red and green colours of the Viet Cong.

By the next day, LBJ was in Sydney. The tickertape fell like confetti, as if to bless the union between the United States and Australia. But demonstrators were waiting with signs as the presidential party reached the National Gallery of New South Wales for a reception. 'CONSCRIPTION MEANS VIETNAM' read one placard, with the

'T' in Vietnam represented by a series of crosses, spreading ever outwards into an unending toll of death.

Despite these blemishes, the visit was a success. Together, Holt and Johnson visited Queensland, then flew on to Manila. Johnson must have been thoroughly talked out following his trip to the Antipodes and Asia, for shortly after his return to Washington he had to be hospitalised for the removal of a polyp on his vocal chords. Holt rang him to wish him well for the operation, which Johnson received warmly: 'Glad to hear you . . . We have most pleasant memories of our visit there and I got some nice pictures I'm gonna send you. You look like a movie star.' Holt reported that his grandson had become a new admirer of Johnson's: 'Young Christopher's got your picture hanging up now in the bedroom. It's an inspiration to him.'

The president chuckled at this news. But he would have to rest his vocal cords for a while after the operation. Lady Bird had never known him to be speechless before, and promised that 'we are going to make the most of it'.

25

Off to the Races

Be thankful, Mr Holt . . . Mr Calwell will keep you in office.
Electorally, he is still sound material. He has gone over as a con-
scientious, hard-working and very human Prime Minister. It is in
Parliament and away from the gaze of much of an apathetic public
that he has fallen down.

—*The Australian*, 3 October 1966

UNLIKE PRESIDENT JOHNSON, HOLT NOW NEEDED TO use his vocal cords more than ever, as a federal election was scheduled for 26 November 1966. The memory of Johnson's visit loomed large in the election campaign, as the American progressive magazine *The Nation* predicted in its issue of 29 October. The author of the leading article argued that Australians had lost a 'father figure' in Menzies, and that his successor was left to deal with 'his unpreparedness in defence' and the problems arising from his Vietnam policy, which were now 'beginning to multiply'. Holt, the author continued, was 'unable to mask the uncertainties in his mind', and was thus 'just one of the children trying to do his best'. The author went on to note the role of Johnson in Australian federal politics:

> It is to be expected that numbers of people in this condition of political orphanhood will, like Mr Holt himself, seek a new father image in Lyndon Johnson . . . Towards the end of his Australian visit Mr Johnson seemed conscious of how the US moral position in Vietnam would be weakened in the event of the Holt government being

defeated in Australia next month. He will be personally involved in these elections in every sense. He will be a force and a presence in them more powerful than Mr Holt.

The final sentence may have overstated the matter – after all, Mr Johnson was not on the ballot in Australia – but the American press captured the importance of Johnson to Holt's campaign.

On 1 November, Holt attended the Melbourne Cup, making an unsuccessful both-way bet on one of the favourite horses, Prince Grant. Then he turned to electioneering, where his prospects of success were much brighter. The economy was strong; unemployment and inflation were low. But foreign, not domestic, matters were paramount, as the main issue of the election was Australian military involvement in Vietnam, especially the use of conscripts there. The government held that the country's involvement was vital to the maintenance of the US alliance, while Labor promised to abolish conscription and withdraw all conscripts forthwith, with the withdrawal of regular troops to follow as soon as practicable. Holt accused the Labor Party of undermining the American alliance and thus threatening Australia's national security, arguing that to bring the troops home would be a wholesale betrayal of our allies. His government campaigned with the slogan 'Keep Australia secure and prosperous – play it safe'.

Holt assured voters that his government was completely united on the issue of Vietnam. But there were signs of dissent within the Liberal Party. In June, Liberal Senator Douglas Clive Hannaford of Adelaide (known universally as Clive) had caused consternation when he made a statement expressing disagreement with the government's policy on conscription, declaring that he was speaking out because 'I had to be honest with myself'.

More recently, a group of Liberals opposed to their party's policy on conscription and the war had formed their own breakaway party named the Liberal Reform Group and announced that they would oppose endorsed Liberal Party candidates at the election.

But these divisions were minor compared with those in the Labor Party. One of the strongest opponents of the war, Jim Cairns, had visited Vietnam and concluded that a complete withdrawal of allied troops might in fact be inhumane as it could endanger many of the South Vietnamese left unprotected. Other Labor MPs had gone to Vietnam and on their return had tactfully suggested that their party might need to reconsider its policy.

Whitlam, envisaging Labor Party seats falling like dominoes, suggested that a Labor government would commit to withdrawing conscripts, but keeping regular soldiers in Vietnam. This was a stance which some Labor members felt might be more palatable to the electorate. Calwell immediately refuted Whitlam, but the electorate was left with the impression of a confused and divided Opposition.

Everyone knew this would be Calwell's last campaign, as well as his last chance to be vindicated publicly for his lifelong stand against conscription. He wanted the election to be a referendum on the issue, as if it could be separated from all the other issues, complications and personalities of the campaign.

Although shaken, he had recovered from the assassination attempt of June and was back on the campaign trail, denouncing the prime minister as 'a grisly warmonger'. After two election defeats, perhaps he was hoping that his third time might be lucky, but the voters were not going to have him as prime minister at any price. Their incumbent prime minister may have been a dull public speaker, but his pleasant face and manner were assets, and he seemed to represent the future rather than the past.

He began his campaign in Melbourne and was greeted at Essendon Airport by mini-skirted young women singing, 'Vote Liberal, vote Liberal, vote Liberal while you can' – a tacit suggestion that this might be the last opportunity for a democratic vote before the advance of Asian communism intervened.

Holt recorded his policy speech in front of a hand-picked audience of three hundred, most of them from his own electorate.

He watched the speech on television in the lounge of his Toorak home, surrounded by family. Two Siamese cats, Cha and Cha-Cha, padded around the room, while Holt smoked three cigarettes during the 45-minute telecast.

He began the speech with optimistic words about Australia's future. The years ahead would be 'years of steady national progress – progress fortifying our security, and strengthening the base of our economy'. Australia was well poised for progress, he told his viewers: 'You must feel it in your bones, as I do, that the next decade may rank as the greatest in our history.'

He continued his speech with a pedestrian account of intended policies, both foreign and domestic. *The Sydney Morning Herald* gave it qualified praise:

> No one can say that Mr Holt's first policy speech was particularly eloquent or inspiring. Its promises are cautious, not to say meagre. Its ideas are few. . . . Yet it has a solid, responsible ring to it which should at least inspire confidence in the voters. It is to the government's credit that it has sought to buy votes neither in its Budget nor in its policy speech.

The following night, Holt took to the hustings at the Astor Theatre in the Brisbane suburb of New Farm. He faced a crowd of 1500, comprising a mix of supporters and opponents, including a contingent from Save Our Sons with a banner reading 'ONLY POLITICAL PROSTITUTES GO ALL THE WAY'. While some cheered their prime minister, anti-war chants also filled the theatre. 'We are lucky that we live in a democracy where we are able to dissent,' Holt began.

His supporters wrestled the SOS banner to the ground. It was raised again, this time upside-down. He shouted over the din: 'I am glad to see so early in the campaign that some of my opponents have gone into reverse.' Slow hand-clapping began. In the middle of the theatre, a policeman karate-chopped a demonstrator. One young man kept chanting 'You chicken-hearted fascist murderer!' until he was hustled out. Another: 'Flip your flippers, Harold!'

The prime minister fielded most of this, until he heard a question shouted from the audience: 'What did you do in the war?' Menzies would have dismissed this question with a few well-chosen words. But Holt launched into a long-winded explanation of his service in World War Two. It was his old habit of trying too hard, feeling he must labour on, proving himself to others, and perhaps to himself. A *Sydney Morning Herald* reporter felt that Holt had 'performed magnificently in the first forty minutes of his speech', but had then 'lapsed into his habit of not knowing when to stop'.

At the end of the meeting an interjector who had been calling out all night asked him a question. The prime minister heard him out and gave him an answer. The interjector marched out of the theatre, but before he reached the exit doors he turned to the stage and shouted: 'You're a sport, Harold.'

The Opposition leader delivered his policy speech for Labor the following evening, appealing to the mothers of conscription-aged sons to help defeat the government:

> There are 600,000 Australian mothers with sons between 15 and 20 years of age, and many of these boys could be sent away to die or be wounded in the long, cruel, dirty war that is raging in Vietnam. I call on those 600,000 mothers to tell Mr Holt that the lives of their eligible sons are too precious to be squandered by the man who has pledged this country to go all the way with LBJ.

When Calwell had finished his jeremiad on Vietnam, he turned to a long list of domestic proposals, from education to health. In reply to these endless promises, Holt quipped: 'When the Russians and the Americans get to the moon they will find they are too late. Mr Calwell will have given it away.'

* * *

William White, a 21-year-old primary-school teacher from the Sydney suburb of Gladesville, had registered as a conscientious objector after his call-up, declaring his opposition to serving in the army in any capacity. He lost his appeal but continued to disobey army orders. Finally, in front of television cameras, four thuggish-looking police officers dragged him unresisting away from his home. His eyes were closed, his shorts falling down to expose naked flesh. Nine uniformed policemen as well as some plain-clothes ones had been summoned to arrest one pacifist.

Seeing this, Holt may have felt conflicted. When he asserted that the individual had a right to live his own life in his own way without being pushed around, he was sincere. But now that push had literally come to shove, his words sounded hollow. The White case plagued Holt throughout the last days of the campaign. At Rockdale Town Hall in Sydney, minutes before his arrival, his opponents started chanting 'Release Bill White!'

In an angry fugue, the voices chased each other, uniting in huge waves of sound. Solid blocks of people kept up continual chants until a man in the front row gave a signal with his arm. Then they all stopped and another block took up the same chant from a different part of the hall. They stood on chairs, waved placards and gave Nazi salutes.

There were quiet protestors, too. When Holt began his speech, several young men wearing black armbands stood in the middle of the hall and remained standing silently with heads bowed. With the thumb of his right hand, Holt compulsively rubbed his index and middle fingers. He felt his shirt sticking to his back in the heat.

The next night in Caulfield, in his own electorate, there was more of the same. As Holt and his wife walked to their car after the meeting, more waves of noise assailed them: *'Kill him! Kill the bastard! Tip the car over!'* The demonstrators wedged themselves between him and the police. Holt threw himself backwards into the crowd from the side of the car to protect Zara. He felt a blow, then a mouthful of spit from a teenage girl. Finally the car pulled away, leaving in its wake a trail of women's shoes, contents of handbags, spilled packets of cigarettes.

In his official photo for the election, the prime minister looked demure and benign, far removed from the world of war and suffering. It was hard to believe that such a man had become the focus of such hostility.

Zara missed the meeting at Rockdale because an abscessed tooth had flared up. She watched the proceedings on television and was relieved when her husband arrived home seeming as cheerful as ever. 'She'll be right,' he reassured her. He felt that most of the electorate supported him on Vietnam, and the opinion polls were showing a strong swing to the government.

On election morning he told the press when and where he and Zara would vote – at the primary school in Canterbury Road. He drove there himself, filled in his ballot paper, folded it in half and dropped it into the box marked A–L.

All year, Vietnam had weighed on Zara's mind and was still troubling her when she entered the voting booth. In the privacy of that space, she made a small non-numerical squiggle on her ballot paper, folded it in half and dropped it into the same box.

The return of the government was predictable, but the size of the swing against the Labor Party surprised many. The government gained nine seats, giving it a record majority of two seats for every one held by Labor. Even supposedly ultra-safe Labor seats changed hands, such as the apparently unassailable seat of Adelaide, where the winning candidate, Andrew Jones, was barely old enough to vote. The writer, producer and radio actress Kay Brownbill won Kingston, another South Australian seat, thus becoming the first woman from South Australia to be elected to the House of Representatives. The following year she took her place as the only female member of the House. 'One woman and 123 men' was the newspaper headline. Labor lost three seats in South Australia, where the swing was a staggering 12.5 per cent.

The government took another three seats from Labor in New South Wales and a couple more in Queensland. In Victoria, Labor lost only one seat, but its position in that state was already so weak it could hardly get worse. The only state where the party increased its share of the vote was Western Australia, where Whitlam had campaigned extensively. It was a debacle for the Labor Party. The government's solid majority of 1963 now looked impregnable.

The electorate was not disposed to create a situation whereby Australia would have three prime ministers in the same year, especially when Holt seemed to be more in touch with the spirit of modern Australia than his opposite number. He was able to exploit the feeling that the Labor leader was a throwback to the past and out of tune with the times; younger people, especially, had strongly favoured government candidates, despite the fact that conscription was affecting the lives of the young. To many of them, Calwell was viewed as a relic of an earlier period of Australian history, with his beliefs in socialism, nationalisation and the White Australia policy. As the *National Service Act* only conscripted twenty-year-olds, 21-year-olds – newly eligible to vote – could vote for Holt's party without the fear of being sent to Vietnam.

Though Holt had been prime minister for less than a year, he had made a strong and positive impression. The mainstream press endorsed his second term, while excoriating the Labor Party over both its domestic and foreign policies.

Once the troops were engaged in Vietnam and casualties were sustained, many voters felt there was no going back. Though the government's policy on Vietnam was hardly attractive, it was deemed by many to be necessary – and a better alternative to Labor's. Those vocal opponents who had disrupted Holt's meetings had certainly made an impression, but they did not represent the majority and their tactics were counterproductive.

Most of the electorate supported the war and Australia's role in it. They believed their government's warnings that Australia faced a real danger from communism in South-East Asia and that the

American alliance was a bulwark against it. Though many who favoured keeping regular troops in Vietnam were unhappy about the use of conscripts there, they often maintained critical support for the government.

Calwell, meanwhile, went into seclusion to mourn the end of his prime ministerial ambitions. For the election, the Liberal Party had produced an advertising leaflet showing a voter's hand with a pencil drawing a heavy line against the menacing downward arrows of Asian communism. Underneath was a statement and a question: 'It's your choice: where do you draw the line against communist aggression?' The electorate had drawn the line not so much against 'communist aggression' as against Arthur Calwell and his divided party.

* * *

On the day after the election, Holt rested at Portsea in a string chair while his daughter-in-law Amanda brought him tea, just as she had ten months earlier when he had first become prime minister. It was a handsome bookend to a successful year which had ended as it began, full of promise. The sun shone on his white slacks and tangerine t-shirt and a light breeze blew from the sea, which looked as benign as his smile. Nearby, Zara relaxed on a chaise lounge. Her husband had the contented and relieved look of a man who had survived some unpleasant surgery.

The troubled waters were stilled for a while, the silence punctuated only by the warbling of magpies and the distant barking of dogs. Holt played some holes of golf with his son Sam. For a few days he could enjoy a slower pace and then look forward to Christmas at Portsea in four weeks' time. 'I feel fine!' he told visiting members of the press.

I'd be very hard to please if I didn't, after a result which on my first election as prime minister gave me such strong support. I'm very gratified that there should have been this endorsement of our policies and I am grateful to the Australian people for this opportunity to give effect to our principles and our policies over the life of this parliament.

He had been buffeted and abused, had endured a level of hate he had never encountered before. But now it had all come right, and he had earned the votes, the respect and perhaps even the love of more of his countrymen than any of his predecessors. Written congratulations came to him from many people, including Johnson, whose own party had lost many seats in the mid-term elections.

At year's end, he was back on the cartoon pages, this time of *The Bulletin*, on a page satirically titled 'Rushton's New Year's Honor's List'. He was one of the honorees. Bill Rushton caricatured him with a beaming face with both rows of white teeth fully exposed. The caption succinctly identified a major theme of his life: 'HE WHO HESITATES – HAS WON'.

The cartoonist suggested that he was to be offered a peerage, as 'elevation to the House of Lords is the only way to get him out of the country'. Calwell was on the list, too, to be knighted 'for services to the Liberal Party'.

Another article in the same magazine aptly declared 1966 to have been 'McMahon's Year'. In the space of a year, he had been married and become a father for the first time; had succeeded Holt as treasurer and deputy leader of the Liberal Party. Further, he had successfully warbled his way through his first budget and had been returned in his own electorate with a record majority.

For Holt, shadows had still fallen over 1966, even though it had been the most successful year of his life to date. Aunt Vera had died on the day he became prime minister, and his brother Cliff had been ill all year, his weight dropping to eight stone. But he had rallied somewhat, regained some weight, and in September wrote to a friend that 'the experts are confident they have patched me up well enough to see me through a good number of years, so maybe I'll be seeing you in May '67'.

Cliff felt well enough to celebrate his brother's election victory, writing to him a few days later:

> What a win! You have now won the office in the way you've always wanted it and have proved you can win votes with the best of them (with a significant margin to spare!) Now that you are back with such a roseate poltical future your health becomes of vital importance to yourself and the party, so do us all a good favour <u>by watching it.</u>

PART THREE

NINETEEN SIXTY-SEVEN

26

The Prime Minister
and the Artists

I didn't paint him as a Prime Minister at all. I just painted him as a
fellow I went skin diving with.
> —Clifton Pugh's description of his portrait of Harold Holt,
> quoted in Traudi Allen, *Patterns of a Lifetime: Clifton Pugh*

OLT HAD ALWAYS GRAVITATED TOWARDS PEOPLE OF
an artistic bent. He had grown up in a theatrical family
and from early in his life, he had built up a wide network of creative people. There was his wife, Zara, his lifelong friend
Johnnie Busst, the art collector and dealer Rudy Koman, and leading
figures in the world of Australian ballet such as Peggy van Praagh,
who enjoyed his company and found his smile 'ravishing'.

Among his artistic friends was Clifton Pugh, and in January
1967, Holt welcomed him to Portsea to paint his portrait. He had a
happy association with the bohemian artist, who lived in a mudbrick house in the suburb of Eltham in Melbourne's north. The
long-haired artist drove down to see his famous friend in a Jeep
carrying wombats and with a rear window festooned with anti–
Vietnam War stickers. He and his wife were friendly with Jean
McLean and shared her vehement opposition to conscription and
the Vietnam War.

Holt's and Pugh's mutual love of art and of the sea, where they
snorkelled together, was stronger than their political differences.

Holt's neighbours and minders had advised him to break off his friendship with Pugh because of his anti-war politics, but he had refused. He knew, as did Pugh, that if you pushed people away because you disagreed with their politics, you would lose the company of many estimable people.

Pugh had been impressed by Holt's physical fitness. Once, they had climbed up a cliff from the beach and Holt had been in far better condition at the top than Pugh, despite being sixteen years older.

During World War Two, Pugh had fought the Japanese in the jungles of New Guinea and had been traumatised by the experience, which had coloured his life and work ever since. More recently the atrocities in Vietnam had provided the subject matter for his art. During 1966, he painted his distress into a new work, *The Vietnam Body Count*, in which he depicted Vietnam as a charnel house. Set against a jungle-green background was the faceless shape of a soldier's body, his gun barrel sticking into the stomach of a pregnant Vietnamese woman whose womb had been ripped open, the dead foetus within still attached to her umbilical cord. Images of a pile of bones, gouts of blood on soft pink flesh, legs rigid in death, were splayed over the foreground. It recalled Picasso's *Guernica* in the jungles of Asia.

Now the artist prepared himself to create an image of his friend after almost a year as prime minister. He decided to paint him not in his official role, but as the friend with whom he went snorkelling. His painting was done in bright colours suggesting the beach, and the sitter wore patterned maroon trousers and a bright orange shirt, the flesh around the collar open to the sun. The painting's background was filled with beach colours in bright horizontal and vertical lines – blue, white, orange, tan, yellow. The man in the foreground seemed far removed from the political world and its formal attire.

But the heaviness of that world showed in his face. The colours could not quite lift it – his smile was gone, his hands lay heavily on his trousers, his eyes reflected the trials of the previous year. He had aged, and Vietnam had much to do with that. In the week before Christmas, he had announced that another 1500 Australians would be sent there in the new year.

Pugh's subject still had good looks, though without the matinee idol glamour of his younger years. The artist described his subject as he posed for him as 'a mixture of smiles and weariness'.

Zara disliked the portrait, especially the attire in which her husband was painted. Nick Holt thought that he was made to look devious and cunning, quite unlike the man he knew. Both of them were unhappy that he had been depicted with a strained and weary look on his face. What Holt himself thought of the portrait remains unknown, but he could hardly have found it as satisfying as the famous portraits he had seen during his travels throughout the world. He looked far from Byronic.

*　*　*

Another of Holt's artistic friends was Marjorie Gillespie, his neighbour in Portsea and near-neighbour in Toorak. She had been born in 1918 into the wealthy Matear family of Melbourne. The family business eventually grew into a company controlling fourteen Melbourne restaurants, forty cake shops in the city and suburbs, and, the jewel in the crown, the Hotel Australia in Collins Street. In February 1940, when she married Winton Gillespie, *The Argus* published a brief report of the wedding, accompanied by a photograph of her in her frock of foaming white chiffon.

Winton Gillespie was a tulip grower and Marjorie was an artist. They had three children, Wayne, a successful Melbourne architect, and daughters Sheriden and Vyner. Members of many prominent Melbourne families attended their cocktail parties, where the prime minister was sometimes present.

Over time, the friendship between Holt and Marjorie Gillespie became romantic. She loved Holt's positivity, his robust sense of life. For his part, Holt was pleased to have secured the love of this beautiful, elegant and sensitive woman. Her voice was pleasant and cultivated and her turn of phrase was sometimes poetic.

Although he was now almost sixty, Holt was still a good-looking man. Marjorie sometimes called him 'Pablo', because in his swimming gear he reminded her of Picasso, the octogenarian artist whose physique was still magnificent.

Harold and Marjorie shared an interest in art and a touch of bohemianism. In Melbourne artistic circles, Marjorie was well known as a painter; she too was a friend of Clifton Pugh. On one occasion, she had visited Pugh's house in Eltham and gone skinny-dipping with the other visitors. Her art was formal but modernist in style, with some abstract elements; one painting of a pomegranate cut in half was particularly sensual. She painted images from nature, such as *Waterlilies*, an oil painting done with simple, elegant lines against a background of varying shades of blue.

On 21 January 1967, her elder daughter, Sheriden, died in a car crash on the Mornington Peninsula. Sheriden's long-term boyfriend, Alan Stewart, was the driver. Holt, in recess from parliament, was present to offer his support to Marjorie. He gave her his heart in sympathy; he also gave something of that strong will to go on in spite of everything.

Sheriden's death had heightened Marjorie's sadness over the deaths of other young Australians in Vietnam. Although Harold had assured her he believed that his government's policy was right, she knew that he lay awake at night worrying about 'the boys in Vietnam'.

Though grieving deeply over the loss of her daughter, she was philosophical and strongly engaged with life and she willed herself to go on. In this respect she was like Holt. She was also forgiving; although Alan Stewart had been the driver at the time of the accident, she still considered him a part of her family.

Holt was complicating his life by sharing it so intimately with Marjorie Gillespie. As they were neighbours in both Toorak and Portsea, it was easy for them to meet, but some form of cover was needed. Playing tennis together, whether at her Portsea house or at those of other neighbours, could provide that. But however one looked at it, the prime minister was living dangerously.

27

Testing the Water

The confidence Mr Holt exuded last week seemed well founded.
—The Age, 24 January 1967

O N THE WEEKEND THAT SHERIDEN GILLESPIE DIED, Harold Holt was at Portsea, stirring up water which had been relatively slack since the November election. He was hosting Prime Minister Nguyen Cao Ky, the controversial leader of South Vietnam. Johnson knew that if Ky came to the US, his presence would trigger mass demonstrations. In February 1966 the two leaders met in Honolulu, but Johnson ensured that Ky did not set foot in any of the mainland states.

By summer, the turbulence of November was still fresh in many people's memories, but having been so successful in the election, Holt felt confident enough to test the waters again. The mainstream press in Australia had supported the re-election of the Holt government, but now they opposed the prime minister's decision to invite Ky to Australia. 'Mr Holt has embarked on a precarious course,' commented *The Age,* concluding that 'most Australians will think it an act of extreme foolhardiness to re-open the divisive community arguments of the Johnson visit and the federal election'.

As the leader of the anti-communist cause in Vietnam, Ky was far from attractive. Calwell excoriated him as 'a miserable little butcher', 'a moral and social leper' and 'a little Quisling', referring to his years in the 1950s when he flew planes in support of French colonialists. Someone else remarked that he looked like a saxophone player in a seedy nightclub. He had once declared that what Vietnam needed to solve its problems was 'five Hitlers'. Shortly after Errol Noack's death, Ky's name appeared on placards held by boys aged no more than twelve or thirteen: 'NOACK DIED FOR KY – I WON'T DIE FOR KY'.

Zara let her husband know she was opposed to the visit. She felt he was bringing him out too soon, before people had time to think deeply enough about why Australia was fighting in Vietnam. It could be physically dangerous for Ky. She thought her husband was slapping the country in the face.

Holt laughed at her concerns. He wanted to invite Ky and his wife to a dance party that was to be held on the grounds at the Gillespies' house at Portsea. But if the press and the demonstrators didn't ruin it, Zara predicted, the security men would. Very reluctantly, he took her advice and changed his plans.

In 1956, as a young officer flying transport planes, Ky had made a ten-day navigation training flight through Australia in a Dakota. Now, like Johnson, he wanted to make a sentimental return visit.

Ky was no Johnson, and there seemed to be no political mileage in his visit. But the Vietnamese leader had played host to Holt in Saigon, praising him as the leader of a friendly country who had come to his country's aid in its time of need. Holt intended to return his hospitality. For Holt, that was what you did for a friend and ally, even if he was far from perfect. With a little goodwill, anyone could work with anyone else.

He intended to enhance Ky's image. He would bring him to Portsea, surround him with his own family and enable the Australian people to see him in a different light. He trusted that the electorate would be with him, just as they had been in November.

Knowing that this would be his last public appearance as Opposition leader, Calwell led the demonstrations against Ky. The protesters gathered under the pylons of the Sydney Harbour Bridge. Young men in short-sleeved plaid shirts burned in effigy a swastika-daubed Ky. Others had brought signs:

LOCK UP HOLT, THROW AWAY KY
GO HOME MURDERER AND TAKE HOLT WITH YOU
Y DY 4 KY?

The summer heat seemed to intensify the bitterness of the occasion. Few of Calwell's colleagues rallied with him for this demonstration. But he predicted that the Labor Party would fight the next election on the issue of the war and that they would win.

Ky came on tour to Australia with his 'secret weapon' – his wife, Mai, clad in a shimmering silk *ao dai*. They were welcomed quite warmly in Queensland, making successful visits to Brisbane and the nearby town of Beaudesert. In Sydney, Sonia McMahon was called up to accompany Madame Ky while Marshal Ky held meetings with South Vietnamese medical students and with the governor of New South Wales. Meeting members of the press in Melbourne, Ky spoke English clearly but tentatively, explaining that 'English is my third language'. Deferentially, he asked if he could, 'with your permission', light a cigarette.

During the weekend he and his wife accompanied Holt to Portsea. Instead of demonstrators burning effigies there were beachgoers waving towels and cheering as the helicopter carrying the two leaders descended. Ky was surrounded by members of the Holt family: Harold, Andrew, Amanda and Christopher. The two leaders tested the temperature of the water with their hands. 'No swim,' decided Ky. 'But of course you're used to water the temperature of the Mediterranean,' concluded Holt, referring to the waters of the South China Sea.

There would be no dance party at the Portsea house, but a reception at the Portsea Officers' Club instead. Wherever Ky went, there were more police than demonstrators. The prime minister had come through again; 1967 was continuing as 1966 had ended, and he was still smiling. 'It's turned out nice again,' he enthused.

28

A New Voice

Mr Holt said he had sent Mr Whitlam a telegram congratulating him on his win. 'I told him I hoped he had a long tenure in his new position – as Leader of the Opposition,' said Mr Holt.
— *The Age*, 9 February 1967

T HOUGH THINGS HAD 'TURNED OUT NICE AGAIN' FOR the prime minister, signs were emerging that he would soon face a more challenging time in parliament. On 8 February 1967, Whitlam finally took over the leadership of the Labor Party; he claimed he had long been 'destined' to be leader. Holt had tried to follow Menzies' advice to 'look after Arthur', but sooner or later Arthur had to go.

The Labor Party had reached its nadir with the election debacle two months earlier. Now its fortunes could only improve. Its new leader was impressive. Much taller than Holt and physically more imposing, he loomed over those around him and had plenty of gravitas – much like Menzies. He was known as 'the brolga', as he displayed some of the grandeur of that native Australian bird which danced and strutted imperiously. He was good-looking, with a face made for television and a voice to match: pleasant, reassuring, never strident. Its distinctive cadences highlighted the key words and phrases of every sentence. His delivery was steady, his syntax smooth and designed to enhance clarity, and, unlike Holt, he paused at all the right places. His voice worked in tandem with an agile mind that could deliver with devastating force a cutting rejoinder or *bon mot*.

Born into a family that thrived on good books and good talk, the new leader was erudite and well educated. His grasp of history, politics, the classics, and literature both sacred and secular left his colleagues reeling. He soon employed a biblical allusion when he accused the Holt government of blindly following the United States in Vietnam, 'like Ruth among the alien corn, saying "where you go, we will go".'

At the same time, Whitlam decided not to outrun public opinion on Vietnam. A realist, he knew how difficult it would have been to bring home all the troops without an armistice, as his predecessor had advocated. Instead, he expressed full support for the troops, while arguing against the American bombing of North Vietnam.

Holt had to rise to the challenge of countering what he disparaged as the Opposition's 'glamorous new leadership'. After parliament reopened in late February 1967, it was clear that he would require a different approach from 1966. It had been easy to shine against an opponent like Calwell, but now he had a new rival whose polish would be harder to tarnish. Whitlam was a peerless parliamentary debater, and while Holt could usually hold his own in the House, his voice and diction lacked the assurance of Whitlam's, who spoke as if the truth of his pronouncements was incontrovertible.

The summer of 1967 was savage in the mainland states and in Tasmania. On 7 February, bushfires hit Hobart, devouring the small town of Snug, which led to many deaths. Holt witnessed the devastation firsthand and said it looked 'like a blitz'.

Early in the same week, New Zealand infantry in Vietnam mistakenly fired on Australian troops, killing six and wounding many more. On 17 February, which would have been Douglas Salveron's twenty-second birthday, Australian soldiers engaged in a major battle with an unexpectedly large Viet Cong force. Eight were killed and twenty-seven wounded. One of the dead was Trooper Victor Pomroy, the first (and only) alumnus from Wesley College to die in Vietnam. His name joined the long list of those to be read aloud each Anzac Day. Pomroy's face was on the front page of the morning paper, along with those of some of the other casualties. Newspaper correspondents again expressed disquiet.

During that month, Senator Clive Hannaford announced that he would resign from the Liberal Party as he could no longer in good conscience support the party's policies on conscription and Vietnam. He had 'read incessantly about the problem of Vietnam and its implications'. On 9 March, he told his fellow senators:

> I want to make it quite clear that this was not a hasty decision. It goes back to June of last year when I first declared that I was not in favour of the government's policy of intervention in Vietnam or of sending conscripts there. I continued to support the government but I felt that continuation of that course might give the impression that I was condoning the policy on Vietnam, and that I will never do. I can assure honourable senators that the night prior to making my final decision to break with the government parties was one of torment to me . . . On the Tuesday morning before the opening of parliament I went along to Senator Henty [leader of the government in the Senate] and explained my position . . . I was treated very sympathetically by Senator Henty . . . He said: 'Where there is a matter of conscience I would not try to influence a member who has made a very serious decision.'

Senator Hannaford would support the government on all issues except Vietnam, but he would sit beside Senator Turnbull on the crossbenches.

Whatever looming challenges faced the prime minister, his stocks within his party were higher than ever. Ray Aitchison of the Canberra Press Gallery was present when the record number of sixty-one Liberal members held their first party meeting since the election. When Holt entered the party room, they gave him a standing ovation. Aitchison described how the cheers from the room reached the Press Gallery upstairs, 'setting the pigeons on the roof nervously fluttering and calling'. This was the high-water mark of his career.

29

Back to Asia

Our greatest dangers and our highest hopes are centred in Asia's tomorrows.

—Harold Holt, address to parliament, 12 April 1967

L ATE IN MARCH 1967, HOLT WAS PREPARING FOR HIS second visit to South-East Asia within a year. He was going to Cambodia, Laos, Hong Kong, South Korea and Taiwan – the first Australian prime minister to visit those countries. At the same time, External Affairs Minister Paul Hasluck would be in Korea and Japan – part of the government's continuing efforts to strengthen Australia's links with the countries of Asia.

On 24 March, a death in his family turned Holt's thoughts from his public to his private life. While at Portsea for the Easter break, he learned that his brother Cliff had succumbed to his illness. He had died at Mater Misericordiae Hospital in Sydney, where eleven years earlier Holt himself had recovered from his car accident.

It was a terrible blow for Holt, and he said as much. He and his brother had been very similar in appearance and very close in age. They had bonded in childhood without the frequent abrasions and jealousies that can characterise the relations between siblings, and in the years after their parents' separation and divorce they had come to rely on each other still more. Later, another branch of the Holt family had taken shape in Sydney, with Cliff, his wife Maura and their three children, Peter, Carol and Susan. When Harold won his election so handsomely just a few months before, Cliff had still been there to add his voice to the chorus of congratulations.

Like his brother, Cliff was well liked and highly regarded, and kindly in his outlook towards other people. As a journalist and editor, he was considered to be 'always good for a new story, a square shooter who pulled no punches'. He had followed his father into theatrical management, and by the time of his death he had his own very successful public relations company.

With his brother gone, Harold perhaps felt ill winds blowing closer to him. Few of the Holts seemed to reach old age, and now he was approaching the age of his father when he had died twenty years before.

After the weekend, he flew up to Sydney for Cliff's funeral mass. As soon as his brother was buried, he set off for South-East Asia, once more willing himself to go on, just as he had after his mother's death forty years before.

*   *   *

Holt's trip to South-East Asia came hot on the heels of the Australian Ballet's tour of the region. At the final performance of Australia's Borovansky Ballet, in 1961, its artistic director, Peggy van Praagh, stepped onstage to persuade her audience of the need for an Australian ballet company. Holt, then federal treasurer, went backstage to pledge his personal support.

With the help of 'Nugget' Coombs, governor of the Reserve Bank of Australia, the Australian Ballet was created, and staged *Swan Lake* as its opening performance in November 1962, at Her Majesty's Theatre in Sydney. In early March 1967, the company set out on a tour of South-East Asia and Japan, performing in twelve cities, beginning in Singapore and continuing on to Malaysia, Thailand and the Philippines.

Several weeks later, the prime minister set out to visit the same region. His visit to Asia was designed to 'make Australia and its policies better known', for 'geography brings us together and, at the same time, there are mutual interests to be served'. He was aiming to develop political and economic relationships between Australia and these countries. He also hoped to create a Festival of Asia arts tour that would visit Australia.

Reporters described him bounding through his engagements in the four countries he visited with the energy of a kangaroo. He was becoming Australia's best ambassador abroad; it was not surprising that he wanted to be Minister for External Affairs when he was no longer prime minister.

In Cambodia, he was delighted by the neat cities, the quiet rural areas and the historical relics, such as Angkor Wat, which few Westerners had seen at that time. He and Prince Sihanouk had their differences over Vietnam, but they still talked amicably. Holt told Sihanouk of his long-held belief that 'geographically, Australia is part of Asia', a very different view from the one which had prevailed during the Menzies years.

In the other countries he was feted as an honoured guest. In Vientiane, Laos's prime minister, Prince Souvanna Phouma, gave him a traditional welcome. The Holts and their hosts sat shoeless and cross-legged on a cushion. The highlight occurred when the Prince tied strings of cotton onto Holt's left wrist, designed to ward off evil spirits and bring good luck. 'You have to keep the cotton on your wrist until it wears out. If you break the strands, you will have bad luck,' the Prince advised him. The Australian prime minister laughed. Later, he attended a meeting of the Laotian cabinet and visited the Royal Capital, Luong Prabang, for an audience and lunch with the Laotian King.

In Taipei he received a gold key to the city in recognition of his becoming the first Commonwealth leader to visit Taiwan. At Songshan Airport he was given full military honours and a nineteen-gun salute. He met with the Taiwanese cabinet and dined with Chiang Kai-shek, who asked him to extend his visit an extra day, an offer Holt declined, as he was expected in South Korea.

While he was there, the University of Seoul conferred on him an honorary Doctor of Letters in recognition of his contribution to the 'furthering of international cultural exchanges and promotion of international economic co-operation'. On the evening of his arrival in Seoul, he was driven through a crowd estimated at half a million people welcoming him in the streets, showering his motorcade with coloured paper.

Though more people had turned out for Lyndon Johnson the previous year, Holt must have been pleased to have been greeted by even a fraction of that number. Perhaps he chuckled inwardly as he remembered the president's anecdote about his own drive from the airport in Seoul:

> Every step, there were people packed ten to twenty deep. I never saw as much humanity in all my years and I've been running around looking for it, advertising for it. I was just so pleased with the reception and I leaned over to the president and said: 'Mr President, how many people do you reckon are here today?' He walked down, got a hold of his aide, and he talked to him a little bit and went down and got a hold of the Chief of Police, talked a little bit, and it took about five minutes and it was holding up the reception and I wished to God I'd never asked the question. Then finally the interpreter came back and said (at this point, Johnson mimicked the interpreter's voice): 'Mr President United States, the President Korea say the best estimate they got is about two million. The President say he very sorry, but that's all the people he got.'

Though it was a smaller turnout for Holt, the spirit was similar – and just as satisfying. Buoyed by the trip, he returned to Australia 'in great heart'. His overseas odyssey had exceeded his best expectations. He discovered that life was often much easier in countries other than your own, where the constant rub of political frictions abraded and eroded. He felt 'overwhelmed with the friendliness experienced wherever I moved' and had not encountered 'one hostile banner or heard one hostile voice'.

On his return, he declared that 'our investment in Asia is deep, developing and permanent'. But what was happening in Vietnam was worrying. Whitlam accused the government of following 'a policy of inflexibility and non-approachability' over the war, and of being reluctant to support peace moves coming out of the US. Australia was supporting 'the worst scorched earth policy in history', he said. 'Our fathers and grandfathers would have squirmed at what is going on – the rest of the world condemns what is going on.'

Protestors continued to gather outside Holt's Melbourne residence. On the evening of 1 May, he arrived home to be greeted by thirty or so student protestors chanting slogans and carrying placards. He was exasperated – hadn't the Vietnam issue been settled at the recent election?

At other times his homecomings were far more pleasant. Across St Georges Road at number 79 lived a young admirer, Nigel Green, a nine-year-old who attended school at nearby Scotch College. When the prime minister arrived home, he waved cheerily to the boy. As the month of May began, Holt still felt assured of the goodwill of many others of his countrymen and of his own party. He was credited with having established himself forcefully in Australian eyes in little more than a year and with making his presence known in six overseas trips. Perhaps, suggested one editorialist, the day might even come when he was no longer remembered for 'that skindiving picture'.

30

The *Voyager* Case

CANBERRA, Wednesday. The Prime Minister, Mr Holt, tonight intervened in the Voyager debate and said the government hoped to decide tomorrow whether it favours a new inquiry.

Tense and obviously under great strain, Mr Holt told the House of Representatives that parliament itself was on trial over attempts to reopen the case.

—*The Sydney Morning Herald*, 18 May 1967

IN MAY 1967, THE MONTH AFTER HIS RETURN FROM ASIA, Holt confronted the lingering fallout from Australia's worst ever peacetime disaster three years earlier. His government suddenly had to deal with lingering doubts about the verdict reached by the Royal Commission that was set up to discover the initiating cause of the disaster.

On the night of 10 February 1964, in Jervis Bay, off the southern coast of New South Wales, HMAS *Voyager*, a radar-controlled – 'push button' – destroyer, was engaged in night flying exercises with the flagship of the Royal Australian Navy, the aircraft carrier HMAS *Melbourne*. At 8.56 p.m., *Voyager* crossed the *Melbourne*'s bows and within three seconds had been cut in half. *Melbourne*'s captain, John Robertson, watched as the severed bow of *Voyager* scraped against the port side of his ship and the stern against the starboard side. On *Voyager*'s bridge, Captain Duncan Stevens and all the officers who were with him there were killed instantly. The bow section of the ship sank within ten minutes, taking with it most of the eighty-two victims of the collision.

217

The collision had been sudden. 'One minute everything was all right,' John Robertson later explained, 'and the next minute everything was not all right, and there was the collision.' Two hundred and thirty-two survivors from *Voyager* were fished out of the water, many injured and most sick from swallowing oil. Just after midnight, some of them gathered on the deck of *Melbourne* to watch the aft section of their ship slowly sink into the 600-fathom-deep water.

At 9.15 p.m. that night, a naval duty officer rang Tony Eggleton, then director of naval public relations: 'Look, I hate to bother you,' the officer apologised, 'but we've just sunk a ship, and it's one of ours.' 'Is it serious?' asked Eggleton. '*Voyager*'s bow has been separated from its stern,' the officer replied.

That was serious indeed. In the next few days the collision was front-page news all over the world. Australian newspapers printed photographs of *Voyager*'s survivors with faces bandaged and bodies blackened with oil, and of *Melbourne* crawling into Sydney Harbour on the morning of 12 February, a long, jagged hole in its bow above the waterline. The scenes of survivors reunited with tearful relatives and of the injured being carried to shore reawakened memories of World War Two – as did the long list of missing sailors from every Australian state and territory.

On the same morning, Sydney's *The Daily Mirror* printed some reactions to the disaster from members of the public. 'It is a terrible thing,' said one, 'but I don't think anyone should be made a scapegoat to save face for the powers that be.'

But the powers that be had other ideas. When Menzies decided to hold a Royal Commission into the disaster, he chose Sir John Spicer as the presiding judge. Spicer was a far from independent choice, having been a well-known Liberal Party senator. It was also known that Menzies was friendly with Sir Jack Stevens, father of *Voyager*'s late captain, a highly influential public servant and former advisor to the prime minister.

With the death of almost all of *Voyager*'s bridge crew, any hope of finding out directly why the ship had turned into the path of

Melbourne was lost. The commissioners found that *Voyager* bore the responsibility for the collision because it had made a turn beyond that ordered by *Melbourne*, but that it was 'not possible to form any firm conclusion as to why *Voyager* did this'. The commissioners concluded that the cause of the collision was 'inexplicable' and 'incomprehensible'; they could identify no specific person on *Voyager* who may have been responsible. Although they found that a proper watch had not been kept on *Voyager*'s bridge, no further investigation was made as to why this was the case. They criticised three of *Melbourne*'s officers, including Captain Robertson, claiming that they should have warned *Voyager* while it was engaged in its fatal turn.

Throughout Australia, many people suspected that the truth of the disaster had been covered up, and the Royal Commission's findings manipulated to scapegoat Captain Robertson. After being demoted to a shore posting, he resigned from the Navy in protest, thereby losing his pension and other entitlements.

The publication of *One Minute of Time: The Melbourne-Voyager Collision* in 1965 reinforced public suspicions about the Royal Commission. The book's author was Vice Admiral Harold Hickling, a British naval officer living in retirement in New Zealand. He had been largely motivated to write the book to defend the reputations of Captain Robertson and two other officers on *Melbourne* whom he believed the Royal Commission had maligned. Hickling put into words what many people already suspected – 'a scapegoat was wanted and the nearest one to hand was Captain Robertson'. Of the Royal Commission, he claimed, 'there was red herring after red herring, and it turned from an enquiry into a trial'. He derided Sir John Spicer's conclusion that the collision was 'inexplicable and incomprehensible', insisting that 'nothing is inexplicable and nothing is incomprehensible'.

Hickling had not known Duncan Stevens personally, but he had heard that he was 'a man of moods – sometimes in buoyant good humour and sometimes in the depths of depression'. He believed that Stevens had 'destroyed his night sight' a few minutes before the collision by putting his head under the bright artificial light of the chart table. Captain Stevens, he argued, had been unable to see when he looked out from his bridge towards the *Melbourne*.

Lieutenant Commander Peter Cabban, second-in-command to Duncan Stevens on *Voyager* during 1963, had felt the weight of the Captain's 'moods' and problems of physical health. Cabban resigned from the Navy a month before the collision, after concluding that Stevens was unfit to command *Voyager* due to his medical condition – a duodenal ulcer causing severe pain which he tried to relieve by drinking brandy, often to excess. Stevens had concealed his medical condition because he feared losing his sea command, and two Navy doctors also concealed their knowledge of his illness. Cabban was convinced that if Stevens ever had a drink at sea he would lose *Voyager*.

A steward on *Voyager* testified that on the fateful night he had served Stevens a triple brandy about ninety minutes before the collision, but the commissioners failed to ask the obvious question. If Captain Stevens had broken his strict rule of never drinking while at sea, why did he do this? Vice Admiral Hickling advanced the theory that Stevens must have been in great pain with his stomach ulcer before the collision. 'That was why he drank a triple brandy when he usually never drank at sea,' he concluded. 'Something must have been worrying him for him to break a lifelong habit.'

Peter Cabban was devastated at the loss of the ship he had loved, along with so many of its crew, and haunted by the thought that the collision may not have occurred if he had still been on *Voyager* at the time. He was convinced that an injustice had been done to John Robertson. In early 1965, following a dinner party at Robertson's home, he made a tape recording of his recollections from 1963, talking until he had exhausted his prodigious memory. The 'Cabban Statement', as it became known, ran to nineteen pages. In his statement, Cabban documented many occasions during the year when Stevens had been the worse for alcohol, sometimes to the point of incapacitation.

Captain Robertson had another ally in John Jess, a forthright and outspoken backbencher from Victoria, whose wife was a cousin by marriage to Robertson. Jess was determined to restore Robertson's reputation. He went to see Robert Menzies about the matter: 'Oh well, my boy, it's all over. Just forget it,' Menzies advised him. 'Great and powerful people are looking after it. You just look after your career.'

But Jess was not persuaded. He believed that the government's aim in setting up the Royal Commission was 'to have an inquiry and never find anything out' – indeed, 'to impede finding out the answers'. He persisted, and after Menzies retired he approached Holt, who urged him to drop the matter until after the November election, when he would look into it. That seemed fair.

But with the election over, the prime minister continued stalling, and Jess requested that a select committee be formed to reinvestigate the case. He asked Holt for permission to take the matter to the party room, telling him that unless he was allowed to do so he would resign and thus create a by-election for his seat. Holt knew Jess well enough to know he was not bluffing.

Holt felt conflicted. He knew that new revelations could embarrass both the government and the Navy, so part of him wished to cooperate with the powers-that-be and have the matter dropped. But at the same time, he began to assist Jess to bring the matter into the open, for his style of leadership valued above all else cooperation among colleagues. The party room tried to thwart Jess's efforts. But soon the Melbourne tabloid *Truth* ran a front-page story about *Voyager*'s captain under a melodramatic headline:

DRUNKEN DUNCAN
THIS IS WHAT IT'S ALL ABOUT
CAPTAIN WITH TRIPLE BRANDY

Holt's cabinet now realised that they would have to settle the matter once and for all. Within a week, it would be debated in the House of

Representatives. Jess had allies for his cause within his party, all back-benchers with seats around Sydney: Ted St John, the newly elected member for Warringah; Harry Turner, the member for Bradfield; and Malcolm Mackay, the member for Evans. All were prepared to back him in parliament in his criticism of the government.

The *Voyager* question was set down for debate on Tuesday 16 May. Attorney-General Nigel Bowen opened proceedings with a statement on behalf of the government. John Jess and Don Chipp, Minister for the Navy, followed him. Then Ted St John was scheduled to deliver his maiden speech, which he would use to argue that the enquiry into *Voyager* should be reconvened through the formation of a select committee. With his pursed lips, chiselled-down face and black-rimmed glasses, he had the air of a stern, slightly prim headmaster. He also had the qualities of an outstanding courtroom lawyer: clarity of thought, forcefulness of expression and fixity of purpose.

Holt had spoken to St John only twice since his election the previous November, for it was hard to find the time to get to know all of his many backbenchers. But he had erred, for St John did not like being overlooked.

On 16 May, people queued for more than an hour to enter Parliament House to hear the speeches; senators were forced to sit on the floor. Over the two days of debate, a record number of people – 4000 – passed through the public gallery of the House of Representatives.

St John's reputation had preceded him into the parliament, and the press knew he would give them a good show. Relatives of the *Voyager* dead filled the public gallery, and many thousands of other people listened to the radio broadcast. Members of Duncan Stevens' family were there, the weight of the disaster again upon them. Sir Jack Stevens, tight-lipped and silent, looking like an ageing reincarnation of his late son, sat with his daughter-in-law, Beatrice Stevens.

Holt was anxious. He had listened uneasily to the debate all afternoon, compulsively rubbing his index and middle fingers with the thumb of his right hand. Then it was St John's turn to speak. The Speaker of the House drew the attention of members to a matter of protocol: 'As this is a maiden speech, I remind all honourable members that it is to be heard in silence.'

St John's opening must have made most of his colleagues uneasy about the direction his speech would take: 'I rise to make my maiden speech conscious of my loyalty to the party of which I am proud to be a member and of my duty to the electors of Warringah who have done me the honour to elect me to represent them in this House, but conscious above all of my sovereign obligation to speak the truth as I see it in the interests of this, my country.' By now Holt was tiring. At six o'clock the Speaker halted the debate for the dinner adjournment.

Just after eight p.m., St John resumed, observing that his speech had been 'bisected'. He was ready to land the knockout blow. He felt it outrageous that Peter Cabban's evidence about Stevens and his drinking had been labelled 'irrelevant' by government spokesmen:

Irrelevant indeed! Is it irrelevant that the captain of a destroyer in port is perpetually drunk, comes back every morning at 8 o'clock under the influence of liquor, sleeps all day and then starts drinking again? This went on day after day after day . . . When they came back from the Far Eastern cruise – before it had finished – from August to January, when the ship went in for its refit, he was perpetually drunk – if not asleep or sick, attempting to recuperate. Is this irrelevant? Is not this one of the facts and circumstances leading up to the *Voyager* disaster? Or have I lost the meaning of the word 'irrelevant'?

As if punched in the back, the prime minister jerked around to face St John. His half-strangled voice startled the House as much as his interjection: 'And what is the meaning of the word "evidence?"' St John struck back, as sharp as a scimitar, 'I did not expect to be interrupted by the prime minister.'

Red-faced, Holt glared across the chamber. But his sentence could never be retracted. All members of parliament knew that he had always been a stickler for protocol. But now he had violated it in the most embarrassing way possible. He had set St John up to make the obvious point: 'The prime minister's interruption demonstrates better that anything else that this kind of matter can be sifted only by a proper judicial committee.' St John continued his defence of Cabban:

> I believe this man is telling the truth. I would not care if the Minister for RAN with all due respect to him, brought along a stack of statements from serving officers saying they could not remember or could not corroborate.

At this, the Minister for the Navy, Don Chipp, leapt from his seat. Billy Snedden, his friend and colleague, put his hand on his shoulder to hold him back.

Holt was the ultimate team player, and the government was the team of which he was captain, but he had collided with colleagues who had become adversaries when they recognised that there were higher loyalties than that owed to the party. First there was Hannaford; now there were Jess, St John, Turner and Mackay. The independent spirit of Reg Turnbull was alive in all of them. Holt had been used to jousting with truculent union leaders or testy voters, but he found fractious colleagues harder to manage.

Four more government backbenchers rose, one after the other, to further St John's attack on the government. Harry Turner alleged that 'the Navy and the government have carried out Operation Cover-up in respect of the whole affair'.

As an exercise in democracy, the debate over *Voyager* was a triumph. The forms of parliament had been used as a means of seeking truth, beyond the usual constraints of partisan politics. But for Holt it was a disaster. His government had been publicly embarrassed, and many of his colleagues were dismayed by what they saw as his failure of leadership. Soon more bad news came to him, this time about one of the country's most powerful newspaper owners,

Frank Packer, who warned him that he could no longer support the government's reluctance to reopen the *Voyager* matter.

Holt's terrible evening finally ended at 1.32 a.m. He was under enormous pressure both to reopen the *Voyager* case and to keep it closed. He was angry with himself over his failure to contain the dissidents in his party. He desperately wanted to avoid another enquiry, to which most of his party were opposed, but now the worms were out of the can. He feared the power of the press to undermine him further. So he decided to try to close the government's ranks in support of a new inquiry.

On 18 May he announced that 'the government has concluded that there should be a further enquiry and that it should be a judicial enquiry conducted probably by three judges'. The terms of reference were to be confined mainly to an investigation of Peter Cabban's allegations about Duncan Stevens, to discover whether Stevens' drinking habits and state of health had contributed to the disaster.

Holt showed some truthfulness with his admission that at the time of the 1964 Royal Commission: 'There was created an atmosphere that the government, in order to avoid some political embarrassment for itself, concealed evidence which should properly have been placed before the Royal Commission.'

He asserted that parliament had to be seen 'to do justice to the living and the dead'. He paid a generous tribute to Peter Cabban, wishing not to prejudice him in the forthcoming Royal Commission.

John Jess considered Holt to be 'a gentleman who gave me every consideration'. He and others gave Holt credit for finally consenting to the reopening of the *Voyager* enquiry, but this hardly comforted him. Many of his colleagues felt that he had yielded too readily to pressure. One night not long after the *Voyager* episode, journalist Ray Aitchison was present at a private dinner when he heard Bill Aston, the Speaker of the House, predict: 'I'll give Harold only another six months.'

It was not just Ted St John's speech which had been 'bisected'. For Holt, everything after his indiscretion in the House had been separated from everything before it. Whitlam felt that the prime minister's behaviour during the *Voyager* debate had destroyed his confidence. 'It was a shambles,' he said.

The last photograph of *Voyager* was taken three hours after the collision, as its severed stern section began to sink. An eerie white mist shrouded the ship, as if the spirits of its dead sailors were surrounding it in its death throes. The *Cheviot* was still yielding up its treasures, the *Voyager* its curses.

31

A Bad End
to a Bad Week

*If it hadn't been for you two, the helicopters would have been out
there on Bass Strait looking for Harold's body.*
> —Zara Holt, thanking her husband's rescuers after his near-
> drowning on 21 May 1967, quoted in Barker and Larkin,
> *The Holt Report*, 1968

OLT MUST HAVE FELT COMFORTED AS PARLIAMENT'S
winter recess was approaching. On the weekend of 20–21
May, he drove down to Portsea to recover. Normally he
could shift almost seamlessly between worlds, cut in and cut out, but
now he was drowning in the backwash of the past week.

The press and the public welcomed the news of a further Royal
Commission. But this was small comfort for Holt. In full view
of the public, the government had split wide-open and many of
its members were angry that their leader had yielded to pressure
by agreeing to a new inquiry. It was barely six months since Holt
had won a record majority for his party, but already that felt like
ancient history.

The Holts had friends from Sydney staying with them for the
weekend – Eric McIlree, managing director of Avis Rent A Car, and
Dianne Lett, a New Zealand–born model. The visit started badly on
the Saturday when McIlree slipped in the house and badly twisted
his ankle.

Sunday's *The Sydney Morning Herald* profiled Ted St John, who was photographed relaxing at home with his two young sons. The writer described the 'sensational government somersault that has again thrown open the *Voyager* inquiry'. Some of St John's colleagues had snubbed him, following his maiden speech. Holt still referred to his rebel colleagues Jess, Turner and Mackay by their first names, but he pointedly called St John 'Mr St John'.

Later that Sunday morning, the Holts and their guests went to Cheviot Beach to go snorkelling. Zara stayed behind in the car, reading. After diving for twenty-two minutes, Holt had already caught four fish and five abalone. Suddenly, he called to the young New Zealander, 'Di, move in a bit.' Then a word he rarely spoke: 'Help!'

She swam across to him. His speargun had sunk to the sand and his lungs were gurgling with salt water. McIlree saw Holt and Dianne struggling to get ashore, their arms interlaced. Holt's face was puce-coloured. He was hyperventilating and barely breathing.

Together, his two friends helped him towards a rock and hooked his hand into a hole. 'Hang on!' they urged. It took a quarter of an hour to get him ashore. He reeled onto the beach, vomiting water. His snorkel had started leaking and he was unable to get back to the beach to change it, for the tide had started to turn. One of the notorious Cheviot rips had caught him, dragged him over rocks and entangled him in kelp.

From the car, Zara saw the trio struggling back towards her. 'I've always dreaded something like this happening,' she told them. She thanked them for saving her husband's life. It was the closest he had ever come to drowning; had he been alone, he almost certainly would have drowned. 'Cat' Holt had been granted another life. After this lucky reprieve, he introduced Dianne Lett as 'the girl who saved my life'.

The cuts on his torso and legs could be masked, as could any public knowledge of what had occurred. This was just as well, as he had to return to the public eye in the coming week, to campaign for a Yes vote in the two referenda to be held the following Saturday, 27 May.

32

Two Referenda

27th of May / Each one say / YES YES YES / For Freedom
— Song advocating 'Yes' vote for May 1967 referendum

SATURDAY 27 MAY IN MELBOURNE WAS COLD AND GREY when Australians went to vote on two constitutional referenda proposals. It was exactly six months since the federal election, and now Harold and Zara Holt returned to vote at the Canterbury Road school.

One of the referenda was political in nature, the other moral. The political one was a proposal to change the constitution to break the nexus between the House of Representatives and the Senate, which required changes in the number of lower-house members to be matched by changes in equal proportion to the number of upper-house members. Both the government and Opposition were arguing for a slow, sensible increase in the size of the House of Representatives without simultaneously creating more senators.

The referendum that was moral in nature was a proposal to grant citizenship to Australia's Aboriginal, or First Nations, people, who in some official publications were still classified as 'fauna'. It proposed to include Aborigines in the national census and to allow the Commonwealth government to make laws on their behalf. Two sections from the existing Constitution were at issue. The first was Section 51 of the Constitution, which contained the following words:

The parliament shall, subject to the Constitution, have power to make laws for the peace, order, and good government of the Commonwealth with respect to the people of any race, other than the aboriginal race, in any State, for whom it is deemed necessary to make special laws.

This would be a small step to start redressing the wrongs committed by white Australia against First Nations people, dating from the British colonisation of Australia almost two centuries earlier. If carried, the referendum would allow the words 'other than the Aboriginal race' to be struck from the Constitution. The proposal would thus allow for the government to legislate for the advancement of First Australians, especially in the areas of health, education and housing. It would help to right longstanding wrongs against Australia's first people by removing from the Constitution language which, as the prime minister had noted, smacked of discrimination.

The second section from the Constitution at issue was Section 127, which prevented Aboriginal people from being included in the census. 'The simple truth is that Section 127 is completely out of harmony with our national attitudes and modern thinking,' said the prime minister. 'It has no place in the Constitution in this age.'

That the referendum was happening at all was a result of much more than Holt's leadership. Faith Bandler was one of the referendum's main drivers. Born in northern New South Wales in 1919, Bandler's father, Peter Mussing, had been kidnapped from Ambryn, an island in what was known as the New Hebrides, and brought to Australia to work on sugar plantations. Bandler's awareness of her father's bitter experience strongly affected her and impelled her towards political activism on behalf of social justice. 'I wanted to understand,' she explained, 'why a man should be an outcast in his own country just because his skin is black.'

In the late 1940s, Bandler met the feminist and peace activist Jessie Street, who later encouraged Bandler to campaign for greater Commonwealth responsibility for Aboriginal Australians. In the early 1950s, a meeting with Aboriginal activist Pearl Gibbs led to Bandler's establishment in 1956 of a new organisation, the Sydney-based Aboriginal-Australian Fellowship, to work for Aboriginal rights by lobbying for legislative change. By 1967, Bandler was secretary of the organisation, and campaigning to change the constitution. 'I think they thought I was mad,' she recalled. 'Here we were, about four or five people, the poorest little group functioning in Australia, I'm sure, talking about having to change the federal constitution.'

At a packed meeting of Aborigines and white people, she was elected to direct the New South Wales campaign for the Yes vote. Shortly afterwards, journalist Kay Keavney described her thus:

> She has fought all her life for what she sees as a question of human dignity. Her own skin is deep café-au-lait. She has not one drop of Aboriginal blood. Her father was Melanesian, from the New Hebrides. Her mother was part-Scots, part Indian. But she is coloured; she knows what prejudice and poverty mean.

In the 1960s, action on behalf of Aboriginal people was also underway on other fronts. In February 1965, Aboriginal activist Charles 'Uncle Charlie' Perkins, of Student Action for Aborigines (SAFA), organised a bus tour, or 'freedom ride', around New South Wales designed to draw attention to the plight of his people, especially in the areas of health, education and housing. The two-week tour was inspired by the 'freedom rides' throughout the southern states of the US during the early 1960s, which sought to raise awareness of the need to win civil rights for black Americans.

In February 1967, Holt met with activists from the Federal Council for the Advancement of Aborigines and Torres Strait Islanders (FCAATSI). Among them was Bandler, who worked nonstop in the weeks leading up to the referendum to help ensure its successful passage, and Douglas Nicholls, well known in Victoria since his days as a star Australian Rules footballer. Members of FCAATSI met with politicians on both sides of parliament to seek bipartisan support for the referendum.

First Nations' politics was new terrain for Holt. Before 1967 he had met few Aboriginal people, and during his time as an MP, there had been few Indigenous people among his constituents. But he was close to the eminent public servant and chairman of the Reserve Bank, Harold 'Nugget' Coombs, a tireless advocate for Aboriginal people. Coombs encouraged Holt to educate himself about Aboriginal history and culture by reading everything he could find.

Like Holt, Coombs was gentle and low-key. He warmed to the prime minister's kindly nature, but felt it worked against him in his role as national leader. Coombs felt that Holt was 'too nice a person to exercise power successfully'. He admired the warmth that in previous years had made Holt welcome in trade union circles, but as prime minister, Coombs felt Holt struggled to assert himself against ruthless colleagues and a large, fractious backbench. He thought Holt lacked the assurance and ability to identify the focus of dissension which had marked his predecessor's command over the coalition.

The Labor Party joined the government in supporting both referenda. Only the DLP opposed the 'nexus' proposal, as it had a vested interest in increasing the number of senators. Whitlam felt that the electorate was not clear about what it was voting for. The 'breaking the nexus' referendum was convincingly lost, winning a majority in favour only in New South Wales. Victoria, with its solid core of DLP voters, rejected it heavily. Both Whitlam and Holt were disappointed, but not surprised, that the proposal was defeated.

On the second referendum, however, an overwheming majority of 90 per cent supported the proposal. Holt felt encouraged by the support for a necessary step towards justice:

On the Aborigine question, I was delighted with the overwhelming vote in every State of the Commonwealth favouring the elimination of those references which smack of discrimination. The grant of power to the Commonwealth in relation to aborigines which follows from the vote will enable it to play a useful part in ensuring justice and social acceptance for people of the aboriginal race.

The vote will not only help the Aborigine, it will contribute to Australia's international standing by demonstrating to the outside world our overwhelming desire to give full acceptance to the aboriginal people within our community.

The Sydney Morning Herald expressed disappointment about the level of the No vote in certain areas:

It is depressing that the No vote on Aborigines was significant in places where the question was a real issue – in other words, in areas where there are Aborigines to resent and be prejudiced about. The No vote was worst in the three States – Western Australia, South Australia and Queensland – that have been most criticised for their treatment of the remaining Aboriginal populations.

Nonetheless, most of the country was united on the Aboriginal question. It had been a campaign in which Aborigines and their white supporters sang together: '*We are going, we are going to freedom . . .*' – reminiscent of the choruses supporting civil rights in the United States. Holt was surprised and pleased by the strength of the Yes vote, but expressed concern and the need for action: 'The referendum indicates that the government should do something about the situation of the Aborigines. Their plight is very distressing.'

Following the referendum, Holt invited Charles Perkins to write a submission for a federal bureau that would give priority to employment and education for First Nation people and advise the government on the formulation of national policies for the advancement of Aboriginal citizens. This was to be the Council for Aboriginal Affairs (CAA). It would be administered by a secretariat to be called the Office of Aboriginal Affairs (OAA). Both the

Council and Office would be given considerable power and would be able to advise the prime minister directly.

Holt appointed 'Nugget' Coombs chairman of the council. Though at first reluctant to accept, Coombs consented after Holt strongly assured him of his genuine desire to enact reform. Later, as chairman of the Australian Elizabethan Theatre Trust, Coombs encouraged Holt to legislate for the creation of the Australian Council for the Arts.

Coombs felt that it was because of the anxieties which Holt was facing in other areas of politics that he was turning to these initiatives in the arts and for First Nations people. They represented work which 'better expressed his own generous and human spirit'.

Charles Perkins described the referendum on Indigenous constitutional recognition as a 'moment of truth', indicating whether or not white Australia was 'interested in our welfare and rights'. On the morning after the vote, writer Rodney Hall described the change he saw on Brisbane streets:

> There were black people on the streets in a way that we had never seen them . . . It was so touching. People were up. Had washed their children, combed their hair and got themselves up in their very best gear and walked the streets of Brisbane, down Queen Street where they never went.

In 1967, Kaye Price was twenty-six years old, living in Hobart, and attending Hobart Teachers' College. She recalled the Aboriginal referendum thus:

> I remember the debates leading up to the referendum, particularly post-referendum, when it was realised that almost all the 'No' votes were in the Top End. I feel that the referendum marked a turning-point in attitudes to Aboriginal rights. At last we were to be counted in the census, which gave us more 'status' as human beings. The referendum also showed that Aboriginal people had been denied

human rights and this was now brought to the attention of voters, the majority of whom were non-Aboriginal.

1967 was a landmark in that we would never get 92 per cent of the population voting in our favour these days. As a teacher and writer, it is very important to me that Indigenous people themselves do not confuse 'counted as citizens' with 'citizens'.

1967 will always be a recognised milestone in Australian history.

33

Shadows in
the Rose Garden

*President Johnson and the Australian Prime Minister were ensconsed
in this mountain-top retreat today for weekend talks clearly marked
by Mr Johnson's preoccupation with the Middle East crisis.*

*Mr Johnson put Mr Holt at ease by saying that he was looking
forward to 'just having a nice Saturday evening and Sunday with
an old and treasured friend.'*

—*The Age*, 19 June 1967

A T THE END OF MAY, HOLT PUT DOMESTIC POLITICS
aside and travelled overseas again, to North America and
London. He was due in Montreal on 7 June, Australia's day
at *Expo 67*, Canada's Centennial Exhibition held to mark the first
hundred years of that country's confederation.

The Holts made a short stop in Honolulu, staying overnight at
the Colony Surf Hotel in a room facing the beach, which naturally
delighted the prime minister. After Hawaii, he stopped in Los Angeles to speak at that city's World Affairs Council luncheon, before
heading east for Washington, DC and the White House.

Johnson was feeling the strain of his job more than ever; he
had aged visibly, even since his visit to Australia just eight months
before. Both president and prime minister appeared burdened when
they were photographed in the Rose Garden of the White House.
In another photograph, taken as the two leaders walked side by

side along a White House path, deep in conversation, they again appeared to be in uncanny synchronicity, as they had been the previous year. This time they were snapped from behind, their shoulders and heads bowed, as if carrying the world on their shoulders.

Their recent shared happiness had diminished and the shadows had deepened. As well as Vietnam, the president was worrying about impending war in the Middle East. Holt downplayed the rumblings in the area as 'huffing and puffing', hoping that another war would not draw America's attention too far from Vietnam. But the so-called huffing and puffing soon flared into the Six-Day War, which culminated in Israeli triumph on 10 June.

Johnson was steadily losing public support for the war in Vietnam; his calls for patience were wearing thin. The American economy was feeling the pinch. At the start of the year, Lady Bird Johnson had written in her diary that a 'miasma of trouble' was hanging over everything. Privately, her husband was considering not seeking re-election in 1968. He had a history of heart trouble and the strain of the job was endangering his health. Moreover, he was feeling the loneliness of his office as acutely as ever. He claimed that the only two friends he had left were the King of Thailand and the prime minister of Australia.

At their best, both Johnson and Holt were healers. Each could work with people who held different points of view; each took seriously the advice to reason together. Both had been successful negotiators: Holt as Minister for Labour and Immigration, Johnson as Senate majority leader and now as president. Johnson believed he could turn any enemy into a friend, but he could not do that with Ho Chi Minh, who was determined to unite North Vietnam and South Vietnam under communist rule.

The war was creating a sea of devastation. Indeed, cartoonists drew Johnson in the guise of a beleaguered sea captain: in one cartoon he was drawn as captain of the battleship *SS Democratic Politics 1968*. While he manned the bridge of the ship, bombs labelled 'Inflation', 'Polls', 'Poverty', and 'Vietnam' exploded around him. His first mate asked, 'Sir, we were wondering if you'd volunteer to go down without the ship.' In another cartoon, he was Captain Ahab from *Moby Dick*, and the white whale he was pursuing was labelled 'Vietnam'.

Johnson himself used maritime imagery to describe his plight. He paraphrased the biblical injunction 'cast your bread upon the waters, and it will return to you' as 'cast your bread upon the waters, and the sharks will get it'. In a surrealistic vision he imagined himself alone, standing in mid-ocean on a newspaper. 'If I go this way,' he said, tilting his hand to the right, 'I'll topple over, and if go this way' – he tilted his hand to the left – 'I'll topple over, and if I stay where I am, the paper will be soaked up and I'll sink slowly to the bottom of the sea.'

A steady stream of his staff members had departed in recent months, including Bill Moyers. Johnson's spiritual son had cut the umbilical cord and broken away to become father to his own life. Soon after his resignation, he had been seen lunching with Senator Robert Kennedy, whom Johnson despised more than anybody else in Washington. Soon Moyers was saying that, painful though it was to contemplate, if Johnson persisted with his Vietnam policies, he hoped he would be defeated in 1968. This would depend on who the Republicans nominated as their candidate, but it was astonishing that he might prefer any Republican as president.

Johnson tried to bring some humanising elements into his life. He happily anticipated the approaching birth of his first grandchild, the child of his daughter Luci and son-in-law Pat. He lavished his love on his little white terrier named Yuki, a lost dog whom Luci had brought home from a Texas gas station. Johnson yodelled duets with the dog and declared that he had never enjoyed sleeping with anyone as much as with Yuki.

He had planned to complete his discussions with Holt at his Texas ranch on the weekend of 17–18 June, but he had to change these arrangements, as he was scheduled to meet the Russian premier, Alexei Kosygin, in New Jersey the following weekend. If anything happened to Kosygin while Johnson was far from Washington, the situation would be diplomatically vulnerable. So Holt and Johnson instead arranged to meet at Camp David, the presidential country retreat situated in the Catoctin Mountains of Maryland and named for Eisenhower's grandson. There, in July 1965, Johnson made the fateful decision to escalate the war in Vietnam beyond the point of no return.

Meanwhile, Holt was on his way to Canada for one of his more pleasant tasks, opening the Australian pavilion at *Expo 67* in Montreal. He met the singing group The Seekers for the second time, as well as Kathleen Collier, the contralto. He was thrilled that members of the Australian Ballet were going to give six performances before continuing on to South America. According to director Peggy van Praagh, he had put on his ravishing smile and given her clear instructions: 'You've got to go for Australia's sake.' He was eager to bring Australia before the rest of the world, especially through his favourite art form. For her part, van Praagh was grateful to him for promoting Australia's image as a cultural nation.

Since helping to establish the company five years earlier, he had taken a special interest in its work. Robert Helpmann – dancer, choreographer and Australian of the Year for 1966 – was chosen to oversee Australia's contribution. He ensured that the Australian Ballet played a major role, performing his own ballet *Yugen* as well as *The Display, Elektra, The Lady and the Fool* and the last act of *Raymonda*. Another ballet, *Melbourne Cup*, was chosen to give a distinctively Australian flavour.

The theme of the Australian pavilion was 'From the Stone Age to the Space Age' and both the Holts were in attendance. 'By some coincidence we each heard our favourite speaker,' explained Zara Holt. 'Mr Holt listened to a talk by Sir Robert Menzies, and from my chair came the voice of Alan Moorehead' – one of her favourite Australian authors.

On 17 June, the Holts travelled by helicopter to Camp David with Johnson and the rest of the Australian and American parties. This time, the two leaders planned to discuss matters of trade and finance rather than Vietnam. Holt intended to present the case for lifting import duty on Australian raw wool, and urged the easing of restrictions on the movement of capital overseas from the United States.

It was fiercely hot at Camp David when Holt arrived. The first thing he wanted to do was swim. An amusing mishap ensued, however, when Holt lost his swimming trunks in the pool. As he explained to reporters:

> Having arrived in the heat of lunchtime without my luggage, I looked at the pool and mentioned wistfully that I would like a swim. President Johnson kindly made a pair of trunks available. But what will gracefully stay on the President's figure was a little too ample for me. Having dived into the pool, the pants would not stand the impact as well as they might have. I don't think any harm was done as I managed to stay under water a little time to restore the situation without too much embarrassment.

After Johnson coaxed the prime minister from the pool, they sweated out the weekend in Aspen, the Camp David lodge situated in a forest of oaks, maples, planes, cedars and aspens. Usually, they would have enjoyed a breathtaking view of the mountains, but this weekend a heat haze blanketed the surrounding valleys. Vertical streams of sunlight filtered through the trees, slashing the plate-glass windows of the room. On the Saturday night, Johnson wrapped his arms around his treasured friend and asked: 'Well, what movie will we watch tonight, pardner?'

The next morning the president awoke to the news that thirty-five more of his 'boys' had died and many more had been wounded in a large battle to the north of Saigon. The previous day, Secretary of Defence Robert McNamara gave instructions for an academic study to begin a documentary history of American involvement in Vietnam, from the earliest days to the present. This later became known as *The Pentagon Papers*. On the other side of the country, in California, the Monterey Pop Festival was underway, one of the main attractions of that year's 'Summer of Love'.

With Johnson, Harold and Zara attended a service at Harriet Chapel, a small historic Episcopal church. After the service, Johnson and Holt spent some time greeting the other congregants. Holt bounced a three-year-old boy on his shoulders, informing him: 'Today is Father's Day, and this is the day you must be nice to us fathers.'

By the time Holt reached Honolulu on the first leg of his return home, the story of his mishap in the Camp David swimming pool had reached the newly formed Hawaiian branch of the America–Australia Society. They presented him with a pair of swimming trunks which he would never lose – if he could get into them. They would provide 'perfect protection in the water', he told the press, 'but for the fact that they would barely fit my grandson'.

Holt returned to Australia on 22 June, feeling fitter and in better spirits than when he had left. As deputy leader of the Liberal Party, Billy McMahon met the Holts' flight at Sydney Airport. The next day, *The Age* reported on a 'government rift' over McMahon's alleged link to an industries group which Country Party leader John McEwen claimed was out to destroy his party.

McMahon had formed a close connection with Maxwell Newton, a Canberra press gallery journalist who was the editor of *The Australian* newspaper when it first published in July 1964. He had a following as an economic theorist among parliamentarians, public servants and journalists. He was also known to be a supporter of the Basic Industries Group, which consisted of about twelve wealthy graziers opposed to the government's policy of protection of rural industries. They also opposed the Country Party and had campaigned against them in six electorates in the previous year's election. According to the newspaper report, McMahon denied having any knowledge of the group's activities. McEwen, for his part, excoriated the men of BIG:

A group, unseen and unknown – its members faceless and nameless but very real indeed – very rich, indeed, and very reckless in misrepresentation. It has one publicly avowed intention – printed and circulated – to destroy the Country Party in favour of the Liberal Party. No names, but score of thousands of dollars spent for this purpose.

The association between McMahon and Maxwell Newton was largely carried on by McMahon's favourite medium, the telephone. Every week he called Newton from a public telephone or from his home phone, and he visited Newton's home often during the first half of 1967. In the newsletter in which he published articles on economic policy, Newton praised McMahon fulsomely, while criticising Holt and excoriating McEwen.

Holt would soon be hearing much more of Maxwell Newton.

34

Far From Lotus Land

The lotus is a most marvellous flower. It's like a gigantic white tulip with pink tips.

—Zara Holt, *My Life and Harry*

WHILE SHE AND HER HUSBAND WERE VISITING Angkor Wat in Cambodia, Zara Holt saw a huge lake surrounding one of the ruins; it was a flagged moat without water. The guide explained to her that in the days when the city was still populated, the moat was filled with water with lotus flowers growing in it.

'This was done for decorative purposes, I assume?' she asked. 'Oh no, crocodiles were kept there also,' the guide informed her. 'The lotus grows a very sharp, hard spike down under the water, and when enemies were attacking the buildings nearby they waded into the water and gashed themselves on the lotus. The crocodiles smelt the blood and came in to finish them off.'

Three months after his visit to Cambodia, Holt was worrying about the recent British decision to withdraw its forces from two other South-East Asian countries: Singapore and Malaysia, known in the region as 'East of Suez'. On 20 July he cautioned his people: 'The British withdrawal from the far East should bring home to the great mass of Australians that they don't live in some kind of lotus land.'

After returning from his most recent overseas trip, Holt was soon back in the thick of domestic politics. Sir Hubert Opperman, his former immigration minister, was vacating his seat of Corio, in the Victorian regional city of Geelong. One of few changes the prime minister had made after the November election was to move Opperman from his portfolio and offer him the position of High Commissioner to Malta. Holt had been the first Australian immigration minister to visit the island since the Second World War and was well respected there.

Opperman, a former Olympic cyclist, was a Geelong local and very popular in the area; he would be missed. The new Liberal candidate, Ronald Hay, was an 'import' from Melbourne. The Labor candidate, Gordon Scholes, was a local man who had unsuccessfully contested the election in the previous November. He was an engine driver and a former Victorian heavyweight boxer.

The Holt government looked very unlikely to lose this seat. In the sixty-six years since its establishment, the seat of Corio had belonged to the Opposition for less than two years. For the other sixty-four, successive Corio MPs had always been in government, no matter what its complexion. The maxim went: 'As Corio votes, so votes the nation.'

Corio's last by-election was in 1940, when Hitler was said to be watching. Now Holt was suggesting that Ho Chi Minh and the North Vietnamese were watching. At his meetings, he affirmed his support for continuing the bombing of North Vietnam, even as more American voices were now being raised against the bombing; one of those voices, Whitlam pointed out, was that of Robert McNamara, the Secretary of Defence.

In a bid to support Labor's campaign for Corio, Whitlam lived in the electorate for a full two weeks before the election, concentrating on local issues. He held meetings at local factories, canvassed for votes door to door and talked to housewives about their problems – he shook hands and kissed babies. He presented the Labor candidate as a local man, not a Melbourne import, declaring that 'Gordon Scholes is the man I want with me in federal parliament'.

Meanwhile, Holt maintained focus on Vietnam and national security, and seemed confident in the outcome of a Liberal victory at the by-election. *The Age*, too, expected no surprises:

Only one thing could make tomorrow's by-election interesting, and that would be a heavy rebuff to the government. Nothing in the Corio campaign or on the national scene suggests that the Liberals will suffer anything worse than a trimming of their majority of 8,000 in the electorate.

But *The Age* was wrong. The Liberal Party candidate was soundly defeated, the first chip off the rock of the government's majority. So the champion cyclist was replaced by the champion boxer. Gordon Scholes looked likely to have a majority of 8000 votes; the seat would not even need to go to preferences. Holt made the usual excuses for losses in by-elections: they were notorious for running against an incumbent government; people often used them to give the government a knock, knowing that it could not be changed. Later, Whitlam looked back on his rapid ascent and declared 'it started in Corio'.

On the Sunday of the following weekend, 30 July, Holt welcomed two distinguished American visitors dispatched by Johnson to South-East Asia, Australia and New Zealand in an effort to encourage his allies in these regions to increase their contributions to the war effort. One of these was Clark Clifford, chairman of the Foreign Intelligence Advisory Board, a wealthy corporation lawyer and White House counsel to Democratic presidents since Harry Truman. The other was General Maxwell Taylor, former ambassador to South Vietnam and chairman of the Foreign Intelligence Advisory Board and chairman of the Joint Chiefs of Staff. The publicly declared aim of these men was to provide an update on the situation in Vietnam, but their real intention was to secure promises of more troops. Clifford admitted that in official statements he and Taylor had disingenuously downplayed this aim in saying that they would not be making 'specific requests of any kind'.

Mindful that 1968 would be a presidential election year, Johnson was desperate to break the stalemate that had developed in Vietnam, and he was still hoping that a lift in troop numbers would do it.

If he decided to run for re-election, his prospects would slump if an end to the war was still nowhere in sight. The American people were growing far less optimistic about the course of the war, as were the Australian people.

The discussions lasted for seven hours. Clifford and Taylor were joined by Ed Clark, the American Ambassador to Australia, and the prime minister was joined by a number of members of his cabinet. Clifford noted that Holt became extremely evasive when he and Taylor told him that Johnson considered Australian participation in the war effort to be particularly critical, and that Australia's actions would strongly affect those of the United States.

Holt responded to Clifford's description of the American political landscape with a comparable portrait of Australian politics, designed to show that he, too, faced a difficult situation at home. He had supported the US as much as he felt he could; he could not increase support further. Clifford returned home somewhat defeated; he was especially disappointed by Australia's attitude:

> Australia, which had given so much during World War Two, dismayed us the most. Johnson, who remembered the country with special affection – from his brief service there in World War Two – had counted on more from Down Under and his good friend Harold Holt.

For his part, Holt used many words to say very little about the meeting:

> The talks ranged extensively over all aspects of the Vietnam situation which the representatives of both groups raised. The exchange of information and views will be helpful to further consideration by the governments of both countries.

He was under heavy pressure to extend his country's commitment to the war, but he was acutely aware of the growing domestic disquiet. During the first half of 1967, there had been little tangible progress in the war, and Australian casualties kept growing.

The next evening, Holt was booked to deliver the annual Alfred Deakin Memorial Lecture at his alma mater, the University of Melbourne. This lecture, which was always given by a prominent member of the Liberal Party in memory of an early prime minister, would take place in the Old Arts Public Lecture Theatre, near the building where he had studied Law.

Before his arrival, there was an air of ferment amongst the mainly student audience. The compere struggled to introduce Holt against the racket. As Holt approached the lectern, he was assailed by a fusillade of paper darts. He opened with a potted history of Deakin's origins and early life, and continued with an account of events leading up to the formation of the Liberal Party.

There was stamping, booing, heckling and slow hand-clapping from the floor, as well as interjections: 'Who wrote this trash?' and an old favourite, 'Did yer bring yer flippers with yer, Harold?'

Against an intensification of jeers and darts and the shouted words 'Vietnam' and 'conscripts', Holt reaffirmed his party's pledge to political liberty and individual freedom. 'And that means freedom to throw paper darts at a democratically elected prime minister, too', he added.

One of the darts found its mark in the middle of his forehead. Then the chanting began, accompanied by whistles and thumping of desktops: 'Bring on Gough! Bring on Gough!'

He struggled on. Life for a politician had grown far more complex, fast-paced and difficult, he noted. He complained that 'ours is a grudging democracy which holds politicians in low esteem'.

In the aftermath of this ordeal, he told the press:

I am a graduate of this university myself. I was not surprised. I am mainly pleased that so many people turned up to hear what I had to say. I managed to say it – that was the main thing. I think people who really wanted to hear me were able to do so.

But the tail of the lotus had given him a sting. The next day the meeting was front-page news in Melbourne and Sydney, with an image of a paper dart flying towards him.

A few days later, he made his usual August trip to Bingil Bay – his own lotus land – to celebrate his fifty-ninth birthday. With Bob Dyer and his wife Dolly, the Melbourne quiz-show hosts, he sailed out to Dunk Island in the Great Barrier Reef in Dyer's boat, *Tennessee 11*. They were photographed in the fish-laden boat, looking like members of an extended family. The prime minister lay back like a sybarite, enjoying his freedom.

Earlier, he had struggled unsuccessfully with a large, defiant fish for twenty-five minutes, treading water, running short of breath, until he had to give up the contest. The episode prompted talk of death: 'Well, if you've got to go, you've got to go, and this would be the way to go,' he explained.

35

Treading Water

*Those Liberal members elected to seats which would normally
be counted as Labor's but for the violence of the reaction against
Mr Calwell's style of Opposition, now are beginning to see just how
short their stay in politics is likely to be. Perhaps unfairly, they are
blaming Mr Holt personally for their impending political extinction.*
—10 October 1967, Newsletter of the
Management Information Group.

I N MID-SEPTEMBER, HOLT FLEW TO WESTERN AUSTRALIA
to open the North West Cape Communications Station to the
north of Perth, built for the US Navy as 'a simple, practical
and logical extension of the ANZUS treaty'. To justify their support
of America in Vietnam, Australia and New Zealand had invoked
this defence agreement between their two countries and the United
States. A new town, Exmouth, had been built as the centre for the
North West Cape station.

In Perth, Holt was photographed on a street bench beside a
small boy who appeared not to realise who he was sitting next to.
A border collie sat at their feet. Wearing his black-rimmed reading glasses, Holt was engrossed in the morning paper. He looked
entirely comfortable, an ordinary citizen among others, free from
self-consciousness and from security personnel. A man in a casual
jacket strolled by with a camera.

An impromptu hotline had been installed by radio from North
West Cape to Washington, so that the prime minister could report to

Johnson, who was asleep when the call from Australia came through at 1.30 a.m. in Washington.

'Tell Harold to call back,' he ordered, as Holt did shortly after.

'Glad to hear you, Harold,' greeted the president.

'Sorry to disturb you.'

'Glad to hear from you any time, Harold.'

'It is a great day for the United States and Australia. It would make your heart glad to see the teamwork here at Exmouth.'

But Johnson could no longer help Holt with the challenges of domestic politics. During the following week, President Giuseppe Saragat of Italy arrived in Australia on a state visit to greet the country's large Italian community. Holt suffered in comparison with the leader of the Opposition at the nationally televised parliamentary luncheon for Saragat. He was judged to have been 'too prone to mouth platitudes'.

On the last day of September, another by-election was due, this time in the North Queensland seat of Capricornia. It was a tall order to expect an incumbent government to win a by-election for a seat held by the Opposition, especially when the government's popularity was already in decline. But once again, Holt was optimistic, and predicted a win for the Liberals.

It is impossible to know why he made such a claim. Perhaps he was so desperate for an electoral success that he put objective judgement to one side. But his prediction flew in the face of history. Only once in the sixty-six years since Federation had a government of any complexion won an Opposition-held seat at a by-election, and that was in quite extraordinary circumstances.

Billy McMahon intervened in the campaign, warning direly that the Labor candidate, Douglas Everingham, was 'a left-winger with way out social, economic and religious beliefs'. Zara accompanied her husband to Queensland for the campaign, and made her own contribution: 'Queensland needs to get with it. Something needs to happen up here. I could shake Queenslanders. They are the nicest people on earth, but so foolish.'

Ultimately, Everingham retained the seat for the Labor Party with an absolute majority. Many Liberals were nervous and interpreted the result as a defeat, rather than as merely the inevitable. Holt made the usual comment about by-elections running notoriously against incumbent governments, but those close to him felt that since the result, something had died in him. He was desperately hoping that the tide would turn in his favour, but, with a Senate election due at the end of November, he had no time to brood. The leading editorial in *The Age* of 9 October asserted that 'Mr Holt is not wearing well as prime minister'.

This made him sound like an old coat that needed patching. The writer described his performance over most of 1967 as having been 'in sad contrast with the assurance he brought to his first year in office'. While acknowledging that the prime minister was obviously a man of capacity and experience, he held that he needed to show that he was also a strong man:

> When he took over from Sir Robert Menzies, Mr Holt at once made it clear that his leadership would not be in the style of benign dictatorship. Rather, he saw himself as the captain of a cricket team, and he was a good captain, able to turn events and the popular mood to his advantage . . . As the November elections proved, he was a captain who knew how to retain the ashes. Now he seems more inclined to wear them.

In her husband's early days as prime minister, Zara had identified what she saw as his most attractive quality: his pleasant personality. But if nice guys did sometimes finish first, they did not always stay there. He had ascended to the top job in part because he was an accommodator who rarely made enemies. His pleasant personality had helped his new backbenchers to win their seats in parliament, but now that same personality was endangering their seats and they were making mischief under his lenient smile.

There had always been sharp divisions within the Liberal Party, its members ranging from reactionary Tories to progressive 'small l' liberals. But to the public and the parliament, Menzies had managed to portray the party as a united, cohesive political force. Don Chipp felt that the party room under Holt was like a family whose strong, authoritarian father had died and been replaced by a kindly, tolerant guardian. The 'children' misread tolerance for weakness and misbehaved. Like recalcitrant school children, the backbenchers took liberties they would never have dared to take with Menzies. Chipp felt that Holt's softness often bordered on naivete. On one occasion, the backbenchers' criticism became so aggressive that John McEwen jumped to his feet, shouting, 'Okay, if you want leadership, I'll give you bloody leadership. This is what the government has decided and this is what we are going to do.' This forceful rebuke had a salutary effect on the rebels, but made Holt look ineffectual in comparison with McEwen.

The prime minister was conflicted. He wanted to operate as he had before he attained the top job, as a democratic captain who sought consensus rather than imposed his own will. But his survival depended on how effectively he could assert his leadership. Well, he would show that he could. His frank and truthful approach to the Vietnam involvement had won him respect. Perhaps now he could embarrass Whitlam over this matter, just as he had embarrassed Calwell. He decided to engineer personal clashes in parliament between himself and the Opposition leader.

He had recently announced that in six weeks another 1700 men would be sent to Vietnam as reinforcements. Australia would thus have over 8000 troops there – more than it had held overseas since World War Two. But he advised Johnson that Australia had now reached the limit of its capacity in Vietnam. Commenting on the prime minister's announcement, Whitlam charged that 'it is wrong for the government to intensify a war to which it does not see an end and to which it will not help put an end'.

The Australian Senate election usually held every three years was forthcoming, and Whitlam's strategy was to divert attention from his party's still-conflicted policy on the war by initiating a debate about the government's attitude to the possibility of peace. Why, he asked, did the prime minister not encourage the United States to take a step towards peace by stopping the bombing of North Vietnam? Holt struck back: 'The Leader of the Opposition slanders us repeatedly as men who have no wish for peace. I slam it in his teeth. No one in Australia wants peace more than we do.'

Whitlam accused Holt of timing his announcement about deploying extra troops just before the Senate elections in order to position it as a referendum on the war. But the situation in Vietnam was no longer as clear-cut as it had been in 1966 when the government won its record majority. At best, the anti-communist allies were progressing impossibly slowly. As the casualties mounted, Holt often lay awake at night, worrying about his troops.

Since becoming leader of the Opposition, Whitlam had successfully fought by-elections by turning the electorate's attention towards domestic policy. Holt believed that Vietnam was still Labor's Achilles heel. He went on the attack. What would the Labor Party do with the troops if it were to become the government? Thumping the table, Holt glared at Jim Cairns, the leader of the left-wing faction in Labor: 'Isn't it true that you are where you were at the last election? Of course you are. You know you are, because you have said you are.'

He was hardly behaving like a leader who commanded a record majority in parliament. His image was suffering in comparison to Whitlam's as a result of their clashes in the House. His anxieties about the war were also fuelling his outbursts. He was especially troubled by the growing number of Australian soldiers who were being killed or wounded. 'Off the record,' he told some members of the Press Gallery, 'I still think I'm right, but these casualties our boys are suffering are terrible. I believe I know how John Curtin felt during World War Two.'

He talked with Whitlam about his many difficulties. The two men liked each other, having bonded when Holt, as leader of the House, and Whitlam, as deputy leader of the Opposition, had worked together arranging parliamentary business. This happy association had lasted for six years. Though Holt could not match Whitlam's intellect, he shared his urbanity. Outside of their parliamentary jousts, their relationship was amicable. A sympathetic Whitlam told him: 'Harold, I'll never do anything to hurt you personally.'

Some of the business of that day's parliament was less unpleasant for the prime minister. Following up from the May referendum, he announced the arrangements for and the names of the members of the new Council for Aboriginal Affairs. 'Nugget' Coombs would be the chairperson because he was 'a financial whiz'; Barrie Dexter would be seconded from the Department of Foreign Affairs; and anthropologist Bill Stanner would be the other member, because of his expertise.

Dexter had been told that the Council would advise the prime minister directly and would be given substantial power. The Office of Aboriginal Affairs would serve the Council and operate largely independently within the prime minister's office. Holt told him that he would personally, as prime minister, be responsible for Aboriginal Affairs and would use his authority to push through the necessary policies for reform.

36

Man Wasn't Made
to Live Like This

My dear Harold,

During the last six months of the parliament and to the present time, various members at all levels within the Party have expressed to me feelings of disquiet. The same feeling seems to be permeating the electorate and is being followed up in the Press.

Do you personally feel that there could be some reason for this attitude? Do you think it is of sufficient importance for me to probe more deeply into these problems? And to make a further report to you?

I am writing to you only in view of what I think is the seriousness of the situation at the moment and leave it to your evaluation and judgment as to whether you would like a summary of the situation.

—Letter from Dudley Irwin to Harold Holt, found in
Holt's briefcase, quoted in Alan Reid, *The Power Struggle*

THE SENATE ELECTION WAS DUE ON 25 NOVEMBER, a year to the day since the federal election of 1966. Since then, everything had changed for Holt and his government, mostly for the worse, with a long string of losses, both electoral and personal.

As the election neared, Holt faced another worry. In the Senate, Reg Turnbull was asking embarrassing questions about the government's use of its fleet of VIP aeroplanes. Along with members of the Opposition, he charged that the families of parliamentarians were rorting taxpayers by using VIP flights for private purposes. Records of these flights were kept and they would prove it. Was the government failing to answer his questions on notice about the VIP flights because it was 'so ashamed of this business that it will not answer them?' Turnbull asked.

Labor senators joined Turnbull and the DLP to question the prime minister's use of the VIP fleet to fly members of his family between Melbourne and Canberra, as well as the practice of hiding the costs in the defence budget. Billy McMahon, too, had been accused of abusing the system. The national press was relishing Holt's discomfort, one paper suggesting that the prime minister should set up his own travel agency in his Canberra home: 'H. Holt's Travel Agency (Book from Here to Anywhere) – as an annexe of the Lodge.'

Did past records of passengers and costs associated with the flights exist, and if so, were they retained? The prime minister had previously told the House that the records did not exist. His Minister for Air, Peter Howson, backed him in this statement. 'I had backed him up loyally throughout the whole of the intervening period, even denying records were available when I knew that they actually were available,' he recalled.

When Richard Casey, the governor-general, asked Howson why he not been more explicit in parliament on the issue, he told him 'that further discussion would have involved Harold Holt and that I had to protect the PM at all costs'. Howson told Casey that he 'felt that the PM was over-worked and over-tired and was giving too much attention to administration and not enough to political issues'.

Holt had underestimated the potential fallout from the matter. He seemed to be developing a predilection for secrecy, born of his insecurity about his own standing and that of his government. The damage following the new revelations in the *Voyager* case must have been prominent in his mind. But compared to *Voyager* this seemed a trivial matter, a storm in a cockpit – at least, that is what it should have been.

Peter Howson was Holt's friend and their electorates were adjacent to each other. The prime minister often found it difficult to discipline personal friends. The minister offered his resignation, but Holt would not accept it.

Holt had been sufficiently worried about affairs in the Senate to replace the government leader there with John Gorton, a fellow Victorian. Gorton cautioned Holt, his circumlocutory diction now direct: 'Any public disquiet over any alleged secrecy would be much greater than any public disquiet over any factual disclosure.' If the public could not trust the government on a matter like this, he asked, how could they be expected to trust it on a larger matter, like Vietnam? Whitlam was asking the same question, and it was a valid one.

Gorton was adamant: the government's losses had to be cut. Before the assembled Senate, he laid on the table a set of papers giving all the requisite details of flights, passengers, dates and destinations. If Senator Gorton could get this information, asked the press and the Opposition, why couldn't Mr Holt and Mr Howson?

In his diaries, Howson later summarised his view of the problem:

> It was clear after the event that Harold had never taken the VIP matter at all seriously because he thought that the opposition would not press for answers. He forgot, however, that the DLP and the Independent Senators would not have been part of the deal, and it was those people who, in the end, made all the fuss.

In the Senate, on Tuesday 24 October, while Country Party Senator Colin McKellar was answering questions about the VIP matter during a heated session of Question Time, the debate came to a sudden and shocking end. Senator Clive Hannaford, who had broken with the Liberal Party over its Vietnam policy, suddenly slumped over on his crossbench, choking sounds coming from his mouth. A few minutes later he was dead.

The previous weekend, against medical advice, he had spoken at a meeting of protest against the war in Vietnam. Just before he collapsed and died, he had addressed the Senate to attest to the peacefulness of that demonstration. When Hannaford first announced his decision to break with the Liberal Party, Senator McKellar called him 'Judas'. In April, in the Senate, McKellar made another scurrilous attack on Hannaford:

> I have no respect for a person who, having been put here by an organisation, turns on that organisation and resigns from the ranks of the government that that organisation supports, and remains in the parliament. That sort of conduct is not befitting any man who has the interests of the country at heart.

McKellar and Holt obviously had different ideas about what constituted 'the interests of the country'. Speaking about Hannaford after his death, the prime minister made a wise and gracious speech:

> We can imagine the anxiety of mind which led him finally to a decision which severed his connection with his colleagues on this side of the House. It must have been a great wrench for him. We respect the moral courage and the deep conviction which led him to that decision. This really is the kind of courage and earnestness which makes democracy function as it should, with people being willing to stand up for what they believe in regardless of the circumstances.

The VIP matter continued to occupy the attention of the Senate after Hannaford's death. In the House of Representatives, the Opposition leader initiated a vote of no confidence in the government. Holt was angry. From time to time he shouted. He oscillated between defence and attack, making extravagant charges: the Opposition was totally unfit to govern, and the leader had less credibility than any Opposition leader in history. After a noisy four-hour debate, the no confidence motion was defeated along party lines.

It seemed that the press coverage could hardly get worse for the prime minister, but in *The Sydney Morning Herald* it did. In one editorial, the prime minister's speech was described as a 'floundering', 'rambling' and 'sad' performance. Jim Cairns also mocked Holt's rambling manner of speech, comparing it to *Blue Hills*, the seemingly endless Australian radio serial. Another Labor member told Holt that he was struggling 'uphill'. 'I have been uphill all my life,' he countered, 'and I got to the summit.'

Despite the fractiousness of the session, Holt concluded his speaking for the day with a return to the courtesies for which he had always been known, assuring the Opposition leader and his colleagues that,

> We have our differences and they are strong differences on many matters, but we maintain for each other a respect as men who have been sent here to carry out as best we can and according to our lights the wishes of those who sent us here to represent them and to interpret what they would have us say in this place.

The parliamentary summer recess was about to begin. At 12.49 a.m., the House adjourned until a date to be fixed by the Speaker. The prime minister left the chamber for the last time.

*   *   *

Though the fuss over the VIP affair was subsiding, the whispering around the corridors of both houses of parliament was growing. More and more of the prime minister's colleagues doubted his capacity to deal with the political crises that were brewing – or that, some felt, he was creating. Perhaps they agreed with Calwell's assessment from the previous year that 'Mr Holt has lived under the branches of the banyan tree for the past seventeen years and cannot stand up to the fierce light of the sun beating on the political scene'.

John Gorton had leadership ambitions of his own. It had been only a matter of weeks since Holt had promoted him to leader of the Senate, but already he had made his mark. Gorton had been in politics for nearly two decades but had hardly been outstanding in his ministries; his personal idiosyncrasies and resistance to protocol had caused difficulties. But during the VIP debate, he had acted like a decisive leader and his standing among his colleagues had grown. His name was being mentioned as a future leader of the party.

Holt knew well the world under the surface of the sea, the internecine war between predators and their victims. Now the world behind the scenes in the corridors of parliament was starting to resemble that watery world, except that the predators were disguised in suits.

The government whip, 'Deadly' Dudley Irwin, was expressing concern about Holt's performance. McMahon was working behind the scenes to try to persuade members to depose Holt. There was no coherent campaign against Holt, but rather a nod here, a whispered conversation there, a leak from cabinet, and most often a telephone call.

McMahon was flexing his muscles. His old friend Richard Kirby, now president of the Conciliation and Arbitration Commission, had described McMahon as 'a magnificent fighter – literally. He could box like a thrashing machine and he was game as hell.' Now McMahon kept his body trim and his mind alert by playing squash. He wielded his racquet like a sword to smite his opponents, who sometimes reeled back clutching a bruised eye or cheek.

Holt had been finding it difficult to manage the ongoing feud between McMahon and McEwen. He could successfully use his skills of conflict resolution with adversaries who retained a modicum of flexibility, but now he was dealing with implacable opponents. McEwen wanted Holt to remove McMahon from Treasury. But if the prime minister were to replace him with someone more congenial to McEwen, this would greatly offend the New South Wales branch of the party, who supported McMahon. It was a no-win situation for Holt.

The feud was now so destructive that, at McEwen's suggestion, Richard Casey took the highly irregular step of offering to intervene. Holt at first turned him down and instead arranged a meeting between the antagonists, to be held on 9 November. McEwen had refused to meet alone with McMahon, telling him, 'I would not talk with you alone because I would not trust you not to spread a false account of what passed between us.' For that reason, five other senior ministers – Paul Hasluck (external affairs), Allen Fairhall (defence), John Gorton, and from the Country Party, Doug Anthony (primary industry) and Ian Sinclair (shipping and transport) – joined Holt, McMahon and McEwen in discussion.

The meeting developed into a verbal brawl of accusations and counter-accusations. McEwen charged McMahon with taking a totally destructive attitude to everything he did. He accused him of leaking material to the media – especially to Maxwell Newton and Alan Reid – to undermine him.

Maxwell Newton was now considered by some observers to be the most dangerous journalist in Canberra. His activities were causing so much concern that the Australian spy organisation, ASIO, was asked to investigate. McEwen accused McMahon of leaking cabinet secrets to Newton, who then, McEwen claimed, passed them on to the Japanese External Trade Organisation, known as JETRO.

McEwen insisted that Newton was not a newspaperman; he was a 'paid agent' of the Japanese government, employed by JETRO to provide information about Australian tariff policies. This would benefit the Japanese at the expense of the Australian manufacturing industry. McEwen had a copy of Newton's contract with JETRO, and quoted from it in detail, arguing that Newton had been hired to serve the interests of the Japanese while working against the interests and policies of the government of his own country.

McMahon denied knowing anything about Newton's Japanese associations. Newton, he said, had not been in his office more than four times. But McEwen was not persuaded, calling McMahon 'a bloody liar'.

Without directly saying so, McEwen also hinted that McMahon was trying to undermine Holt's support within the Liberal Party. After the meeting, Holt 'spoke feelingly' about McMahon's disloyalty to him. But the conflict between McEwen and McMahon was no closer to resolution. Finally, Holt agreed to have Casey meet with McMahon, whom the governor-general considered to be the major cause of the conflict:

> 'Your notorious relationship with John McEwen is damaging the relationship between the two government parties,' the Governor General began. 'An attack on Mr McEwen,' he contended, 'is an attack on the whole Country Party.'

At this point the treasurer interjected to say that he challenged the governor general's constitutional right to discuss the matter with him, as this was a right reserved only for the prime minister. Casey continued, confronting McMahon over his association with his journalist friend: 'Your close relationship with Maxwell Newton is also harming the government.' McMahon claimed that he had never had a close relationship with Newton, but Casey noted that throughout the interview McMahon had kept referring to Newton as 'Max'.

*   *   *

For years, Holt had alternated a couple of hours of sleep followed by a couple of hours of work. His briefcase was always beside the bed so he could go on working, long after Zara had put aside her copy of Patrick White, Alan Moorehead, or another of her favourite novelists. Now he was finding it almost impossible to sleep.

In 1967 his appearance had changed perceptibly; he now looked distinctly unwell. The ghosts were gathering around him: his brother, Senator Hannaford, the soldiers in Vietnam. The dead were many, and they were exerting a gravitational pull on his mind and spirit.

One day he stumbled while climbing the steps to Parliament House. His colour was bad and he looked ill. This mishap turned out to be the result of a vitamin deficiency, but his colleagues began to speculate that he might have been suffering from more serious health problems. Was he having a heart attack? Was he still fit enough to lead them?

As the Senate election approached, Holt's minders argued that, in order to acquire some of the authority of Whitlam, he needed to update his image. They told him that he smiled too much. He was too nice; he had to collar the rebels and lead his party more forcefully.

He made an effort to adjust his image, but this only made him look wooden, disingenuous. His friend Lyndon Johnson also had an image problem, not that anyone ever accused him of being too nice. He had genuine charm, but in front of the TV cameras he became mannered and sententious, stopping the flow of his natural personality. Zara Holt was saddened that her husband had been advised to try to change his true personality. 'He tries very hard not to smile,' she said, 'and he's not that kind of man.'

On the morning of 11 November, after his election policy speech, *The Age* television critic weighed in: 'Please, Prime Minister, will you smile next time?' His voice, she complained, was completely lacking in force. All four Melbourne television stations had broadcast the policy speech, so viewers had no way of avoiding quadruple boredom:

Mr Holt delivered his party policy speech straight-faced, with clutched hands and occasionally shaking shoulders. It was difficult to see the Prime Minister on camera as he really appeared because, somehow, one saw him as the cartoonists do. No doubt that is why his advisors – knowledgeable people of course – had clearly told him not to smile. It was, let's face it, one of the most boring party political broadcasts we have suffered: on all four channels at once, so we had no choice.

On the day before the election, the same newspaper unenthu-siastically advocated a vote for the government, and was equally unenthusiastic in its assessment of the campaign:

> The present campaign looks like turning into a poll to determine which man has the more attractive presence, the Prime Minister or the Opposition Leader. Because of this, many voters are prob-ably toying with the idea of rebuking the presently unsparkling Mr Holt, though they might not actually want to turn him out of office. Unable to bring themselves to vote Labor, they could be tempted to vote informally.

Holt was attending a St Andrew's Day dinner at the Australia Hotel in Melbourne when the first election returns came in. The government had suffered a swing of about 8 per cent against it and had lost its majority in the Senate. It looked as if the DLP would hold the balance of power. Already there was speculation that Holt might lead the government to defeat in 1969.

The next day he retreated to Portsea. The weather was wet, with strong, squally winds and temperatures much lower than the November average. He made no attempt to hide his disappointment at the result:

> It does not make very good sense in a democratic argument for the government to be in this position. The DLP now has the balance of power, but can't win a single seat in the House of Representatives.

He spent time with his grandson Christopher, who had recently turned eight, and ten-year-old Andrew Hiskens, the son of one of Zara's cousins. The boy was visiting for the weekend; his parents had sent him to the Holts' to give him some experience of spending time away from home. In the morning, Harold Holt drove the two boys into Portsea village to collect the morning newspapers. Andrew was thrilled to share a ride with Christopher in the prime minister's

Pontiac Parisienne, which to a ten-year-old boy was an exotic car indeed. Later, Holt took the boys to the beach, Christopher carrying an umbrella, perhaps meant as a shelter from rain rather than sun.

Monday's *The Age* ran with a front-page story of the swing against the government. Turning to Shakespearean tragedy to represent Holt's plight, cartoonist Les Tanner depicted the prime minister as a black-clad Hamlet in a graveyard, morosely contemplating a Yorick-like skull. Whitlam was the grave digger, eagerly digging a trench with the date 1969 carved above it. Overhead a dark sky glowered, while Mrs Holt peered out from behind a tree, lamenting: 'Poor Harry – they should let him smile more.'

In real life, too, Holt was downcast. It was true that he did not have much to smile about. But if, as *The Age* had observed, he was 'presently unsparkling', that was partly because he was denying his inner spark. If he had allowed himself to be himself, he would have been happier and would have wasted less energy.

On the matter of 'being yourself', his wife had her own feelings.

> How can you be anyone else? You can't be! You'd be brilliant if you could. D'you know what I mean? I just can't walk in and be a different person. The only thing I've changed in ever since I married Mr Holt is I'm no longer late.

On the Monday after the 1966 election, the front page of *The Age* had featured a photograph of Holt at Portsea relaxing and smiling on a chaise longue, attended by a proud daughter-in-law. Exactly one year later, the front-page story in *The Age* was accompanied by a poignant snap of the prime minister with his grandson and Andrew Hiskens at the bluestone wall above the beach. Holt had the air of a solid father-figure, his hand resting protectively on Andrew's shoulder, but he looked diminished. Most of his face was caught in shadow. Despite their tender years, both boys looked pensive, serious, as if some of his worry had rubbed off even onto them.

*   *   *

In dark times, Holt sought the counsel of wise and sympathetic people. He now approached two distinguished public servants with whom he had long been associated. One was 'Nugget' Coombs, who had recently retired from the position as governor of the Reserve Bank and was set to take up the position of chairman of the new Council for Aboriginal Affairs. Coombs found Holt mortified that he had been seen to mislead parliament over the VIP aircraft matter. The prime minister seemed to him more burdened than ever by the demands of his job, as well as by ill-health and personal worries.

Holt also approached Lenox Hewitt, who until a year earlier had been deputy secretary of the treasury. One of the most unpopular men in Canberra, Hewitt was informally known as 'Doctor No'. But he had known Holt since he had been treasurer and had always given him a sympathetic ear. Holt knew that Hewitt disliked McMahon and would understand his difficulties with him. He outlined his problems, especially McMahon's treachery and the feud between the treasurer and McEwen. As he took his leave, his parting words echoed in Hewitt's ears: 'Len, man wasn't made to live like this.'

On the second weekend in December, Holt again took some rest at Portsea, visiting Cheviot Beach with Christopher and his mother, Paulette. The beach was at its best; the water was calm as the family group swam together in a favourite rock pool. But, the weekend over, a new problem confronted the prime minister, this time from the other side of the world. Prime Minister Harold Wilson announced that the British government intended to devalue the British pound. Holt responded by explaining that, after due deliberation, his government would not follow by devaluing the Australian dollar. He and the treasurer set out the reasons clearly.

But John McEwen, overseas in Geneva, deplored the decision, complaining that it would adversely affect his rural constituents and create a political crisis between the coalition parties. The decision, he felt, was 'deep enough to be of political consequence' and struck very selectively at Australia's wealth-producing industries, both primary and secondary.

Holt read McEwen's statement and dropped it onto his desk, outraged that the Country Party leader had taken a contrary public position without discussing it with him first. 'McEwen has gone too far this time! He must be repudiated,' he told his staff. When he was warned that repudiation might lead to the break-up of the coalition, he replied that, 'He's going to be repudiated, even if it does mean the breakup of the coalition.'

Now he had the spur to assert his leadership. He summoned McEwen and in a 75-minute private conference systematically refuted his claims. The press reported that Holt had 'virtually repri-manded' McEwen for criticising the government's decision.

In Brisbane's *The Courier-Mail*, Wallace Brown commended the prime minister: 'Mr Holt took the tough line which a tough situation demanded. He deliberately, calmly and completely rebuked Mr McEwen in public and in private.' Reflecting later on the tough line Holt had taken, the veteran journalist Alan Reid later pointed out that

> though the fact tended to be obscured by his good nature and an irritating verbosity, Holt was a courageous man who was immova-bly stubborn once he had persuaded himself that a course of action was in the national good.

Holt had decided to enlarge Australia's military commitment in Vietnam, which he thought to be to the country's benefit. He decided that repudiating McEwen was to Australia's benefit, so he repudiated him. His anger had focused his mind and sharpened his powers of leadership. 'Tiger' Holt had triumphed over Holt the 'Puss'. Having exercised his authority effectively again, he felt satisfied.

Christmas was approaching. Compared to the previous year, Holt was diminished. In his diary entry of 13 December, Peter Howson reflected:

Looking over the events of the last fortnight, I have been stressing the trials that we have had after the Senate election because our public image has slipped. I've tried to analyse the reasons for this, and it all points back to the organization around the Prime Minister himself. He has been too tired because he has taken too much on his own shoulders. He has not had time to reflect on the major issues and to segregate the important from the unimportant. I feel that he doesn't delegate sufficiently, and that he is too surrounded by civil servants and not sufficiently by politicians so that we take administrative decisions instead of examining the politics of important issues.

But in spite of his debilitated condition, he was still prime minister. He was looking forward to 'the refreshment' at Portsea and a fresh start in 1968. Despite the mutterings about his leadership, there was encouragement from colleagues such as Bob Katter, who praised his courage and tenacity and his way of reaching out and showing appreciation to his colleagues for their work. It had been a quite abnormally difficult and stressful year, he replied to Katter, but he was looking forward to the change of scene and refreshment which he hoped to find over Christmas and New Year.

He and Zara had family and friends staying with them at the Lodge. As well as Paulette and Christopher Holt, Alison Busst was visiting from Bingil Bay. As the first president of the Innisfail branch of the Wildlife Preservation Association of Queensland, Johnnie Busst was intensifying his efforts on behalf of marine conservation. This association had been formed by Judith Wright, an eminent Australian poet. While Alison was at the Lodge, Johnnie rang his old friend to talk about saving the Great Barrier Reef from Queensland government proposals to mine there. 'Look, it's a difficult situation,' Holt replied. 'But I will promise you this, that if the Queensland government starts to mine the reef, or starts to attack the reef, I will come in and bring the Federal parliament behind me.'

On the evening of Thursday 14 December, Holt invited some journalists to the Lodge for Christmas drinks. One of them, Allan

Barnes, watched him as he moved from group to group, making sure that everyone was being looked after. He was smiling again, beaming with friendliness as he took the journalists' wives on conducted tours of the redecorated Lodge.

How nervous he seems as he shows his guests around, thought Barnes. *How much he needs the approval of those around him. That abalone he caught while diving last weekend – he's showing it off the way a small boy would. The way his eyes light up as he urges us to try it! But how tired he looks. His back must be giving him trouble again.*

Barnes recalled Holt's complaints about his back pain during the Senate elections, and his instructions: 'Don't write anything about it. I don't want any sympathy vote.'

Now he was worried that during the Christmas break some of his colleagues would be on tenterhooks about possible cabinet reshuffles. 'All this speculation must make the boys terribly nervous. I hate to think of them spending Christmas wondering whether they're going to be dumped or elevated.'

37

Down to Portsea

Shortly before 1.15 p.m., Mr. Holt arrived back at his Toorak home.
Mrs Lawless recalls that he dashed inside, changed his clothes, and
said to her: 'It's such a lovely day, Tiny, I'll go down (to Portsea)
quickly and see you there.'

—John Larkin and Geoffrey Barker, *The Holt Report*

THE NEXT MORNING, HOLT PREPARED TO LEAVE CANberra for a weekend at Portsea. Alison Busst was going to stay with Zara at the Lodge. As he left, he gave his wife a farewell kiss. 'Before God, you're a rose of a woman,' he told her. Then he was gone.

The weather in Canberra was warm and benign. 'It's a beautiful morning, Prime Minister,' one of his colleagues noted. 'Perhaps it is, outside,' he replied. He stopped on the steps of Parliament House for tourists to photograph him, his eyes tired, but his smile warm.

He met briefly with Sir John Bunting, Head of the Prime Minister's Department. Bunting had been reminiscing about Joseph Lyons and John Curtin, two prime ministers who had died while in office. Holt remarked: 'I hope my own life expectancy isn't cut short.'

'Of course, sir, you are talking of political life expectancy?' asked Bunting.

The prime minister corrected him. 'No, I'm speaking in human terms. Nobody can live for ever.'

His physical health must have reminded him painfully of his own mortality. His right shoulder was giving him trouble, and at times he lost feeling in the fingers of his right hand. He had recently consulted Dr John Cloke, an orthopaedic surgeon, who found that one of his patient's vertebrae had narrowed to half its normal size, causing severe pain. To alleviate this, Dr Cloke prescribed morphine tablets, which Holt now always carried with him. Before he left Canberra, Dr Marcus Faunce looked him over. He advised him to cut down on his swimming and tennis in order to give his shoulder a rest.

At about 11.30 a.m., Holt took a VIP Mystere jet to Melbourne, with Paulette and Christopher Holt, Pat de Lacy, his secretary, and Tiny Lawless. He worked for less than an hour in his Melbourne office. Before leaving, he wrote to his skindiving friend Ben Cropp, who lived on the Gold Coast, made films about the sea and had a history of tangling with sharks. Like Holt, he loved foraging in shipwrecks, of which he had discovered more than one hundred.

Cropp had been nagging Holt about saving the Great Barrier Reef from mining, as had Johnnie Busst. Holt wrote to Cropp as one skindiver to another, referring to their discussions about the matter, and reminiscing about his most recent birthday at the Reef. He was 'all for' protecting it: 'I'm putting it in the hands of one of my ministers, and away we'll go.' He decided it would be John Gorton's responsibility.

Soon Holt was back at St Georges Road, where he shed his public persona and quickly changed into casual clothes, including the blue cloth cap he usually wore for the drive to the Mornington Peninsula. As food for the journey, he picked up a crayfish sandwich which Tiny Lawless had made for him in Canberra. She would follow him down in a government car to keep house for him while he was there.

He packed his brown leather briefcase with his personal monogram, the initials HEH interlocked on the closing flap. For many years now, the briefcase had been his constant companion. Its interior was a microcosm of his public and private worlds, a space within which the odds and ends of those worlds rubbed together.

The briefcase contained objects from both hemispheres: bank-deposit books; tax returns; papers relating to power of attorney; his driver's licence; American Ambassador Ed Clark's business card; a pass to the Amateur Turf Club's Members' car park. In a zip pocket were coins, combs, cigars, a fountain pen and other personal effects. There were sunglasses; a bottle opener; two small colour plates of seagulls on the lawn of the house at Portsea; empty metal cylinders that had contained Romeo y Julieta and Henri Wintermans cigars; books of matches, one of them from the Hotel Bel Air in Los Angeles, a souvenir of his last trip to America.

There were headache tablets – disprin and aspirin – and documents relating to matters that might have been causing headaches. There was an October copy of *Inside Canberra*, carrying a lead story claiming that the

> decision of the Deputy Prime Minister, Mr McEwen, to go overseas while the Senate election is in progress is being interpreted in parliamentary circles as evidence that he is refusing actively to cooperate in the government until his differences with the Treasurer, Mr McMahon, are resolved.

The report continued:

> It is most unusual for a party leader holding Mr McEwen's senior position in a government to be absent during a vital election campaign, but Mr McEwen told the Prime Minister weeks ago that he was not prepared to aid the government while Mr McMahon continued to undermine him.

Then came a section that the prime minister had underlined heavily:

> Mr McMahon said privately on his arrival in Canberra this week that he could not understand why Mr McEwen was going abroad. His own just completed tour had resolved all Australia's immediate trade problems.

The briefcase also contained a long typed letter marked 'Personal and Confidential' from Mr McMahon to the prime minister, describing the treasurer's one and three-quarter hour meeting with the governor-general on 8 December. The discussion, McMahon reported, had been 'frank and wide-ranging'. As for the allegation that he had criticised McEwen's decision to go overseas at an election time, he claimed that this was 'totally false'.

The briefcase contained another troubling letter, from the government whip, Dudley Irwin, expressing 'disquiet' about the current political situation and the direction of the government under Holt's leadership. The prime minister planned to reply in a day or two, when he hoped to feel more at ease. In the meantime, the sea was waiting for him.

He closed the briefcase, gathered his weekend things together, and put everything in the boot of the maroon Pontiac that resembled a boat as much as a car. It carried the palindromic registration number *HOH 111*, perhaps the nearest available to his own initials. He climbed into the driver's seat and eased the car into the traffic on Toorak Road.

From Williams Road he turned onto Nepean Highway, past a string of bayside suburbs and on southwards towards Frankston. Perhaps he pictured the familiar western end of the peninsula as it appeared on the map, a long arm outstretched in welcome; perhaps images of the previous weekend at Cheviot flashed before his inner eye. The tea-trees lining the highway waved in the wind, as if beckoning him on. From Frankston, he travelled along the Moorooduc Highway and re-entered Nepean Highway outside Dromana.

At Sorrento, close to his final destination, he stopped at Jack Shepherd's fish shop. Marjorie Gillespie was there. He paid Mr Shepherd the $3 he owed him for some fish he had bought the previous weekend. The talk turned to crayfish and he teased Jack about the size of the ones in his shop: 'You call those crayfish! You should have seen the ones I caught last weekend!'

Tiny Lawless and her driver arrived at the house around 5.30 p.m. to find him absent, but before long the Pontiac nosed down the

273

driveway. He had been swimming. Then he went to the Gillespies' house for drinks, returning for dinner with Tiny. They read the evening newspapers together before he retired at 9.30 p.m.

The next morning, Saturday, he ate a light breakfast of tea and toast and read the newspapers. One of the front-page stories in *The Age* concerned Alec Rose, the around-the-world solo yachtsman who was following in the wake of Sir Francis Chichester, who earlier in the year had completed his own around-the-world voyage. Rose had set out from Portsmouth in July in his thirty-foot sloop *Lively Lady*, and was now battling his way across the southern Victorian coast on the last leg of his 14,500-mile voyage. The literary section contained a poem entitled 'The Tide Also Turns'. *The Australian* contained an article reporting on the prime minister's health; his doctor had advised him to cut down on tennis and swimming because of his shoulder injury.

Paulette Holt was there with Christopher, and the prime minister worked in the garden with his grandson, pruning and clearing some saplings that were beginning to obscure the view from the house over Port Philip Bay, as well as an overgrown tea-tree.

In the afternoon, he disregarded Dr Faunce's advice and played tennis at his friend Bruce Edwards' grass tennis court, ignoring the twinges from his sore shoulder. At about five p.m., Nick and Caroline arrived from Melbourne with their daughter, Sophie. She was a little scared of her grandfather and sometimes ran away from him. But now she seemed to be overcoming her fear as she waltzed around the garden with him. 'I've made a new friend,' he told her parents.

The front page of that evening's Melbourne *Herald* reported on a recent disaster in the US. A 1920s suspension bridge in West Virginia had collapsed, plunging bumper-to-bumper traffic into the icy Ohio River below, killing sixty. Next to this story was a report of Alec Rose's voyage, accompanied by a large photo of *Lively Lady*, the main headline welcoming the yachtsman: 'Nice To See You, Mr Rose'.

A smaller headline announced 'He's Due In Tomorrow'. The prime minister decided to go and try to see the yacht when it passed through the heads late the next morning, Sunday 17 December.

38

The Last Day

I'd like to get away from earth awhile,
And then come back to it and begin over.
May no fate wilfully misunderstand me
And snatch me away, never to return.
Earth's the right place for love,
I don't know where it's likely to go better.

—Robert Frost, 'Birches'

The Rip is the momentous meeting place of two domains of water.
One mass of water comes in and out of the bay as a tide. The other
is the heave and swell, the fetch that has come all the way up from
the Antarctic. The two seas in the act of meeting and exchange cre-
ate a turbulence as dangerous as anywhere in the world. For the
force from the outside, with the Southern Ocean behind it, is coun-
tered by the lunar propulsion of the Bay – a huge bay, as we know,
that must find its way out through the narrow Heads.

—Barry Hill, *The Enduring Rip: A History of Queenscliffe*

O N SUNDAY MORNING, HOLT WAS UP EARLY AS USUAL.
At 6.30 a.m. he asked Tiny Lawless for a light breakfast of
orange juice, toast and tea. 'The weather doesn't look too
good for spear-fishing today,' he told her. 'But we don't need any fish
today because we've got some whiting.'

Going out to buy the Sunday papers, he saw *The Sydney Morning*
Herald had a banner headline about the disaster in West Virginia.

Another article told of the departure the day before from Adelaide of the Third Battalion, the new troops to leave for Vietnam as part of the last increase of Australian troop levels announced in October. There was another report on Alec Rose, due to sail into Port Philip Bay in *Lively Lady* some time after noon. Holt decided to take Marjorie Gillespie with him to get a glimpse of the boat.

It was Clifton Pugh's birthday. He and Holt had arranged to go snorkelling that afternoon, but Pugh's wife, Marlene, arranged a surprise birthday party for him and so the excursion was called off.

By 9.30 a.m., Holt needed more sustenance, so he went to the kitchen for a plate of rhubarb and cream.

He rang Jock Pagan, federal president of the Liberal Party, and informed him that the tides were forecast to be high. Meanwhile, at the nearby Portsea back beach, lifesavers were calling for the beach to be closed to swimmers. The surf looked dangerous; they feared that there might be drownings or near-drownings.

Shortly afterwards, the telephone rang. Tiny answered it and called the prime minister. It was Billy McMahon.

The telephone was McMahon's Excalibur. Johnson described the telephone as a great healer, but for McMahon it was an instrument through which he inflicted himself on both friends and adversaries. Holt heard the nervous quavering voice which was like no other and thus needed no introduction. Billy was worked up.

Tiny heard the edge of tension in the prime minister's voice, the volume and pitch rising at times. And then finally: 'All right, Billy, if that's the way you want it, have it that way. That's that.' He hung up the phone and turned to Tiny. 'That's it then, Tiny.'

The housekeeper wondered to what 'it' might refer and what McMahon might have been saying on the other end of the line. She was struck by the agitation in Holt's voice; it sounded as if he had reached some point of finality, but was most unhappy about it.

The two men had quarrelled earlier in the week, and the conversation had clearly not resolved their differences. Perhaps Gorton, or another colleague, had warned Holt that McMahon was working against him, and this was the source of the quarrel. But the substance of the conversation remained undisclosed.

He rang Marjorie to invite her to go with him to the headland to see *Lively Lady* sail through. She explained that she had with her Alan Stewart, her daughter Vyner, and Vyner's boyfriend, Martin Simpson. 'That's all right, bring them all.' Sophie came to Holt's car and he laughed as he said goodbye to her.

Martin Simpson found it hard to believe that he was going on an excursion with the prime minister. But he was happy to be there. He had met Holt for the first time at a cocktail party at the Gillespies'. Considering himself to be a young 'leftie', he had many reservations about Holt, but, almost in spite of himself, he was charmed.

The weather was overcast and humid as the prime minister led the way in his Pontiac, Marjorie Gillespie beside him, dressed for the beach in a bikini covered by a loose chiffon blouse. Holt was wearing light blue shorts, a dark blue shirt, a green bush hat and old sandshoes without laces. To get to the headland they had to enter the Quarantine Station. This time there was a one-man gauntlet to run, in the form of a young cadet from the Officer's School.

'Halt! Who goes there?' he asked.

'Holt,' replied the prime minister.

'You can't come in here.'

'Don't you know who I am?'

'No, I don't.'

'Well, I'm prime minister.'

Some flurry behind the scenes, and at last the gates were opened.

They caught a glimpse of *Lively Lady* coming through the heads. The yacht, white etched against blue, was crossing Bass Strait on its way to Melbourne. Alec Rose's solo feat of endurance embodied the spirit of courage and adventure which the prime minister greatly admired. To the party watching it, the yacht was just a speck on the ocean.

The heat was rising; the talk turned to swimming. Marjorie suggested that they go to Geyser Beach nearby, but Holt demurred. 'No, let's go to Cheviot. It's always more fun.' And so the party set off for there, the prime minister leading in his Pontiac with Marjorie, the others behind them. Once above the beach, they climbed down the track through the tangle of tea-tree. The gnarled arms of the trees looked brittle but menacing. The wind wailed through the trees and shook the tussocks of grass. Etched against the sky were the bare branches of she-oaks.

After clambering down a steep sand dune, the party walked onto the beach, its ochre rocks awaiting them. The spray off the surf was spectacular as the wind lifted it clear of the waves. The tide was high and the water was no more than about ten metres from the foot of the sand dune. White water foamed towards the beach across the limestone ledge which separated the sand from the ocean.

Very quickly, Holt trotted ahead, the others far behind. He was carrying a string bag with the Sunday papers, two tins of flyspray and two cans of beer. Catching up, Alan Stewart offered to carry the bag. 'Perhaps the boys would like some beer?' the prime minister suggested. There were chuckles of amusement when he related the story of the hold-up at the gates to the quarantine station.

Heavy chunks of driftwood were being lashed against a cliff nearby and piling up on the beach. As the party reached it, they saw the rest of the sea's detritus – broken shells and cuttlefish and clumps of kelp. The party stood together in the shallows, discussing the big tide and the driftwood which was battering their legs.

The waves kept pounding in, soaring and crashing onto the rocks on the sea floor. It was like the Ancient Greeks' image of the sea in full cry, an embodiment of Chaos, beautiful in its ferocity. 'Not a good day for snorkelling,' Holt informed the others. 'The tide needs to be out.' And then: 'I know this beach like the back of my hand.' He dived behind a rock to change, emerging in swimming togs and sandshoes.

Marjorie had never seen surf like this at Cheviot. The waves were boiling up, ten to fifteen feet high, into huge hills. Uphill, embodying his personal myth. *I have been uphill all my life and I got to the summit.*

He would still accept any challenge that sent him uphill, even though he was not as strong as he had been in those early days as prime minister when he had posed on the beach with his daughters-in-law, glowing with vitality. Even though he reminded Marjorie of Picasso, his body was not as it had been even a year ago, when he considered himself fit enough to be a jet pilot. St Paul was wrong: the body was not a temple, it was a museum – a museum of the accumulated scars, scratches and infirmities of a lifetime. But the morphine gave him confidence to keep going, always one step further.

Holt had often been in the presence of death and had always survived, had gone it alone throughout his life. Alone again, he stepped out, cavalier as usual. Marjorie felt her first moment of shock. 'Surely you're not going in?' He answered her by striding towards the water. She blanched as he took the first steps, for she felt he was risking his life by entering surf as wild as this. 'The PM must be fitter than we are,' said Alan Stewart. 'There he goes, striding out like Marco Polo.'

He was without flippers, but he wore sandshoes as protection against the rocks. He stopped at a rock, climbed onto it, dived off and started swimming straight out to sea. 'Well, if the PM can take it, I'd better go in too,' said Stewart. He waded into the water up to his knees but no further. The undertow was alarmingly powerful. He felt the run-outs as the tide rushed out in irresistible surges between the rocky outcrops and the sandbars. After a short time in the shallows, he decided to leave the water.

He returned to Marjorie, frowning. After a while, he asked her: 'Does he always swim this long?' 'No,' she replied. By now, Holt was being sucked out irresistibly through the deep blue section of water which was being channelled through the space between the rocks. Marjorie was alarmed by the speed and force of the water. *It's taking him out like a leaf*, she thought.

He got out into a line of breakers. She hoped he could catch one and ride it back in. But soon she could barely see his head, its silver hair blending with the silver of the waves as if it belonged to them.

'Come back!' she called, though she knew he could not hear. But perhaps he could see. She began to mime her command.

Suddenly, the tide turned. The water boiled up and engulfed him. She watched the body she had loved vanish beneath the waves. It was so quick, like one of Houdini's disappearing tricks. The fates had misunderstood him, after all. Alan Stewart raced up the beach, back to his car, and hurtled off towards the Officer's School to get help.

Vyner and Martin had been walking with their backs to the water. They returned to see Marjorie standing on a rock in her bikini, her chiffon blouse billowing in the wind. She was shielding her eyes and looking out to the water, a tear glistening on her cheek.

'Mum, what's wrong?' asked Vyner.

'He's gone. He went out to the rock and he's gone, like a leaf on the tide.'

She returned to the car with the others. They kept looking back at the sea as if he might magically reappear. A sudden shaft of sunlight broke through, lighting up the scene.

*   *   *

At 12.45 p.m. in Melbourne, Inspector Lawrence Newell was showering at his home, getting ready for duty at Russell Street police headquarters. His wife called to him that Inspector Hildebrand was on the phone.

'Is it important?' he asked her.

'It is. He said it's very important.'

Wrapped in a towel, he listened to Hildebrand.

'One of us has to go off to Portsea. The report we have at the moment is that the prime minister has gone for a swim. He's gone out and he can't be found.'

'Stop bulldusting me, Hildebrand. What's the matter?'

Hildebrand assured Newell that he was deadly serious.

In Canberra, Zara Holt was at a luncheon when Ray Coppin, the Holts' driver, was sent to speak to her.

'Mrs Holt, I'm afraid I have some very bad news. The prime minister is missing, presumed drowned.'

'Good God, no. He could be washed up on the rocks. He often goes off for a swim and sits on a rock in the sun and doesn't come back. We won't worry too much.'

But a little later, she asked:

'Do you know if he was wearing his sandshoes or his flippers?'

'It was probably his sandshoes,' she was told.

'Oh. Then he's gone.'

A housemaid gathered some things together for her to take with her on the flight to Melbourne. Alison Busst would go with her, as would Marcus Faunce, the doctor.

On the way to Melbourne, Zara braced herself for the landing. Her sister, Genevieve Home, was there to meet her. 'The only thing now is to find him,' Zara told her. 'This waiting is terrible.'

She was still clinging to a shred of hope that he would be found alive. But she had enough knowledge of Cheviot Beach to know that within minutes, perhaps within seconds, he would have been lost.

Sam Holt heard on a transistor radio at Portsea front beach that a VIP was missing in the area. He suspected it was his father. He could hear the buzz and throb of helicopters overhead. He found a public phone box and rang the house. Tiny answered, motherly but direct: 'I'm sorry, darling. He's gone.'

* * *

The news of Harold Holt's disappearance spread quickly. In Melbourne, Don Chipp heard the news at Black Rock beach in his electorate, where he was attending a lifesaving carnival. His wife Monica rushed to the beach in distress to tell him.

Shortly after the Chipps reached their home in Bluff Road, Don received a call from Billy Snedden, who had been crying in his bedroom for half an hour after hearing the news. He sounded inconsolable: 'Chippy, I've loved this man for more than twenty years, ever since I was a boy. I don't think I can ever get over this.'

That afternoon, the phone rang hot in Chipp's household. Soon after the initial calls about the news of Holt's disappearance, another flurry of calls began to reach him. To his disgust, many were from colleagues seeking support for the leadership and trying to get in quickly to shore up the numbers. One of them was Snedden, who had recovered sufficiently from his grief to consider standing for the leadership. Chipp agreed to support him, but was shocked by the speed of his appeal. Holt had been Snedden's mentor, had encouraged Menzies to make him attorney-general, and had made him Minister for Immigration in his own government.

When asked to make a television appearance to discuss Holt's disappearance, Snedden demurred, as did most of his ministerial colleagues. Holt's image had been tarnished; in all the circumstances, they felt it might be unwise to emphasise their connection with him. As no colleagues more senior in rank were willing to speak about Holt, Chipp agreed to do so, although he ranked very low in the ministry at the time.

Robert Menzies heard the news about his friend and protégé at his home in Haverbrack Avenue, Malvern. Throughout 1967, Menzies had been disappointed in Holt, as he went from one blunder to the next. He felt that Holt had succumbed to his 'besetting sin' – the need for everybody to love him.

He later expressed some of his feelings about the tragedy in a letter to his daughter, Heather Henderson:

I will never quite understand why Harold Holt, who was a skin-diver but who was not a particularly strong swimmer, should have gone out suddenly into a raging surf into which no experienced surf swimmer would have ventured. This, so far as I am concerned, remains a mystery.

Menzies felt that Holt had become 'vastly worried' about events during 1967 'because he was too experienced a politician not to realise that he had made errors . . . I think he ended the year very worried and anxious and in a very poor state of nervous health.'

*   *   *

On the other side of the world, in Washington, DC, Lyndon Johnson was getting ready for bed when he received the news of Holt's disappearance, from Tony Eggleton by phone. The president was deeply grieved. He sprawled on his bed and pondered his movements for the next few days. Early the next morning he instructed his pilot: 'We may want to go to Australia tomorrow. You better get my big plane out and make sure it's ready to go.'

Sue Holt, Holt's niece, was spending a year working in London and travelling the continent. During the early shift at the Royal Lancaster Hotel in Kensington, she was serving a customer his bacon and eggs. He noted her accent: 'Oh, it looks like your prime minister has gone for one too many swims,' he informed her.

She looked at him questioningly. 'What do you mean?' she asked. 'Your prime minister's gone. They think he's dead.' She dropped her notepad and ran upstairs. The telex machine confirmed the news about her uncle Harry. She began to make plans to fly to Australia. Eventually she managed to secure a seat on the plane which brought Harold Wilson and Prince Charles to Melbourne for the memorial service.

*   *   *

Back in Australia, by late afternoon on 17 December, about one thousand holiday makers had gathered along the Nepean Highway at Portsea, waiting for Zara Holt to arrive. They were standing with heads bowed in silent tribute to her. The extended Holt family had gathered at the house, waiting for the search to resume the next morning. During the night, a boisterous electrical storm hit the town. Zara got up and moved around the living room, making sure everyone was comfortable, before returning to her bed.

In the final hours of Sunday and first hours of Monday, the sea at Portsea was dark, dramatic and windswept. The waves were still up to fifteen feet high as they thundered towards the shore. Night closed over the now deserted beach and the waves told their tales, just as they had eighty years before, on the night when the *SS Cheviot* sank.

39

Missingness

Death defines life . . . Our deaths illuminate our lives . . . Each of us
dies the death he is looking for, the death he has made for himself.
If we did not die as we lived, it is because the life we lived was not
really ours; it did not belong to us, just as the bad death that kills us
does not belong to us.

—Octavio Paz, *The Labyrinth of Solitude*

People are much more interested in seeing things disappear than
seeing them appear . . . When you make things appear they say 'Oh,
he had it on him all the time!' But when you make things disappear,
they are amazed.

—Harry Houdini, quoted in Ruth Brandon,
The Life and Many Deaths of Harry Houdini

THE NEXT MORNING, MONDAY 18 DECEMBER, NEWS
that the prime minister had vanished was the lead
story not only in Australian newspapers but around the
world. In *The Australian*, Alan Ramsey concluded his obituary by
reflecting on the changes in Holt's fortunes since becoming prime
minister:

Two years later the heady brew had gone a bit flat, and in some
ways the novelty had worn off. It had become obvious Mr Holt
had to 'make it' in his own right, particularly with such a goer as
Mr Whitlam now leading the Opposition ranks.

It was in these circumstances that Harold Edward Holt, trier extraordinaire, went swimming against his doctor's orders, off Portsea yesterday morning.

'Trier extraordinaire' was an apt phrase. All his life, Holt had desperately tried to 'fill the unforgiving minute': he had slept too little, worked too hard, worried too much – in short, he had tried too hard. Finally, he had overestimated his ability in his favourite element. Sam Holt later said of his father: 'His courage exceeded his wisdom.' Holt had indeed dared, as his school's motto urged, but not always wisely.

The sea and the sky were grey and squally on Monday morning, when Zara Holt joined her sons and their wives at Cheviot to thank the searchers for their efforts: 'It has been reassuring to know that so much is being done and I want to thank everybody for their kindness and help,' announced Zara. 'I have been deeply touched by the many hundreds of messages of sympathy, so many of them paying warm tribute to the prime minister.'

By now she had accepted that her husband was dead and that the ongoing search was to recover his body. She had a suggestion for Colonel John Bennett of Southern Command: 'Please search *Pope's Eye* and *Chinaman's Hat*, two swimming holes along the shelf. He often swam there, and there is a westward rip. He might have been washed into there.'

There was another task for Marjorie Gillespie and the party that had been at Cheviot – to re-enact, step-by-step, the events of Sunday afternoon. Paulette Holt accompanied them. They started with the walk down to the beach to the exact spot where Holt had entered the water. It was almost too much for Marjorie. But she still had to undergo an interview with members of the Federal Police, outlining her connection with the prime minister and the events that had transpired the day before. To her, this felt like a violation: 'The contents of my heart are not the property of the Australian Federal Police.'

'Nobody can live for ever,' Holt had reminded the head of his department. He may have had an intuition that he would not reach sixty. His father and his brother had both died before then, and his mother had died at forty. In 1967 the gravitational pull of death had been strong. Sheriden Gillespie had died in January, then Cliff had died in March. His old school friend Norman Mussen, who had introduced him to Zara, had died in April, also not yet sixty. Apart from Aunt Leila, who was in her eighties, all of Tom Holt's siblings had died, all of them around the age of sixty. In October, Clive Hannaford had died suddenly in the Senate.

According to Peter Howson, in his last week of life the prime minister had told the governor-general that he could not manage another year like the one he had just endured. On 18 December, the day after Holt's death, he described in his diary his recent poor health:

> Certainly in these last few weeks Harold has been ill. His shoulder has been giving him a lot of trouble – it has been stiff, which shows that if he did get into trouble in the sea he was not as well able to cope with troubles as he had been in the past . . . The same sort of symptoms had emerged in his final Cabinet only at the end of last week. So a picture emerges of a Prime Minister worn out after two tremendously hectic, difficult and industrious years; he was certainly not well.

Perhaps Harold Holt had an intimation that his end was bound up with the element that had given him delight in life. If it's going to happen, then it's going to happen – that was his philosophy. So, take the risks; you have nothing to lose.

* * *

Holt shared the same initials as Harry Houdini. The magician's specialty was escapology, and water was the element from which he made his escapes. Apart from his self-deliverance from the Yarra and Detroit rivers, among others, he had introduced the 'Chinese torture cell' into his repertoire. These acts spoke of a desire to reach another world, while still remaining in this one. This he shared with the Australian HH; when seeking to reach that other world, they risked their lives in this one.

Thus Harold Holt became the most famous of the long list of people lost at sea without trace in Australia, presumed dead, yet categorised as missing. This is a haunting and peculiarly Australian motif, not only in our history, but in our literature. In 'Five Bells', one of Australia's best-known poems, Kenneth Slessor ruminates on the story of the disappearance of his friend Joe Lynch, a black-and-white cartoonist for *Punch* magazine, who, on the night of Saturday 14 May 1927, drowned after falling from the ferry *Kiandra* in Sydney Harbour. He had been drinking steadily that afternoon and his coat pockets were filled with bottles of beer for the party to which he was travelling. He disappeared over the side of the boat near Fort Denison and drowned. Though his body was never found, it was certain that he had perished.

In the year that Holt went missing, Joan Lindsay's novel *Picnic at Hanging Rock* was published. This novel told the story of the inexplicable disappearance of three schoolgirls and their mathematics teacher at Hanging Rock in Victoria. In Peter Weir's film adapted from the novel, the faces of the missing are displayed on a noticeboard near the scene of their disappearance, their grainy, fuzzy images embodying the liminal space between life and death.

Disappearance threatens the corporality of the world, haunts us by blurring the line between life and death. The Vietnamese believe that if a loved one's body is not found, his spirit will roam restlessly for eternity. Perhaps Zara Holt had something of that feeling as she contemplated her loss.

The next of kin of the sailors lost in HMAS *Voyager* received a dreadful official letter from the assistant secretary of the Navy informing them that their relatives 'became missing' while engaged in naval operations and were thus 'for official purposes presumed to be dead'. Became missing – that curious phrase suggests that the missing have entered a liminal state somewhere between life and death, but belonging to neither.

Death may indeed be presumed 'for official purposes', as the bureaucratic phrase went, but not necessarily for the purposes of those whose association with the deceased was more personal. So it was for May Usas, the mother of sailor Tony Syaranamual, who was lost with *Voyager*. For years afterwards, she still expected him to walk through the front door. Douglas Salveron's sister could not believe that her brother was really dead because his face was bandaged and could not be identified.

Harold Holt's body was never found. But some weeks after his disappearance, the tide that enters The Rip and circles to Cape Cook carried a thigh bone and another leg bone into the scallop boats' nets. These human remains were not identified.

40

In Memoriam

Oh you who bow your heads now at mention of me,
Hear this: It wasn't kelp, current or shark
That finally hauled me down under,
But the voluminous waste of your minds,
The effluence pumped from the shore, against which
Only a god could contend. I, being human,
And having, in plain proof of this,
Sought in the water escape from the poison of office,
Drowned, three days out,
And entered the bloodstream of myth.
　　　　　　　　　—Bruce Dawe, 'Reverie of a Swimmer'

A CROWD HAD GATHERED AT 112 ST GEORGES ROAD ON the morning of Thursday 21 December, waiting for Zara to return for her husband's memorial service the next day. When she arrived, she was accompanied by Paulette and Christopher Holt, John and Alison Busst and Marcus Faunce.

Among the crowd was the Holts' young neighbour Nigel Green, whom Holt had often greeted with a cheery wave of his hand. Like many other Australians, Nigel had heard the news of the disappearance at about 2.30 p.m. on the Sunday, amidst the domestic routine of that weekend.

That evening he followed the television coverage of the search for the missing prime minister, as Tony Eggleton briefed the public on the progress of the search. Nigel probably knew nothing of Cheviot

Beach or of Mr Holt's penchant for risk. Perhaps nothing before had rippled his pond like this. But eventually he was convinced that his neighbour would not be coming back, and his thoughts turned towards Mrs Holt.

He worked his way through the crowd and approached her with a small bunch of jasmine picked from his family's garden and tied with a piece of cord. 'I'd like you to have these,' he told her. She put her arm around him, smiled and kissed him, like a grandmother. 'Mrs Holt looked so sad,' he explained, 'and I wanted to make her happy.'

Next morning, a photograph of Nigel presenting the flowers to Mrs Holt appeared in the newspapers. It was Friday 22 December, the morning of the memorial service. With Christmas decorations in the city and the summer holidays on the horizon, the sudden disappearance of the country's leader seemed incongruous.

He had been admired for his reliability. When Lyndon Johnson arrived in Australia to attend the Memorial Service, he spoke briefly to the welcoming party, naming what he saw as the late prime minister's most outstanding virtues: 'He was steady. He was courageous. He was there when he said he would be there.'

Outside the cathedral was his photo, with a caption underneath: A GREAT AUSTRALIAN. The photograph provided no insight into what might have led to the circumstances of a few days before. His face usually let people in, but here there were no clues.

Apart from the immediate family, Johnson was perhaps the chief mourner. He had arrived in Canberra in the early hours of Thursday the 21st, the day before the service, in time for discussions with other heads of government who had come to Melbourne. The next day, immediately before the service, he went to St Georges Road to meet with the family. He told Nick, Andrew and Sam: 'Your father was a fine man. Be proud of him.'

Then he turned to Christopher, extolling his grandfather's influence in public life and urging him to follow his example: 'You have a great reputation to uphold. You are following in the steps of a great man – a world statesman. We are looking to you to uphold that name.'

He made this sound like Christopher's immediate task in life. It must have been puzzling to an eight-year-old.

The president met with Zara in the study of the house and they shed tears together. Within an hour, he arrived at the Great West Door of St Paul's Cathedral, the Gothic Revival Anglican church at the corner of Swanston and Flinders streets. Then Zara arrived with her family, a black veil shrouding her usually happy face, now in grief. She put one foot in front of the other and willed herself onwards.

A panoply of South-East Asian heads of government arrived around the same time – leaders from South Vietnam, the Philippines, Singapore, Thailand – countries that Holt had visited during his term of office.

Archbishop Philip Strong gave the eulogy. His presence was designed to be reassuring, with his grey hair, glasses and commanding voice with marked English vowels. When the archbishop spoke of the prime minister's capacity for 'stewardship', the president leaned forward, straining to understand a word that seemed not to translate to American ears.

'Stewardship' means reliability, the capacity to be where one is meant to be. The archbishop had identified the importance of Holt's knack of being there. Though he had found a place in the world of public service, in recent days and months that place had become increasingly uncertain. It was fitting that the music of the service emphasised the idea of the need for security. From Brahms' *German Requiem*, there was 'How Lovely is Your Dwelling', referencing Jesus' assurance: 'In my father's house are many dwellings. If it were not so, I would have told you.'

The last hymn was 'O God, Our Help in Ages Past', with its words that speak of finding 'our eternal home'. It was fitting that the prime minister's 'eternal home' was also the one he had chosen as his favourite element. Now, in memory, he would always belong to it.

After the service, Acting Prime Minister John McEwen stood beside Johnson at the top of the west steps as the assembled mourners waited for the Holt family to depart. McEwen's face was that of a man who had endured and would keep enduring. He and the president exchanged the occasional word and sage nods of the head. Apart from those few words, the hint of a tear trickling from the president's eye was the only utterance from this usually voluble man. Perhaps he remembered the last time he and his friend had been together, in June at Camp David. Even since then, he had aged and the burdens and loneliness of his office had grown.

The foreign visitors had upstaged the local politicians, including Holt's erstwhile colleagues, who were present in body if not entirely in spirit. For some of them, this was a working memorial service, an opportunity for more urgent business. Don Chipp was distressed to observe far more lobbying for votes than expressions of sympathy or quiet reflection, on what should have been regarded as an important national and spiritual occasion, above party politics. He regarded it as the most sickening public service he had ever attended. Among those doing the lobbying were men who had been plotting Holt's downfall at the time of his death. Chipp later denounced them as 'unspeakable bastards'.

In the days following Holt's disappearance, some of the warmest tributes came not from his Liberal Party colleagues, but from representatives of other parties. One of the most expressive was from Whitlam:

> The period he spent in Opposition gave him a tolerance and an understanding of an Opposition's duties, which I found immensely valuable when he, as Leader of the House, and I, as Deputy Leader of the Opposition, arranged the parliamentary business together for six years. That tolerance, together with a very deep and genuine urbanity, enabled him to avoid or modify many of the acerbities inseparable from political life. He was in the truest sense a gentleman.

After the service, the canvassing for votes got into full swing, as Harold Holt's colleagues filed out of the cathedral, ambition moving forward in black suits.

41

Enduring Memorials

'Now, how may I perpetuate my name?'
'Carve it . . . Deep into a ponderous stone and sink it, face down-
ward, into the sea, for the unseen foundations of the deep are more
enduring than the palpable tops of the mountains.'

—Herman Melville, *Mardi*

SHORTLY AFTER THE START OF THE NEW YEAR, ZARA Holt flew with Alison Busst to London for another memorial service for her late husband, this time in Westminster Abbey, where they had attended the Queen's coronation almost fifteen years before. She and Alison sheltered from the rain under a black umbrella before entering the abbey. Afterwards she met with the Queen Mother, who herself had lost a beloved husband prematurely. She patted Zara's hand.

'I know how you feel, my dear,' she told her. 'You have a pain in the heart, don't you?'

'Oh yes. How long does it last?'

'It lasts forever.'

'I'm not going to let it last forever in me,' Zara assured her.

From London, she went on to Greece, where she was the guest of Joe Gullett, the Australian ambassador. He took her to a Piraeus restaurant, world-renowned for its seafood. The proprietor recommended the specialty of the evening, a giant lobster on death row in a saltwater tank. Zara shook her head. 'Oh dear no,' she protested. 'I couldn't have him. Lobsters are the scavengers of the sea. He might have eaten my Harry.'

In May, Zara greeted the Indian prime minister, Indira Gandhi, who was making good on a promise from the previous year to visit Australia at the late prime minister's invitation. Though Mrs Gandhi had excoriated the Americans and their allies over Vietnam, she had warmed to Holt. Now Zara met the leader of the country where she had spent some of her earlier years. She had brought Christopher with her. Mrs Gandhi beamed when she saw him, placing her hand on his shoulder: 'What a beautiful child he is, isn't he?' Mrs Gandhi used the rest of her time in Australia meeting with the cabinet, encouraging them to support a total halt to the American bombing of North Vietnam.

As if to establish the sincerity of her vow not to let the pain in her heart last forever, Zara – now Dame Zara – remarried in February of the following year, with Sam Holt as best man. Her new husband was Jefferson Bate, a Liberal Party MP from New South Wales. Fell, Holt, Bate – now she had a third husband with a monosyllabic last name. It was an unconventional union, marked by long periods of separate living. There were still the dress shops to manage and a growing family of grandchildren. Every so often her activities came under scrutiny from the press but, for the most part, her life was no longer lived out on the public stage.

In May she went to California to launch a new American destroyer, the USS *Harold E. Holt* at the shipyards in Long Beach. Eight times the champagne bottle refused to break as she swung it against the body of the ship. Some of those watching hoped it was not a bad omen.

A few months earlier, Lyndon Johnson had left office and returned to his ranch in Texas. Lady Bird Johnson, their two daughters and their grandson Lyndon were with him for the flight. Like Holt, he had longed for the freedom to live his own life. He said he had missed smoking every day since 1955, when a heart attack compelled him to stop. 'I'd rather have my pecker cut off,' he told his doctors.

As soon as he had settled into his seat on the plane, he put a cigarette in his mouth. Alarmed, Luci grabbed it away:

'Daddy, what are you doing! You'll kill yourself.'

'I've raised you two girls, and I've been president. Now my time's my own.'

On 22 January 1973, his heart finally gave out. A few days later, his successor, Richard Nixon, announced that the war in Vietnam, which had ended Johnson's presidency and hastened the end of his life, had finally been settled with the signing of a peace treaty in Paris. A few months after Holt's death, Johnson had announced that he would not run for re-election.

In Australia in the late 1960s and early 1970s, opposition to involvement in Vietnam had gradually gathered strength, as it had during the same period in the United States. Jean McLean, of the Save Our Sons movement, described how the change in public opinion over the war had been reflected in the change in attitude towards the movement:

> There were newspaper articles saying the *Save Our Sons* women were probably 'communists.' Then they started saying we were just 'naïve.' Eventually, as opinion about the war shifted, they started referring to us as 'dedicated' women.

*   *   *

Zara Bate continued her visits to Bingil Bay to see Alison Busst after Johnnie died in April 1971. His fellow conservationist and friend, poet Judith Wright, remembered him as 'a slender, enthusiastic man full of laughter, a compulsive smoker and lover of good company, a friend of the then prime minister, Harold Holt'. Since Holt's death, Johnnie Busst had become a Councillor of the Australian Conservation Foundation to promote environmental issues, especially in North Queensland. In 1968 he wrote to Lyndon Johnson calling on him to back a move to set up adjoining marine and wildlife parks throughout Australia in memory of their mutual friend. After Busst's death, a plaque was attached to rocks at the northern end of

Bingil Bay, with words of tribute from Judith Wright: 'JOHN BUSST, ARTIST AND LOVER OF BEAUTY, WHO FOUGHT THAT MAN AND NATURE MIGHT SURVIVE.'

Holt, too, was remembered with a number of plaques, one of them bolted to the ocean floor near the place where he had disappeared:

> IN MEMORY
> OF
> HAROLD HOLT
> PRIME MINISTER OF AUSTRALIA
> HE LOVED THE SEA AND
> DISAPPEARED HEREABOUTS
> ON 17 DECEMBER, 1967

In late April 1973, Zara Bate was invited to Wesley College. It was almost fifty years since Holt had been there as a pupil, though he had visited from time to time in his various ministerial roles to speak to the boys about politics and public service. Wesley boys were often encouraged not only to dare to be wise, but also to be inspired by the thought that the school had 'produced' two prime ministers of their country.

Now the school had a new principal who was embarking on a program of rebuilding and redevelopment. As part of this, two wings of the school were to be renamed for the two alumni who had become successive prime ministers of Australia. Sir Robert and Dame Pattie Menzies were among the guests of honour. The ceremonies took place in front of the school's façade, with the grey towers that were left intact during the extensive rebuilding program of the 1930s. The participants and audience faced St Kilda Road and the front turf where Holt had played cricket and football as a boy nearly half a century before.

Menzies was now frail and confined to a wheelchair. Dame Zara's hat and dress were dark, but her smile was bright as she leaned over the elderly man in the wheelchair and clasped his arm, like a mother.

Dame Pattie and Dame Zara unveiled the plaques in honour of their husbands. In one of the speeches, Holt was described as 'a capable, kind, courteous and gentle man, whose life was cut short in circumstances causing grief to us all'. For a moment, Zara might have returned in her memory to that day five years earlier when the fabric of her life had been so savagely ripped.

Though Harold Holt was gone from Zara's life, on this day his presence was everywhere. As a husband, he had often been less than faithful, but her love for him had remained intact, like the material for her dresses which she hated to cut up. That afternoon at Wesley must have brought him back to her with immediacy. She must have felt his presence, memories of the body she had known and loved, the smile that had enchanted many others. She would try to remember him as he had been at his best: capable, kind, courteous and gentle.

Acknowledgements

I would especially like to thank the staff at La Trobe University Press, my publisher. I owe a special debt to Chris Feik, who read my manuscript appreciatively and offered me a contract for publication. Many thanks to Emma Fajgenbaum for her skilful editing, which helped to add pace and fluency to the narrative, and to Jo Rosenberg and Lauren Carta, who made further careful readings of the manuscript. Thanks, too, to Iryna Byelyayeva and Stephanie Whitelock for their publicity work, and to Amelia Willis for her work on the pictorial section of the book.

Relatively little has been written about Harold Holt and his life. The only previously published full length biography of him is Tom Frame's *The Life and Death of Harold Holt*. I am especially grateful to Professor Frame for the information in this fine biography, as well as in his book *Where Fate Calls*, the definitive account of the *Melbourne–Voyager* collision. Martin Simpson, Andrew Hiskens and Tom Griffiths all shared with me their firsthand experiences of meeting Harold Holt. Peter Fitzpatrick passed on to me useful knowledge of Harold Holt's father, Thomas Holt, and his circle.

I made extensive use of the Archives at Wesley College, Queen's College and the National Archives, Canberra, and I thank the archivists who provided me with invaluable material, especially Margot Vaughan at Wesley for helping with photographs. Frank Opray, of the Old Wesley Collegians' Association, has enthusiastically helped to publicise the book at Wesley and has helped me access archival materials from the college related to Harold Holt.

I am also deeply grateful for the help of friends. Paula Roberts very conscientiously read an early draft of the manuscript (twice!) and made many helpful suggestions. Debbie Reid, another sensitive reader, offered to proofread later drafts and passed on recollections of Harold Holt and his colleagues from her late father, Don Chipp. Anne Mancini has always believed in my writing, suggesting projects I could undertake with her characteristic words 'Why doncha?' I also thank John Gellie, her partner, for his long-term interest in the book and his total confidence that I would find a publisher.

Bibliography

BOOKS

Aitchison, Ray. *From Bob to Bungles*. Sun Books, Melbourne, 1970.

Albinski, Henry S. *Politics and Foreign Policy in Australia: The Impact of Vietnam and Conscription*. Duke University Press, Durham, North Carolina, 1970.

Allen, Traudl. *Clifton Pugh: Patterns of a Lifetime*. Thomas Nelson, West Melbourne, 1981.

Anderson, Ross. *Wrecks on the Reef. A guide to the historic shipwrecks at Port Phillip Heads*. Heritage Council, Victoria, 1997.

Arnold, John, and Morris, Deirdre. *Monash Biographical Dictionary of Twentieth-Century Australia*. Reed Reference Publishing, Port Melbourne, 1994.

Arnott, Georgina. *Judith Wright: Selected Writings*. La Trobe University Press, Melbourne, 2022.

Attwood, Bain, and Markus, Andrew. *The 1967 Referendum: Race, Power and the Australian Constitution*. Aboriginal Studies Press, Canberra, 2007.

Australian Commonwealth Police Force, *The Report of the Commonwealth and Victoria Police on the Disappearance of the Prime Minister the Right Honourable Harold Holt, Cheviot Beach, Portsea, Victoria, Sunday 17 December 1967*, Canberra, 1968.

Australian Dictionary of Biography, Volume 7. Melbourne University Press, Melbourne, 1979.

— *Volume 13*. Melbourne University Press, Melbourne, 1993.

— *Volume 17*. Melbourne University Press, Melbourne, 2007.

Barker, Geoffrey, and Larkin, John. *The Holt Report*. An *Age* 'Insight' Book, Melbourne, 1968.

Biographical Dictionary of the Australian Senate, Volume 3, 1962–1983. University of New South Wales Press, Sydney, 2010.

Blainey, Geoffrey, Morrissey, James, and Hulme, S.E.K. *Wesley College: The First Hundred Years.* Robertson and Mullens, Melbourne, 1967.

Blazey, Peter, and Campbell, Andrew. *The Political Dice Men.* Outback Press, Fitzroy, Victoria, 1974.

Bramston, Troy. *Robert Menzies: The Art of Politics.* Scribe, Brunswick, Victoria, 2019.

Brandon, Ruth. *The Life and Many Deaths of Harry Houdini.* Secker and Warburg, London, 1993.

Brookes, Dame Mabel. *Memoirs.* Macmillan, South Melbourne, 1974.

— *Crowded Galleries.* Heinemann, Melbourne, 1956.

Brown, Noeline. *Noeline: Longterm Memoir.* Allen and Unwin, Crows Nest, NSW, 2005.

Brown, Wallace. *Ten Prime Ministers: Life Among the Politicians.* Longueville Books, Double Bay, NSW, 2002.

Buckley, Brian. *Lynched: The Life of Sir Phillip Lynch, Mastermind of the Ambush that Ended Gough's Run.* Salzburg Publishing, Toorak, Victoria, 1991.

Burton, Mirranda. *Underground: Marsupial Outlaws and Other Rebels of Australia's War in Vietnam.* Allen and Unwin, Crows Nest, NSW, 2021.

Cabban, Peter, and Salter, David. *Breaking Ranks: The True Story Behind the HMAS Voyager Scandal.* Random House Australia, Milsons Point, NSW, 2005.

Calwell, A. A. *Be Just and Fear Not.* Lloyd O'Neil Pty Ltd, Hawthorn, Victoria, 1973.

Cameron, Clyde. *The Cameron Diaries.* Allen and Unwin, North Sydney, 1990.

Cameron, David. *The Battle of Long Tan: Australia's Four Hours of Hell in Vietnam.* Penguin Random House Australia, Melbourne, 2016.

Caro, Robert A. *The Years of Lyndon Johnson: The Path to Power.* William Collins Sons and Co., London, 1982.

— *The Years of Lyndon Johnson: Means of Ascent.* Knopf, New York, 1990.

Carroll, Brian. *The Menzies Years.* Cassell Australia, Stanmore, NSW, 1977.

— *From Barton to Fraser: Every Australian Prime Minister.* Cassell Australia, Stanmore, NSW, 1978.

Chipp, Don, and Larkin, John. *The Third Man.* Rigby, Melbourne, 1978.

Chipp, Don. *Keep the Bastards Honest.* Don Chipp Enterprises, Brighton, Victoria, 2004.

Clark, Manning. *A Short History of Australia.* Macmillan, South Melbourne, 1981.

Clifford, Clark (with Richard Holbrooke). *Counsel to the President: A Memoir.* Random House, New York, 1991.

Coombs, H.C. *Trial Balance*. Macmillan, South Melbourne, 1981.

Cross, James U. (with Denise Gamino and Gary Rice). *Around the World with LBJ: My Wild Ride as Air Force One Pilot, White House Aide, and Personal Confidant*. University of Texas Press, Austin, 2008.

Crowley, F.K. *Modern Australia in Documents. Volume Two, 1939–1970*. Wren Publishing, Melbourne, 1973.

Dapin, Mark. *The Nashos' War: Australia's National Servicemen and Vietnam*. Penguin Random House, Melbourne, 2014.

Davie, Michael. *LBJ: A Foreign Observer's Viewpoint*. Duell, Sloan and Pearce, New York, 1966.

Deery, Phillip. *Lock up Holt, Throw Away Ky: The Visit to Australia of Prime Minister Ky, 1967*. Labour History, Victoria University, Melbourne, November 2015.

Duly, Nell. *A Question of Loyalty: The Effect of the American Alliance on the 1966 Australian Federal Election*. (Honours Thesis.) University of Sydney, Sydney, 2011.

Evans, Carla. *Voices from Voyager*. New Holland Publishers, Sydney, 2006.

Fitzpatrick, Peter. *The Two Frank Thrings*. Monash University Publishing, Clayton, Victoria, 2012.

Forward, Roy, and Reece, Bob (eds), *Conscription in Australia: Yes or No Which?* University of Queensland Press, St Lucia, 1968.

Frame, Tom. *The Life and Death of Harold Holt*. Allen and Unwin, Crows Nest, NSW, 2005.

— *Harold Holt and the Liberal Imagination*. Connor Court Publishing, Redland Bay, Queensland, 2018.

— *Where Fate Calls: The HMAS Voyager Tragedy*. Hodder and Stoughton, Rydalmere, NSW, 1992.

— *The Cruel Legacy: The HMAS Voyager Tragedy*. Allen and Unwin, Crows Nest, NSW, 2005.

Freudenberg, Graham. *A Certain Grandeur: Gough Whitlam in Politics*. Sun Books, Melbourne, 1978.

Fricke, Graham. *Profiles of Power: The Prime Ministers of Australia*. Houghton Mifflin, Ferntree Gully, Victoria, 1990.

Gaylard, Geoff. *One Hundred and Fifty Years of News from The Herald*. Portside Editions, Port Melbourne, 1990.

Giorgione, Rear Admiral Michael. *Inside Camp David: The Private World of the Presidential Retreat*. Little, Brown and Company, New York, 2017.

Golding, Peter. *Black Jack McEwen: Political Gladiator*. Melbourne University Press, Melbourne, 1996.

Gordon, Harry. *An Eyewitness History of Australia*. Rigby, Melbourne, 1976.

Grattan, Michelle (ed.). *Australian Prime Ministers.* New Holland, Sydney, 2001.

Grosskurth, Phyllis. *Byron: The Flawed Angel.* Hodder and Stoughton, London, 1997.

Grey, Anthony. *The Prime Minister Was a Spy.* Weidenfeld and Nicolson, London, 1983.

Gruening, Senator Ernest. *Many Battles: The Autobiography of Ernest Gruening.* Liveright, New York, 1973.

Ham, Paul. *Vietnam: The Australian War.* HarperCollins, Sydney, 2007.

Hancock, Ian. *John Gorton: He Did It His Way.* Hodder, Sydney, 2002.

— *The V.I.P. Affair, 1966–67: The Causes, Course and Consequences of a Ministerial and Public Service Cover-up.* Australasian Study of Parliament Group. Instant Colour Press, Belconnen, ACT, 2004.

Hasluck, Paul. *The Chance of Politics.* Text Publishing, Melbourne, 1997.

Henderson, Anne. *Menzies at War.* University of New South Wales Press, Sydney, 2014.

Henderson, Heather (ed.). *Letters to My Daughter: Robert Menzies, 1955–1975.* Murdoch Books Australia, Millers Point, NSW, 2011.

Herman, Arthur. *Douglas MacArthur: American Warrior.* Random House, New York, 2016.

Hickling, Vice Admiral Harold. *One Minute of Time: The Melbourne–Voyager Collision.* A.H. and A.W. Reed, Sydney, 1965.

— *Postscript to Voyager. The Melbourne–Voyager Collision.* A.H. and A.W. Reed, Sydney, 1969.

Hill, Barry. *The Enduring Rip: A History of Queenscliffe.* Melbourne University Press, Melbourne, 2004.

Hocking, Jenny. *Gough Whitlam: A Moment in History.* The Miegunyah Press, Carlton, Victoria, 2008.

Holt, Zara. *My Life and Harry.* The Herald and Weekly Times, Melbourne, 1968.

Howson, Peter. *The Howson Diaries: The Life of Politics.* Viking, Ringwood, Victoria, 1984.

Hurst, John. *The Walkley Awards: Australia's Best Journalists in Action.* John Kerr, Melbourne, 1988.

Johnson, Lady Bird. *A White House Diary.* Weidenfeld and Nicolson, London, 1970.

Johnson, Lyndon Baines. *The Vantage Point: Perspectives of the Presidency 1963–1969.* Holt, Rinehart and Winston, New York, 1971.

Johnson, Rebekah Baines. *A Family Album.* McGraw Hill, New York, 1965.

Jones, Benjamin, Bongiorno, Frank, and Uhr, John (eds). *Elections Matter: The Federal Elections that Shaped Australia.* Monash University Publishing, Melbourne, 2018.

Kalush, William, and Sloman, Larry. *The Secret Life of Houdini*. Atria Books, New York, 2006.

Karnow, Stanley. *Vietnam: A History*. Century Publishing, London, 1983.

Kemp, Rod and Stanton, Marion. *Speaking for Australia: Parliamentary Speeches that Shaped Our Nation*. Allen and Unwin, Crows Nest, NSW, 2004.

Keneally, Thomas. *Australians: Flappers to Vietnam*. Allen and Unwin, Crows Nest, NSW, 2014.

Kiernan, Colm. *Calwell: A Personal and Political Biography*. Thomas Nelson, West Melbourne, 1978.

Killen, James. *Inside Australian Politics*. Methuen Haynes, North Ryde, NSW, 1985.

Ky, Nguyen Cao (with Marvin J. Wolf). *Buddha's Child: My Fight to Save Vietnam*. St Martin's Press, New York, 2002.

Langmore, Diane. *Prime Ministers' Wives*. McPhee Gribble, Ringwood, Victoria, 1992.

Laughton, Verity. *Long Tan*. Currency Press, Strawberry Hills, NSW, 2018.

Lawson, Valerie. *Dancing Under the Southern Skies: A History of Ballet in Australia*. Australian Scholarly Publishing, North Melbourne, 2019.

Lemon, Andrew. *A Great Australian School: Wesley College examined*. The Helicon Press, Wahroonga, NSW, 2004.

Lewis, Steve. *Stand and Deliver: Celebrating Fifty Years of the National Press Club*. Black Inc., Collingwood, Victoria, 2014.

Manchester, William. *American Caesar: Douglas MacArthur, 1880–1964*. Hutchinson, Richmond South, Victoria, 1978.

MacCallum, Mungo. *The Good, the Bad and the Unlikely: Australia's Prime Ministers*. Black Inc., Collingwood, Victoria, 2012.

McCarthy, Elizabeth. *John Jess, Seeker of Justice: The Role of the Parliament in the HMAS Voyager Tragedy*. Sid Harta Publishers, Glen Waverley, Victoria, 2015.

MacDougall, A.K. *The Illustrated History of Australia*. Five Mile Press, Scoresby, Victoria, 2011.

McMullin, Ross. *The Light on the Hill: The Australian Labor Party, 1891–1991*. Oxford University Press, South Melbourne, 1991.

Meyer, Felix (ed.). *Adamson of Wesley: The Story of a Great Headmaster*. Robertson and Mullens, Melbourne, 1932.

Miller, Merle. *Lyndon: An Oral Biography*. Ballantine Books, New York, 1980.

Mullins, Patrick. *Tiberius with a Telephone: The Life and Stories of William McMahon*. Scribe, Brunswick, Victoria, 2018.

Oakman, Daniel. *Oppy: The Life of Sir Hubert Opperman*. Melbourne Books, Melbourne, 2018.

Ormonde, Paul. *A Foolish Passionate Man: A Biography of Jim Cairns.* Penguin Australia, Ringwood,Victoria, 1981.

Parnaby, Owen. *Queen's College: A Centenary History.* Melbourne University Press, Melbourne, 1990.

Pemberton, Gregory. *All the Way: Australia's Road to Vietnam.* Allen and Unwin, North Sydney, 1987.

Pugh, Judith. *Unstill Life: Art, Politics and Living with Clifton Pugh.* Allen and Unwin, Crows Nest, NSW, 2008.

Reid, Alan. *The Power Struggle.* Shakespeare Head Press, Sydney, 1969.

Renouf, Alan. *The Frightened Country.* Macmillan, South Melbourne, 1979.

Solberg, Carl. *Hubert Humphrey: A Biography.* Norton, New York, 1984.

Starr, Graeme. *The Liberal Party of Australia: A Documentary History.* Heinemann, Richmond, Victoria, 1980.

Stevenson, Adlai. *Major Campaign Speeches of Adlai E. Stevenson.* Random House, New York, 1953.

Strangman, Denis. *The Defeated 1967 Nexus Referendum.* Lecture given at Parliament House, Canberra, May 2017.

St John, Edward. *A Time to Speak.* Sun Books, Melbourne, 1969.

Tink, Andrew. *Air Disaster Canberra.* University of New South Wales Press, Sydney, 2013.

— *Australia, 1901–2001: A Narrative History.* University of New South Wales Press, Sydney, 2014.

Trengove, Alan. *John Grey Gorton: An Informal Biography.* Cassell, North Melbourne, 1969.

Van Straten, Frank. *Tivoli.* Thomas C. Lothian, South Melbourne, 2003.

Warhaft, Sally (ed.). *Well May We Say … The Speeches that Made Australia.* Black Inc., Collingwood, Victoria, 2004.

Watson, Don. *Brian Fitzpatrick: A Radical Life.* Southwood Press, Marrickville, NSW, 1978.

Wells, Deane. *The Wit of Whitlam.* Outback Press, Collingwood, Victoria, 1976.

Wesley College Songs. Eleventh Edition. Melbourne, 1968.

Whitington, Don. *Twelfth Man?* Jacaranda Press, Melbourne, 1972.

— *The Rulers: Fifteen Years of the Liberals.* Cheshire–Landsdowne, Melbourne, 1964.

Williams, Peter J. and Serle, Roderick. *Shipwrecks at Port Phillip Heads, 1840 – 1963.* Maritime Historical Productions, Melbourne, 1967.

Woods, Randall B. *LBJ: Architect of American Ambition.* Simon and Schuster, New York, 2006.

NEWSPAPERS AND JOURNALS

The Age

The Atlantic

Australasian Post

The Australian

Australian Jewish News

Australian Women's Weekly

The Bulletin

The Cairns Post

The Canberra Times

The Courier-Mail

Current Affairs Bulletin

Daily Mirror

The Daily Telegraph

The Guardian (Australia)

Hansard, 1935–1967

Home Beautiful

Life (Australia)

The Nation

The New York Times

The Observer (Queensland)

Smith's Weekly

The Sun, Melbourne

The Sun, Sydney

The Sydney Morning Herald

Time

Townsville Bulletin

Truth

Wesley College Chronicle 1925, 1926, 1966, 1968

The Wyvern (Queen's College) 1928–1931

NEWSPAPER AND JOURNAL ARTICLES

· Bateman, Daniel. 'Why Ben Cropp is a pioneer in Great Barrier Reef conservation'. *The Cairns Post*, 31 August 2014.

Carbone, Suzanne. 'Holt's lover at beach swim dies'. *The Sydney Morning Herald*, 30 November 2012.

Emerick, Matt. 'Long Tan 50th: Soldier's sister remembers his death and legacy'. *Catholic Leader*, 1 April 2021.

Foley, Gary. 'Harold Holt's death and why the 1967 referendum failed Indigenous people'. *The Guardian (Australia)*, 27 May 2017.

Griffiths, Tom. 'How Harold Holt was lost'. *Inside Story*, 17 December 2017.

Hocking, Jenny. 'Harold Holt: The legacy is evident, 50 years after his disappearance'. *The Guardian (Australia)*, 17 December 2017.

Jones, Ann, and Borschmann, Gregg. 'Harold Holt, the poet and "the bastard from Bingil Bay": How reef conservation began'. ABC News, 11 August 2018.

Kearsley, Jonathan. 'Harold Holt's family gather to mark the 50th anniversary of his disappearance at sea'. 9News.com.au, 17 December 2017.

Lee, David. 'Issues that swung elections: the "credit squeeze" that nearly swept Menzies from power in 1961'. *The Conversation*, 30 April 2019.

Sharp, Annette. 'Silence of Harold Holt's secret lover, Marjorie Gillespie'. *The Daily Telegraph*, 14 September 2013.

NATIONAL ARCHIVES OF AUSTRALIA, HOLT COLLECTION

Press Cutting Books of Harold Edward Holt, 1926–66, A 1728

Personal papers of Harold Edward Holt, 1941–67, M4299

Personal papers of Harold Edward Holt, 1943–68, M4295

Correspondence (H), 1967, M2684, 84

Correspondence (P), 1967, M2684, 93

Overseas visit – USA, Canada, Britain, 28 May – 22 June 1967, M2684, 120

Papers contained in the briefcase of the Prime Minister (Harold Edward Holt) at the time of his disappearance, M1945, 1

Papers about Mr Holt's car accident, 22 November 1955, M2606, 12

Personal letters – family, 1929–68, M2684, 121

Personal correspondence – family, 1943–67, M4295, 10

Prime Minister – Report on overseas visit, April 1966, A4940, C4359

Prime Minister's Visit to USA and UK, June/July 1966, A4940, C4391

TRAVEL DIARIES AND LETTERS OF HAROLD HOLT, 1952 – 65. M2608

Official visit, 24 July – 2 October 1952, M2608, 1

Coronation diary, 9 May – 23 July 1953, M2608, 3

Travel diary, 1957, M260, 5

PERSONAL PAPERS OF DAME ZARA HOLT, 1946–89, M4296

Travel diaries and letters, 1949–60, M4296, 1

Personal correspondence, 1965–89, M4296, 2

Photographs – family and friends, 1920–86, M4294, 1

Photographs – family and friends, 1946–81, M4297, 1

Photographs – Dame Zara Bate (Holt) and H.J.P. (Jeff) Bate, 1969, M4297, 4

Photographs – Mrs Zara Holt, 1955–65, M4297, 5

ONLINE SOURCES

The American Presidency Project. 'Remarks of welcome to Prime Minister Holt of Australia on the South Lawn of the White House'. https://www.presidency.ucsb.edu/documents/remarks-welcome-prime-minister-holt-australia-the-south-lawn-the-white-house

Australian War Memorial. www.awm.gov.au

Berliner, Eve. 'The moral core of Bill Moyers'. http://www.evesmag.com/moyers.htm

'Conversation with HAROLD HOLT, OFFICE SECRETARY and TELEPHONE OPERATOR'. Secret White House Tapes: Lyndon B. Johnson Presidency. Miller Centre, University of Virginia, 11020. 7 November 1966. https://millercenter.org/the-presidency/secret-white-house-tapes/conversation-harold-holt-office-secretary-and-telephone

Hawkins, John. 'Harold Holt: An urbane treasurer'. *Economic Roundup* 1. National Library of Australia, Canberra, 27 April 2012. https://treasury.gov.au/publication/economic-roundup-issue-1-2012-2/economic-roundup-issue-1-2012

Holt, Harold. 'Alfred Deakin – his life and our times; the Liberal tradition in Australia'. Deakin Memorial Lecture, Melbourne, 31 July 1967. https://pmtranscripts.pmc.gov.au/release/transcript-1634

Holt, Stephen. 'Alan Reid and the thirty-six faceless men'. Speech to the Sydney Institute, 9 June 2010. Republished by the Australian Society for the Study of Labour History, https://labourhistorycanberra.org/2015/alan-reid-and-the-thirty-six-faceless-men/

Korff, Jens. 'Australian 1967 referendum'. Creative Spirits, 12 August 2020. https://creativespirits.info/aboriginalculture/history/australian-1967-referendum

Marsden, Oliver C. 'The writing principles of Robert A. Caro'. The Writing Co-operative, 22 February 2021. https://writingcooperative.com/the-writing-principles-of-robert-a-caro-87c82797bc50

National Australian Archives. '1967 referendum results – Prime Minister Harold Holt responds in press release'. NAA: A1209, 1967/7251. https://www.naa.gov.au/learn/learning-resources/learning-resource-themes/first-australians/rights-and-freedoms/1967-referendum-results-prime-minister-harold-holt-responds-press-release

National Library of Australia. 'Timeline – Events that led to the 1967 referendum'. https://www.nla.gov.au/digital-classroom/year-10/the-1967-referendum/timeline

National Museum of Australia. 'Faith Bandler'. https://www.nma.gov.au/ explore/features/indigenous-rights/people/faith-bandler

State Library of South Australia. 'Aboriginal Australia – referendums and recognition: The 1967 referendum'. https://guides.slsa.sa.gov.au/ Referendum

Turnbull, R.J.D. National Library of Australia. 'Reginald Turnbull interviewed by Suzanne Walker (sound recording)'. 4 December 1974. National Library of Australia. https://catalogue.nla.gov.au/Record/682407

Wesley College. 'Archives, art and collections'. https://www.wesleycollege.edu. au/about-wesley/our-history/archives-art-and-collections

Whitton, Evan: 'The bureaucracy: The *Voyager* cover-up'. From *Can of Worms II*. Fairfax Library, Broadway, NSW, 1987. Republished at Netk. net.au/Whitton/Worms22.asp

Woollahra Municipal Council. 'Rudy Komon MBE'. https://www.woollahra. nsw.gov.au/library/local_history/woollahra_plaque_scheme/plaques/ rudy_komon_mbe

DOCUMENTARIES

The Harold Holt Mystery. Ten Network Australia, 1985.

The Liberals: Fifty Years of the Federal Party. ABC Entertainment and Specialist, 1994.

LBJ. PBS American Experience. A Kera Production in association with David Grubin Productions Inc., 1991.

The Prime Minister Is Missing. A Screen Australia Production in association with Blackwattle Films, 2008.

The Prime Ministers' National Treasures. National Film and Sound Archive of Australia, 2011.

Unfit to Command. ABC Commercial, 2003.

Image Credits

Harold in 1921, posing in football jumper: Photographer unknown. From [Personal Papers of Prime Minister Holt: Volume 1 of press cuttings relating to his early public life], 1926–1946, NAA: A1728, 429675

Reginald John David 'Spot' Turnbull and Harold Holt: photo taken 1922: Courtesy of Wesley College Melbourne

Wesley College football team, 1926: Harold Holt (back row, second from right); Spot Turnbull (middle row, fifth from left): Courtesy of Wesley College Melbourne

Young Harold Holt [c 1930s]: Photographer unknown. Image courtesy of the National Library of Australia

Holt as Minister for Immigration, greeting two girls with wife Zara: ART Collection/Alamy

Holt at home in August 1960, preparing for the federal budget as treasurer: Photographer unknown. From [Personal Papers of Prime Minister Holt: Volume 8 of press cuttings as Treasurer], 1960–1961, NAA: A1728, 429682

Harold and Zara Holt, on the day Harold became prime minister of Australia: Central Press/Hulton Archive/Getty Images

Harold with his daughters-in-law at the beach: Keystone Pictures USA/Alamy

Harold and Zara with their grandson Christopher: Keystone Pictures USA/Alamy

A candid snap of Harold's daughters-in-law bringing him a cup of tea at Portsea, as seen on the front page of *The Age*, 24 January 1966: Courtesy of *The Age*

Sir Robert Menzies and Harold Holt [c 1950s]: L.J. Dwyer. Image courtesy of the National Library of Australia

Harold Holt and Lyndon Baines Johnson, president of the United States: PictureLux/The Hollywood Archive/Alamy

John and Alison Busst: photo taken 1968: Herald & Weekly Times Limited portrait collection

Holt at Cheviot Beach: Historic Collection/Alamy

Marjorie Gillespie and policeman looking at where Holt went missing: Evening Standard/Hulton Archive/Getty Images

Four witnesses on beach. Left to right: Marjorie Gillespie, Vyner Gillespie, Alan Stewart, Martin Simpson: Evening Standard/Hulton Archive/ Getty Images

The front page of *The Age*, 18 December 1967, reporting the disappearance and assumed death of the prime minister: Courtesy of *The Age*

Map of where Harold Holt went missing: Evening Standard/Hulton Archive/ Getty Images

Index

3XY radio station 58, 149

Abbotsholme College, Sydney 20
Aboriginal Australians *see* First
  Nations Australians
Aboriginal-Australian Fellowship 231
Adamson, Lawrence Arthur ('Dicky')
  23–9, 31, 33–5, 50, 154
    father substitute to Harold 27
Adelaide 17, 19, 50, 159, 193, 276
Advisory War Council 70–1, 73, 75
Aitchison, Ray 211, 225
America–Australia Society 241
American Federation of Labor
  Convention, 1952 96–8
American forces in Australia 73–9
Andrews, John 134
Anthony, Doug 261
ANZUS Treaty 249
Ashworth, Fred 62–3
Asia 123, 145, 153, 189, 212; *see also*
  South-East Asia
Asian Development Bank 145
Asilturk, Kemal 109
ASIO 261
Assisted Passage Migration Scheme
  87
Aston, Bill 225
Australian Ballet 213, 239
Australian Communist Party 86, 91
Australian Conservation Foundation
  296

Australian Council for the Arts 234
Australian Council of Trade Unions
  90
Australian Imperial Force 66–7
Australian Labor Party
  Capricornia by-election 250–1
  Corio by-election 243–5
Australian Labor Party (ALP)
  Calwell 142–4, 146
  Chifley's death 94
  divisions, and formation of
    Democratic Labor Party 107,
    110, 118–19
  elections 94, 107, 110, 112, 119,
    142–3, 146, 188–9, 193–4, 209
  Holt as UAP candidate in safe
    Labor seats 53–4
  Labor governments 73, 83
  support for 1967 referenda 232
  Turnbull 155
  Vietnam War 127, 208, 253
  Whitlam 143, 145–6, 209
  World War Two 67, 70–3

Bandler, Faith 230–1
Bangkok 102
Banks, Ralph C. 25
Barnes, Allan 268–9
Basic Industries Group (BIG) 241–2
Bate, Jefferson 295
Bedarra Island 113
Bennett, John 286

Bingil Bay, Cassowary Coast 113–14, 116–17, 158, 163, 175–6, 248, 268, 296
Borman, Frank 144–5, 173
Bowen, Nigel 222
Bradman, Sir Donald 185
Brisbane 76–7, 79, 88, 125, 151, 208, 234
Britain
    devaluation of the pound 266
    relations with Australia 164, 173–4
    withdrawal from Singapore and Malaysia 243
    see also England
Brookes, Cynthia 59
Brookes, Elaine 59
Brookes, Hersey 59
Brookes, Mabel 59–60, 75, 78, 142–3, 169, 184–5
Brookes, Norman 59, 75, 78, 184–5
Brown, Wallace 267
Brownbill, Kay 193
Bryant, Gordon 181
Bunting, Sir John 270
Busst, Alison 113, 116, 175, 268, 270, 281, 290, 294, 296
Busst, John (Johnnie) 29, 36–7, 40, 43–5, 113–14, 116, 158–9, 175–6, 201, 268, 271, 290, 296
Busst, Phyllis 113
Byron, Lord 100–1
    'Childe Harold's Pilgrimage' 101

Cabban, Peter 220, 223–5
Cairns, Jim 189, 253, 259
Calwell, Arthur
    career 142–3
    Labor Party leader 118–19, 143–4, 146, 194–6
    Minister for Immigration 86–90, 142
    position on conscription and the Vietnam War 123, 125, 148, 151–3, 159, 162–3, 189, 191, 206–8
    relationship with Holt 135, 141–2, 146–7, 259

    relationship with Menzies 119, 135, 142–3
    relationship with Whitlam 143, 145–6
    shot at in Sydney 162–3, 189
    United States visit, 1963 123
Calwell, Arthur jnr 142
Calwell, Davis 123
Cambodia 213–14, 243
Cameron, Clyde 159
Camp David 238–41, 293
Canada 96, 171, 236, 239
Canberra 55–6, 75, 103–4, 114, 137–9
    plane crash, 13 August 1940 67
Canton (Guangdong), China 99
Capricorn Wharf, Brisbane 76
Capricornia by-election 250–1
Casey, Richard 65, 256, 261–2
Cerutty, Percy 140
Charles, Prince 283
Charlton, Andrew ('Boy') 29
Cheviot Beach 13–14, 120–1, 228, 266, 273, 278–81, 284, 286, 290–1
Cheviot shipwreck (1887) 13–14, 226, 284
Chiang Kai-shek 214
Chifley, Ben 83–4, 87, 94–5, 137
Child Endowment Act 1941 69–70
China 123, 147, 148
    Cultural Revolution 178
Chinaman's Hat, Port Phillip Bay 14–15, 286
Chipp, Don 222, 224, 252, 281–2, 293
Chipp, Monica 281
Church, Ann 105
Churchill, Winston 71, 95–6
Clark, Ed 246, 271
Clifford, Clark 245–6
Clifton Hill by-election 54
Cloke, John 271
'cold war' 86
Colombo Plan 145
Commonwealth Bank Bill 1940 94
Commonwealth Court of Conciliation and Arbitration 45

Commonwealth Parliamentary
   Association 96, 99, 111
communism 86, 91–2, 98, 107, 144,
   147, 156, 189, 194–5, 237
Communist Party Dissolution Bill 86
conscription 125–6, 142, 148–9, 151,
   154, 158–9, 180, 188–9, 191, 194–5,
   201, 211, 247
Constitution
   change to break nexus between
      House of Representatives and
      Senate 229
   Section 51 229–30
   Section 127 230
Coombs, Harold ('Nugget') 213, 232,
   234, 254, 266
Coppin, Ray 280–1
Corio by-election 243–5
Council for Aboriginal Affairs (CAA)
   233–4, 254, 266
Country Party 66, 71, 82–3, 112,
   132–3, 135, 146, 241–2, 261–2, 266
   coalition government with
      Liberal Party 82–3, 133,
      266–7
Cremean, John 54
Cropp, Ben 271
Cumpston, John 31, 36, 37
Curtin, John 67, 69–72, 75, 82, 86, 92,
   142, 253, 270

Dacomb, Beatrice and Clara 62–3
Dann, Robert 178
Davey's Bay, Mount Eliza 59–60
Davie, Michael 168–9
Dawson electorate, Queensland 146
de Gaulle, Charles 173–4
de Lacy, Pat 271
decimal currency 119–20, 145
Democratic Labor Party (DLP) 110,
   112, 118, 156, 232, 256–7, 264
Department of Immigration 88
Department of Labour and National
   Service 126
Department of Supply and
   Development 65

Depression, 1930s 41–2, 45–6, 53, 91,
   135
devaluation decision, 1967 266–7
Dexter, Barrie 254
Dickens, Charles 40
Dickerson, Sue 99
Dickins, Sydney 9, 39–41, 82, 84–5
Dickins, Violet 9, 39–41, 48–9, 84–5
Dickins, Zara see Holt, Zara Kate
   (née Dickins)
Diem, Ngo Dinh 122, 156
'Dig for Victory' campaign 82
Diggers Rest, Victoria 25
Don Isidro 76–7, 79
Downer, Alick 131
Dyer, Bob and Dolly 248

education policy: state aid to non-
   government schools 118, 146
Edwards, Bruce 274
Efftee Studios 46–8, 57–8
Eggleton, Tony 138, 172, 218, 283, 290
Eisenhower, Dwight 75, 97, 99, 124,
   174
elections, federal for by-elections, see
   under name of the seat, e.g. Corio
   by-election
   1934 53
   1940 67
   1943 82
   1946 83
   1949 84–5, 89
   1951 94
   1954 107
   1955 107–8, 110
   1958 112
   1961 116
   1963 119
   1966 177, 187–97
Elizabeth, Queen, coronation 99
England 96; see also London
Europe 96
Evatt, H.V. 107
Everingham, Douglas 250–1
Expo 67, Montreal 239

Fadden, Arthur 71–3, 112
Fairbairn, James 67
Fairhall, Allen 261
Faunce, Marcus 271, 274, 281, 290
Fawkner by-election and electorate 54–6, 64, 83, 85
Federal Council for the Advancement of Aborigines and Torres Strait Islanders (FCAATSI) 231–2
Fell, James 49–51, 61, 65, 83, 295
Festival of Asia arts tour 214
First Nations Australians
    colonisation impacts 230
    inclusion in census 229–30
    referendum on citizenship 229–35
    see also Council for Aboriginal Affairs (CAA); Office of Aboriginal Affairs (OAA)
Fitzpatrick, Brian 92
Flanagan, Noel 95
Forde, Frank 71, 74
Fort Nepean 13
Fowler, Henry 127
France 171, 173–4
Fraser, Allan 179
Fulbright, William 157

Gair, Vincent 156
Gajic, Nedeljko 163
Gamboa, Joyce (née Cain) 88
Gamboa, Julie 88
Gamboa, Lorenzo 87–90
Gamboa, Raymond 88
Gandhi, Indira 295
General Motors, United States 93
Gibbs, Pearl 231
Gillespie, Marjorie 203–5, 207, 273–4, 276–80, 286
Gillespie, Sheriden 203–4, 206, 287
Gillespie, Vyner 203, 277, 280
Gillespie, Winton 203, 207, 274
Glaser, Johan and family 61, 63–4
Goldwater, Barry 125, 168

Gorton, John 257, 259–61, 271–2
Gray, Lorraine 79
Great Barrier Reef 114, 117, 176, 248, 268, 271
Great War see World War One
Green Club 70
Green, Nigel 216, 290–1
Gribble, Cecil 42
Grounds, Betty (née James) 44, 104
Gullett, Joe 294
Gullett, Sir Henry 67

Hacking, William 122
Hall, Rodney 234
Hannaford, Douglas Clive 188, 211, 224, 257–8, 262, 287
Harold E Holt launch, California 295
Hasluck, Paul 157, 178–9, 212, 261
Hay, Ronald 244–5
Healy, 'Big Jim' 92
Heilster, Gustav 108–9
Hellespont 101
Helpmann, Robert 239
Henderson, Heather 282
Hernández, Amalia 174
Hewitt, Lenox 266
Hickling, Harold, One Minute of Time 219–20
Higgins, Arthur 48
Higgins electorate 85, 94, 110, 116, 119, 192
Hiskens, Andrew 264–5
Hobhouse, John 100
Holt, Amanda 139–40, 195, 208
Holt, Andrew (Andy) 9–10, 65, 81, 83–5, 99, 149, 208, 291
Holt, Caroline 139–40, 274
Holt, Christopher 10, 145, 186, 208, 264–6, 268, 271, 274, 290–2, 295
Holt, Clifford Thomas (Cliffie, Cliff) 17–20, 22, 29, 32, 38, 41, 45, 57–8, 81, 134
    illness and death 141, 159, 196–7, 212–13, 262, 287
Holt, Frances 81

Holt, Harold Edward
  awards, honours and recognition
    Companion of Honour 99
    Queen's College Oratory Award
      43, 113
    University of Seoul honorary
      Doctor of Letters 215
    Wesley College awards 34, 154
  disappearance
    events of the day 275–80
    memorial plaque 297
    memorial service in Melbourne
      283, 290–4
    memorial service in Westminster
      Abbey, London 294
    news of disappearance 280–3, 290
    obituary and tributes 285–6,
      291–3, 297–8
    other Australian disappearances
      288–9
    re-enactment of the events 286
    search 283–4, 286, 290
  early years
    lack of family 32–5, 38–9, 48, 81,
      135
    life with a succession of relatives
      17–20, 28, 39
    loneliness 35, 135, 172
    nicknames 28, 110, 116, 133, 267
    parents 16–20, 22, 32–3, 38–9,
      47–8, 58, 135, 212
    sports 29–31, 48
  education
    primary schools 16–17, 20
    Queen's College, University of
      Melbourne 36–7, 41–4, 90
    school captain 34
    Wesley College, Melbourne
      22–37, 44, 47, 50
  health
    back and shoulder pain 269–71,
      287
    car accident, 1955 108–10
    general ill-health 266, 287
    hit-and-run accident, 1941 70
    lack of sleep 115, 138, 166, 262

    nervous exhaustion 114–15, 283
    travel sickness 95
    vitamin deficiency 263
  homes
    2 Parliament Place, Melbourne 44
    50 Washington Street, Toorak
      81–3, 95, 99
    112 St Georges Road, Toorak 10–11,
      110, 145, 190, 216, 271, 290–1
    Bingil Bay, Cassowary Coast
      116–17, 158, 163, 175–6, 248
    flat over garage in Toorak 70
    hotels and boarding houses 45,
      55–6, 82–3
    the Lodge, Canberra 137–9, 165,
      268–70
    Weeroona Estate, Portsea 10–11,
      120–1, 163, 195, 201–2, 206–8,
      227–8, 264–6, 270–1, 283–4
  law career
    Fink, Best and Miller 44
    practice as solicitor 44–5, 60, 135
  marriage and family
    absences from Zara 103–4
    early involvement with Zara
      37–41, 43, 45–7, 49–51
    infidelities 103, 203–5
    marriage to Zara 9, 65, 81–4, 104
    reconnection with Zara 61–2,
      64–5
    see also Holt, Amanda; Holt,
      Andrew; Holt, Caroline; Holt,
      Christopher; Holt, Nicholas;
      Holt, Paulette; Holt, Sam; Holt,
      Sophie; Holt, Zara Kate (née
      Dickins)
  personal interests
    ballet 105, 114, 166, 174, 201, 213,
      239
    cinema 45, 166, 181
    cricket 29–30, 37
    debating 42–3, 210
    fine arts 10, 36, 95, 100, 110, 166,
      201
    football 29–31, 37
    horse racing 45, 188

personal interests, cont.
  squash 260
  tennis 29, 37, 271, 274
  theatre 29, 37, 44, 48, 52, 70,
    98–9, 102–3, 166, 201
  see also underwater sports; water
personal qualities
  charm 17–18, 45, 52, 60, 110, 172,
    263
  deep feeling 8
  desire to be liked 17–18, 28, 169,
    269, 282
  frankness of manner 110
  friendliness 17, 38, 42–3, 269
  good looks 8, 17, 37, 52, 70, 111
  oriented towards harmony and
    union 8
  physical skill and fitness 8–9,
    140–1, 202
  pleasant personality 251, 263
  popularity 43, 47, 60
  risk-taking 9, 12, 60, 120–1,
    175–6, 291
  seeing and sympathising with
    different points of view 90
  team player 24, 224
politics
  attitude to politics 165
  belief that government should not
    curtail human freedoms 97–8
  budget, 1960 and mini budget
    ('Holt's Jolt'), 1961 114–16
  cabinet member 65–6, 68–70,
    85, 90–3, 95, 107–8, 112–18,
    132, 135, 237 (*see also* Labour
    and National Service portfolio;
    treasurer)
  consensus-seeking 12, 252
  deputy leader of the Liberal Party
    110
  dispute settlement 165
  early views 45–6
  first elected to parliament 54–5
  first political campaigns 52–4
  image for the outside world 65,
    83, 121, 139–40, 253, 263–4

leader of the House of
    Representatives 110–11, 133
  middle-of-the-road solutions 12
  negotiating ability and dispute
    resolution 43, 68, 90, 112, 165,
    237
  in opposition 75–6, 89–90, 293
  public profile 111
  wartime roles 71, 75–6, 79, 191
prime minister
  1966 election 187–97
  appointment 134–6
  assassination attempt 163
  capacity for work 138, 165–6, 262
  doubts about capacity to govern
    245, 247, 249, 251–60, 263–5,
    268, 273, 282–3
  early days 137–50
  image problem 263–4
  no confidence vote, 1967 258
  portrait by Clifton Pugh 201–3
  position on the Vietnam War
    127, 144, 147–9, 151–3, 155–7,
    158–60, 165–6, 183–4, 188,
    193–5, 203–4, 244–7, 252–3, 267
  referenda, May 1967 229–35
  relationship with Lyndon Baines
    Johnson 164–74, 182–8, 196,
    236–41, 249–50, 291, 293
  relationship with Nguyen Cao Ky
    206–8
  relationship with Whitlam
    253–4, 258–9, 285, 293
  and Turnbull 155–7, 255–6
  VIP fleet use 256–60, 266, 271
  Voyager disaster 221–8, 256–7
  workload 266, 268, 286
travel
  1950s 102–3
  Europe and the US, 1952 95–9
  London and Europe, 1953 99–100
  as prime minister 153–4, 164–74,
    212–16, 236–42
  Washington, DC, 1965 127
  a widely known Australian
    politician 135

Holt, Maura 212

Holt, Nicholas (Nick) 9–10, 62, 65, 81, 83–5, 203, 274, 291

Holt, Olive (née Pearce) 17–20, 22, 32–3, 38–9, 47–8, 58, 81, 134, 286

Holt, Paulette 139–40, 266, 268, 271, 274, 286, 290

Holt, Sam 9–10, 65, 81, 83–5, 195, 281, 286, 291

Holt, Sophie 10, 274, 277

Holt, Sue 283

Holt, Thomas (Tom) 16, 18–20, 22, 32–3, 38–9, 45–8, 52, 57–9, 81, 213, 286

Holt, Viola (Lola, née Thring) 47–9, 57–9, 81

Holt, Zara Kate (née Dickins) 8–9
  art 10–11, 39–40, 102, 104, 106, 110, 201
  ballet interests 105
  bracelet with Queens College Orator medal 113
  children 61, 65, 103, 104
  divorce from James Fell 83
  early involvement with Harold 37–41, 43, 45–7, 49–51
  early years 8–9, 39–41
  embroidery 105–6
  fashion business 8–9, 40, 43–4, 48–9, 104–6, 139, 295
  'Gown of the Year' fashion award, 1961 116
  Harold's disappearance 280–1, 283–4, 286, 288, 290–1, 298
  Harold's memorial services 292, 294
  Harold's near-drowning, 1967 227–8
  at holiday homes 10–11, 113, 116–17, 175–6, 195
  in India 49–51
  interior design 104
  marriage to Harold 65, 81–4, 103–4, 298
  marriage to James Fell 49–51, 61–2
  marriage to Jefferson Bate 295
  overseas travel 95–104, 164–5, 214, 236, 239, 241, 243
  political views 46
  position on Vietnam 160, 207
  prime minister's wife 137–40, 160, 164, 192–3, 203, 214, 236, 239, 241, 250–1, 263, 265, 268
  reading 239, 262
  reconnection with Harold after breakup of first marriage 61–2, 64–5
  war work 82
  see also Holt, Amanda; Holt, Andrew; Holt, Caroline; Holt, Christopher; Holt, Nicholas; Holt, Paulette; Holt, Sam; Holt, Sophie

Holyoake, Keith 96

Home, Genevieve (née Dickins) 40–1, 62, 65, 281

Honolulu 206, 236, 241

Hotel Australia, Melbourne 84

Hotel Australia, Sydney 84

Hotel Canberra 55–6, 83, 137

Houdini, Harry 25–6, 74, 285, 287–8

House of Representatives 15, 75–6, 94, 110, 114, 126, 133, 178, 193, 221–3, 258
  referendum on increase in size to match Senate 229, 232

Howes, Bobby 62

Howson, Kitty 105

Howson, Peter 105, 256–7, 267–8, 287

Hoyts theatres 45–6

Hughes, A.A. 110

Hughes, Billy 71

Humphrey, Hubert 144

Hungarian community, Sydney 180

immigration policy 95, 118, 145, 250; see also White Australia policy

Immigration portfolio
  Calwell 86–90, 142
  Holt 90, 107–9, 112, 123, 135, 165, 181, 237

India 49, 65, 295

Indonesia 123

Irwin, 'Deadly' Dudley 255, 260, 273
Isaacson, 'Uncle' Alex 69

Jago, June 103
James, Bert 76, 152
Japan 103–4, 212–13
Japanese External Trade Organisation
(JETRO) 261
Jensen, Nadine 160–1
Jess, John 221–2, 224–5, 228
Johnson, Lady Bird 167, 182, 185–6,
237, 295
Johnson, Luci Baines 167, 170, 238,
295–6
Johnson, Lynda Bird 167, 295
Johnson, Lyndon Baines 124–5, 131,
144, 206, 215, 245–6, 252, 263, 283,
296
'all the way with LBJ' 172, 174,
183–4
death 296
Holt's memorial service 291–3
relationship with Holt 164–74,
182–8, 196, 236–41, 249–50,
291, 293
retirement 295–6
visit to Australia, 1966 182–8
World War Two, time in Australia
77–9
Johnson, Rebekah Baines 166–7
Jones, Andrew 193
Jorgensen, Justus 45

Katter, Bob 268
Keavney, Kay 231
Kennedy, John F. 119, 122–4, 169, 174,
182, 185
Kennedy, Robert 238
Kingston Hotel, Canberra 118–19
Kirby, Richard 260
Knox, George E. 116
Kocan, Peter 162–3
Koman, Rudy 201
Kooyong electorate 148–50
Korean War 86, 124
Kosygin, Alexei 238–9

Kreitmayer, Olive 47–8, 59
Kristallnacht 64
Kurneh, South Yarra 75, 78
Kurrajong Hotel, Canberra 55, 94, 137
Ky, Mai 208
Ky, Nguyen Cao 156, 206–8

Labor Party *see* Australian Labor
Party (ALP)
Labour and National Service portfolio
68–9, 71, 85, 90–3, 112, 132, 135, 165,
237
labour policy 90–2, 95, 98, 112
Laos 213–14
Lawless, Mary Edith ('Tiny') 83, 95,
99, 270–1, 273–6, 281
Lett, Dianne 227–8
Liberal Party of Australia 85–6, 107,
121, 148–9
Basic Industries Group support
242
Capricornia by-election 250–1
coalition government with
Country Party 82–3, 133,
266–7
Corio by-election 243–5
dissent within the party 188
Holt's membership and
leadership 110–11, 113–14, 116,
211, 252
Menzies' leadership 82, 84, 108,
144, 252
policies on conscription and
Vietnam 126, 160, 195, 211, 257
Liberal Reform Group 188
the Lodge, Canberra 137–9, 165
London 95–6, 102, 173, 236
Long Tan, Battle of 178–81
Lynch, Joe 288
Lyons, Joseph 270

MacArthur, Arthur 74
MacArthur, Douglas 74–80, 88,
123–4, 182
MacArthur, Jean 74
Mackay, Malcolm 222, 224, 228

Magg (Zara Holt's fashion boutique) 104–5, 139
Malaysia 123, 213, 243
Malta 244
Martin, Ethel 17, 20, 33
Martin, Harold 17, 19–20, 32–3
Maxwell, George 54
McClelland, Douglas 162
McEwen, John ('Black Jack') 64, 72, 112, 132–3, 135–6, 241–2, 252, 266–7, 292–3
    feud with McMahon 260–2, 266, 272–3
McIlree, Eric 227
McIntosh, Harry D. 19
McKellar, Colin 257–8
McLean, Jean 160, 177, 181, 201, 296
McMahon, Sonia (née Hopkins) 133, 208
McMahon, William ('Billy') 20–1, 85, 132–3, 196, 241–2, 250, 256, 276–7
    feud with McEwen 260–2, 266, 272–3
McManus, Frank 156
McNamara, Robert 240, 244
Melbourne 28–9, 32, 41–5, 54–5, 57, 61–2, 64, 74–5, 78, 88, 142, 159, 177–8, 184–5, 203, 208, 291–2; see also names of suburbs, electorates and organisations
Melbourne 217–20
Menzies, Douglas 53
Menzies, Pattie 71, 297
Menzies, Robert
    conscription and Vietnam War 125–6, 132
    elections, cabinet and policies 94–5, 107–8, 110, 115–19, 125–6, 137, 141, 145, 154, 251–2, 282
    Liberal Party 82, 84, 108, 144, 252
    the Lodge, Canberra 137–8
    re-election as prime minister 84–6
    relationship with Holt 53, 68, 90, 116, 139, 144, 167, 282–3
    resignation, 1941 72–3, 82
    retirement, 1966 131–2, 134, 187
    status and air of grandeur 135, 140, 144, 187, 209
    United Australia Party 53, 65
    views on Arthur Calwell 119, 135, 142–3
    views on communism 86, 92
    views on McMahon 132–3
    Voyager disaster 218, 221
    Wesley College 53, 297–8
    World War Two 66–8, 70–3, 82, 191
Middle East 237
Milne, A.A., The Man in the Bowler Hat 37, 44
Mission Beach, Cassowary Coast 113–15
Monk, Albert 90–2
Montsalvat artists' colony, Eltham 45, 114
Moorehead, Alan 239, 262
Moyers, Billy Don (Bill) 168, 182–3, 238
Munday, Arthur 44–5
Mussen, Norman 37–9, 287
Mussing, Peter 230
Mydans, Carl 80

National Unity, proposed wartime government 67, 70, 72
Nazism 62–4
New South Wales 194, 217, 231–2; see also Sydney; and other place names
New York 96–8
Newell, Lawrence 280
Newton, Maxwell 241–2, 261–2
Nicholls, Douglas 231–2
Nixon Fund Crisis 97
Nixon, Pat 97
Nixon, Richard 97, 296
Noack, Errol 159, 207
Northwest Cape Communications Station 249–50
Nubba, New South Wales 16–17, 33

Office of Aboriginal Affairs (OAA) 233–4, 254
O'Leary, Frances (Frankie, née Salveron) 79, 124, 180–1
Opperman, Sir Hubert 243–4
Opposition Spokesman for Immigration 89–90
Opposition Spokesman on Industrial Matters 75

Paarl, Vladimir 119
Pacific War 73–80, 86–8
Packer, Frank 225
Pagan, Jock 276
Parliament House, Canberra 55, 71, 75, 184, 270
Patterson, Rex 146
Peacock, Andrew 148
Pearce, Vera 19, 32, 37, 40, 52, 62, 99, 131, 134, 196
Pearl Harbor 73, 99
The Pentagon Papers 240
Perkins, Charles ('Uncle Charlie') 231, 233–4
Permanent and Casual Wharf Labourers Union 75–6
Philippines 74–7, 79–80, 88–90, 161, 182, 186, 213, 292
Phillips, Arthur 30
Piaf, Edith 98
Picnic at Hanging Rock 288
Pius XII, Pope 95
Pope's Eye, Port Phillip Bay 14, 286
Porritt, Barbara 107–8
Porritt, Dennis 107–8
Port Phillip Bay 8–9, 13, 139–40, 274, 276
Portsea 10, 13, 84, 139–40, 158, 203–5; *see also* Cheviot Beach; and under Holt, Harold Edward – homes
Preece, Alex 161
Price Kaye 234–5
Pugh, Clifton 201–4, 276
Pugh, Marlene 276

Queen's College, University of Melbourne 36–7, 41–4, 90
  At Home subcommittee 43
  College Sports and Social Club 43
  Oratory Award 43
  Willie Quick Club 42–3
Queensland 66, 76, 116–17, 146, 156, 158, 186, 194, 208, 233, 250, 268; *see also* Brisbane; and other place names

Raleigh, Sir Walter 100
Ramsay, Alan 285–6
Rankin, Annabelle 146
Rapke, Trevor 154
Reid, Alan 118–19, 132, 261, 267
Reid, Rex 105
The Rip (or The Heads), Port Phillip Bay 13, 275, 289
Robertson, John 217–21
Roosevelt, Franklin Delano 55, 73–4, 77, 82, 167
Rose, Alec 274, 276–7
Rossi, Mario 170–1
Rubinnoci, Leopoldo 95
Rushton, Bill 196
Rusk, Dean 127, 157
Ruyton Girls School, Kew 39

Salveron, Clarissa (née Willmett) 79–80, 124, 180–1
Salveron, Douglas Javing 80, 124–6, 161, 179–81, 289
Salveron, Francisco 76–7, 79–80, 87, 124, 161, 180
Saragat, Giuseppe 250
Save Our Sons (SOS) 160, 180–1, 190, 296
Schirra, Walter 144–5, 173
Scholes, Gordon 244–5
Scott, Margaret 105
Scullin, James 53, 137
Senate 15, 94, 156, 256–9
  election, 1967 251–3, 255–6, 263–5, 268, 272

referendum on matching size
with House of Representatives
229, 232
Shepherd, Jack 273
Sihanouk, Norodom 214
Simpson, Martin 277, 280
Sinclair, Ian 261
Singapore 123, 243, 292
Six-Day War 237
skindiving 7, 12–14, 121, 228, 271,
282
Slessor, Kenneth, 'Five Bells' 288
Snedden, Billy 224, 281–2
snorkelling 7, 11, 13, 117, 120, 201–2,
228, 276, 278
socialism 46, 53, 168, 194
South Australia 47, 193, 233; see also
Adelaide
South-East Asia 123, 125, 147, 153, 158,
194, 212–16, 292
South Korea 214–15
South Yarra 62, 75, 104
Souvanna Phouma, Prince 214
spearfishing 7, 9–13, 117, 120, 175–6,
228, 275
Spender, Percy 72
Spicer, Sir John 218–19
St Catherine's Anglican school for
girls, Toorak 47
St John, Ted 222–4, 228
St Kilda Beach Sea Baths 29
Stanner, Bill 254
Stevens, Beatrice 222
Stevens, Duncan 217, 219–23, 225
Stevens, Sir Jack 218, 222
Stevenson, Adlai 97–9, 174
Stewart, Alan 204, 277–80
Stewart, Michael 171
Street, Geoffrey 67
Street, Jessie 230–1
Strong, Philip 292
Student Action for Aborigines (SAFA)
231
Sukarno 123
Summer of the Seventeenth Doll
(Lawler) 102–3

swimming 13, 29, 60, 117, 271, 274, 282
Sydney 16–17, 20, 32–3, 55, 66, 84,
108–9, 139, 160–1, 185–6, 208

Taiwan 213–14
Tanner, Les 265
Tasmania 155, 210
Taylor, Maxwell 245–6
'Ten Pound Poms' 87
Thailand 145, 153, 213, 292
Thanom Kittikachorn 145, 153
Thellefsen, Enos Soren 30
Thring, Frank 46–8, 57–8
Thring, Grace 47
Tivoli theatre, Melbourne 19–20, 32,
52
Tomasetti, Glen 159
Toorak, Melbourne 47, 59, 84, 105,
203–4; see also under Holt, Harold
Edward – homes
Toorak Village Theatre 105
Townsville 78, 158, 180, 184
treasurer 112–20, 122, 132, 135, 154,
266
Truman, Harry S. 124
Turnbull, Reginald John David
('Spot') 30–2, 34, 36–7, 155–7, 211,
224, 255
Turner, Harry 222, 224, 228

underwater sports 7; see also
skindiving; snorkelling; spearfishing
United Australia Party (UAP) 53–4,
58, 65–6, 71, 82, 155
United States
'all the way with LBJ' 172, 174,
183–4
defence communication base,
Western Australia 118–19,
249–50
military bases in Philippines 161
relations with Australia 123, 127,
147, 164, 169–74, 182–8, 210,
238–40, 245–6, 249–50, 252–3
see also New York; Washington,
DC

University of Melbourne
  Alfred Deakin Memorial Lecture
  247
  Queen's College 36–7, 41–4, 90
Usas, May 289

van Praagh, Peggy 201, 213, 239
Victoria 91, 107, 110, 194, 231–2;
  see also Melbourne; and other
  place names
Victorian Cinematograph Exhibitors
  Association 45, 52
Vietnam War 122, 124, 126–7, 144, 161,
  165–6, 182, 276, 295
  Calwell's position 123, 125, 148,
    151–3, 159, 162–3, 189, 191,
    206–8
  casualties 159, 177–81, 210–11,
    240, 247, 253, 262
  election issue, 1966 187–95
  escalation by Johnson, 1965 126,
    170–1, 239, 245–6, 252
  Holt's position 127, 144, 147–9,
    151–3, 155–60, 165–6, 183–4,
    188, 193–5, 203–4, 244–7,
    252–3, 266
  opposition and protests 132,
    158–61, 171, 173–4, 181, 185–6,
    190–3, 201–2, 207–8, 216,
    246–8, 258, 296
  peace treaty, 1973 296
  The Pentagon Papers 240
  Turnbull's position 155–7, 211
  visit of Nguyen Cao Ky to
    Australia 206–8
  waning support in the United
    States 237–8, 244, 246
  Whitlam's position 210, 216,
    252–3, 257
VIP fleet, use for private purposes
  256–60

Voyager disaster 217–28, 256–7,
  288–9

war cabinet 71, 73
Wartime Refugees Removal Act 1949
  87
Washington, DC 98–100, 164–5, 174,
  236–7
water 7–9, 11–15, 29, 100; *see also*
  swimming; underwater sports
waterside dispute, Bowen, 1953 92
waterside regulations 75–6
Waterside Workers' Federation of
  Australia 92
Wesley College, Melbourne 22–37,
  44, 47, 53, 154
  Dame Zara Bates' visit 297–8
  motto: *Sapere Aude* 28, 60
Western Australia 118–19, 194, 233, 249
White Australia policy 87–90, 145, 194
White, William 192
Whitlam, Gough 116, 118–19, 143–6,
  189, 194, 209–10, 226, 232, 247, 263–5
  position on Vietnam War 210,
    216, 252–3, 257
  relationship with Holt 253–4,
    258–9, 285, 293
  rise in popularity 245, 252–3
Wildlife Preservation Association of
  Queensland 268
Willoughby, General 78
Wilson, Harold 164, 173, 266, 283
World War One 24, 148
World War Two 62–4, 66–7, 70–80,
  82, 86–8, 92, 103, 124, 142, 191, 202,
  218, 246, 253
Wright, Judith 268, 296

Yarra 53
Young Nationalists Association 53, 59
Youngblood, Rufus 185